IMAGES
of America

BOWLING GREEN
A TOWN AND GOWN HISTORY

IMAGES
of America

BOWLING GREEN
A TOWN AND GOWN HISTORY

Stephen M. Charter

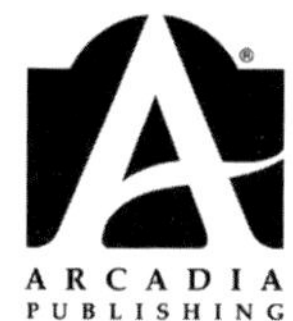

ARCADIA
PUBLISHING

To all of those who have contributed to strengthening the town and gown relationship between Bowling Green, Ohio, and Bowling Green State University

CONTENTS

Acknowledgments

The Center for Archival Collections (CAC) was established in 1969 as the Northwest Ohio-Great Lakes Research Center. The original mission of the center was to collect, preserve, and make accessible primary-source material related to the history of Northwest Ohio, the Great Lakes, and Bowling Green State University. Rare books and special collections were added later. The center's diverse holdings include archives, manuscripts, newspapers, and photographs. Unless otherwise noted, all images appearing in this book were graciously provided by the Center for Archival Collections.

I wish to thank my editor, Liz Gurley, for her kind assistance, guidance, and patience. I would like to especially thank my devoted colleagues Samantha Ashby, Melinda Charter, Kathy Gardner, Bob Graham, Libby Hertenstein, Eric Honneffer, Mike Intranuovo, Annie Land, and Marilyn Levinson, as well as my former staff members Lee McLaird and Dana Nemeth, for their encouragement and support. Thank you to Richard Wright, Paul Yon, Ann Bowers, and Ann Jenks for contributing greatly to my career pursuits. Janet Parks and other close friends, thank you for encouraging me to move onward and upward. Lastly, I wish to thank my family.

INTRODUCTION

Bowling Green, Ohio, began as a small settlement on the sand ridges of the Great Black Swamp of Northwest Ohio and became the county seat of Wood County at the center of a flourishing agricultural region. It developed into a prosperous boomtown following the discovery of natural gas and oil in the surrounding area, and when most of these natural resources were nearly exhausted, it was selected as the home of Bowling Green State Normal College, now Bowling Green State University.

At the tail end of gas- and oil-boom-spurred prosperity, a group of concerned, enthusiastic Bowling Green citizens met on the evening of April 7, 1907, at the Wood County Courthouse to discuss strategies for securing their town as the site of a planned Northwest Ohio normal school. If successful in their efforts, they would insure the future growth and expansion of their town. It was thought that in addition to economic benefits, the school would bring cultural enrichment to the community. Bowling Green was centrally located and easily accessible by various modes of transportation. One of the significant initiatives of the group was the publication of an attractive souvenir booklet that highlighted the exceptional advantages of Bowling Green as a location for the school. The booklet included 28 halftone photographs of streets and public buildings taken by local photographer James A. Walker. Copies were sent to members of the state legislature and sold to the public for $1 each. The collaborative work of the local community was successful in bringing the school to Bowling Green. The foundation of a mutually beneficial town and gown relationship had been laid.

The community continued to serve as local advocates through the years. In 1929, a Bowling Green resident, state representative Myrna Reece Hanna, cosponsored a bill to enlarge the scope of Bowling Green State Normal College. A liberal-arts program was established in addition to a college of education with four-year bachelor of science degree-granting status. In 1933, during the Great Depression, local community advocacy in the form of the Northwestern Ohio Educational Protective Association saved Bowling Green State College from closure and conversion into a state welfare institution. In 1935, a bill was passed that authorized the creation of colleges of business administration and liberal arts. Graduate instruction leading to a master of arts degree was also authorized. Bowling Green State College became Bowling Green State University at that time. During World War II, when enrollment declined, the university became the home of the V-5 and V-12 naval training programs. The university purchased a 120-acre site for the construction of an airport to meet the needs of the V-5 naval pilot training program. Local high school teachers were hired as supplemental instructors for both programs, due to a wartime shortage of faculty members.

The influx of V-5 and V-12 cadets provided stability to the local economy. The wartime prosperity for city and university was sustained by the arrival of veterans who came to take advantage of their GI Bill educational benefits. The campus expanded to meet the needs of an expanding enrollment. Bowling Green businesses, including bars, gas stations, motels, restaurants, retail stores, and theaters have benefited significantly from the increased student population. Families and friends visiting their students, attending commencement ceremonies, or participating in athletic and cultural activities have been vital in boosting the local economy, as visitors patronize local businesses. Many local businesses have had contracts with the board of trustees to provide goods and services. Some of those included A. Froney & Company, Hankey Lumber, Home Steam Laundry, and Maas Brothers Grocery.

Diverse university-sponsored cultural, educational, and recreational activities enrich the lives of Bowling Green residents. Cultural activities have included School of Art exhibits and educational programs, dramatic presentations or productions at various performance venues such as the Joe E. Brown Theatre, Lillian Gish Film Theater, and Eva Marie Saint Theatre, and the Wolfe Center for the Arts, Ice Horizons at the Ice Arena, and musical concerts and educational programs at the Moore Musical Arts Center. Recreational activities held at the Anderson Arena, Ice Arena, Doyt L. Perry Stadium, Perry Field House, Stroh Center, and Student Recreation Center have enhanced the physical wellbeing of local residents.

Bowling Green State University has been a major employer in the community since its founding. Employees who have been transplants, as well as those who have been longtime residents, have helped to improve the community as they have shared their expertise, interests, and talent in collaborative activities or initiatives. The first annual May Festival in 1915 and the Not in Our Town Movement in 2013 are just two examples of such enterprises.

Students, even though in the community for a short time, have always provided service to their temporary home. Alumni in diverse occupations or pursuits in all parts of the world have brought recognition to both town and gown. Included are actors, actresses, authors, artists, business executives, civic leaders, educators, journalists, Olympic athletes, and politicians. Some alumni have become permanent residents, or townies, who have contributed to Bowling Green in various walks of life.

The town and gown relationship that exists between Bowling Green, Ohio, and Bowling Green State University has developed into a resilient, mutually beneficial association of community and college.

One

BOOMTOWN TO UNIVERSITY TOWN

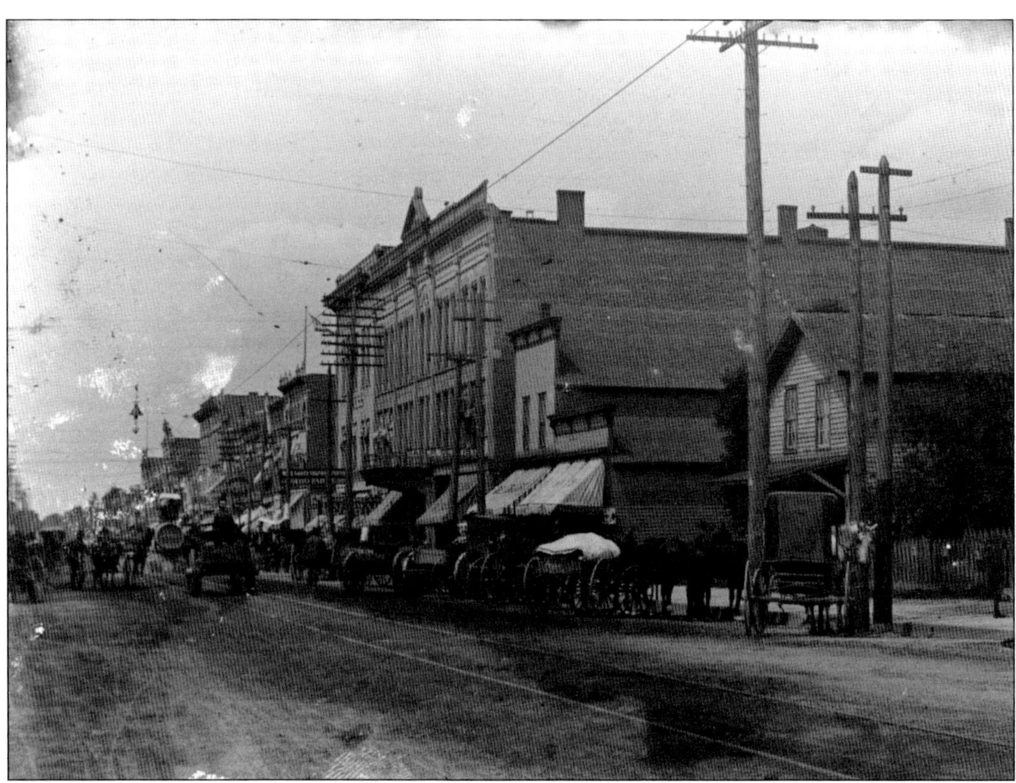

This c. 1900 view of a bustling South Main Street looking north shows the three-story Hankey and Hankey-Taber Opera House Blocks in the foreground. The Chidester and Del-Mar Theatres, respectively, occupied the site of the Hankey-Opera House Block. The Del-Mar Theatre was destroyed by fire in 1926. Several businesses have occupied the site of the Hankey Block at 163 South Main Street, including Kaufman's Tavern & Restaurant. SamB's Restaurant is currently located at the site.

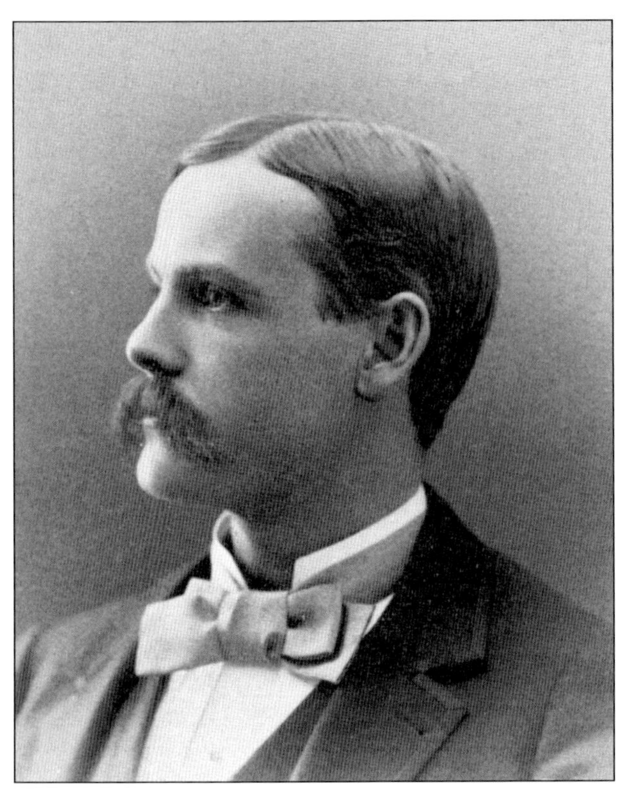

Several local residents served as strident normal school proponents, among them Benjamin F. James and Jacob N. Easley. Attorney James (left) was involved in the early campaign to secure the school for their town and hosted the visiting normal school commission in September 1910. Impressed by the support of the local community, the commission chose Bowling Green. Attorney and businessman Easley (below) purchased the 82.5-acre site selected by the commission for the future school at auction for $10 on October 26, 1911. He then transferred the land to the state for $1. (Both images courtesy of Familiar Faces of Wood County.)

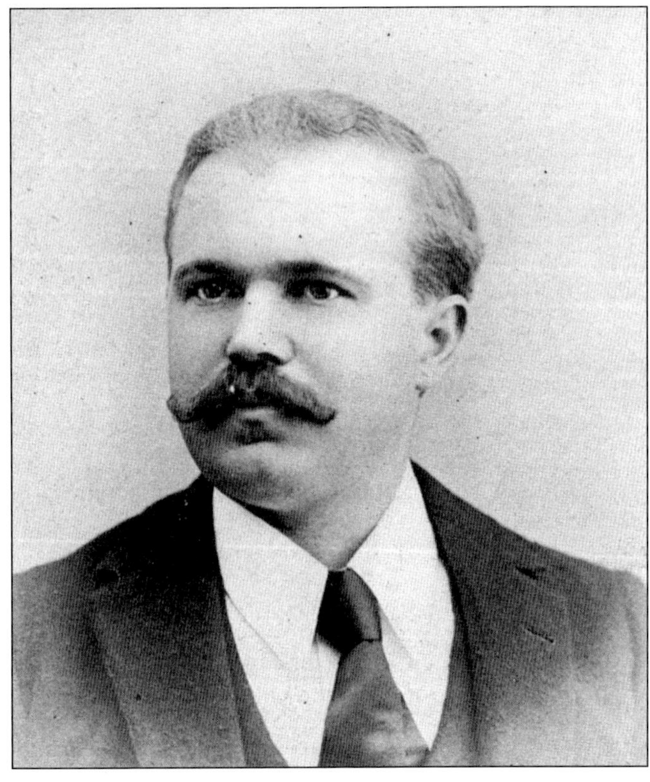

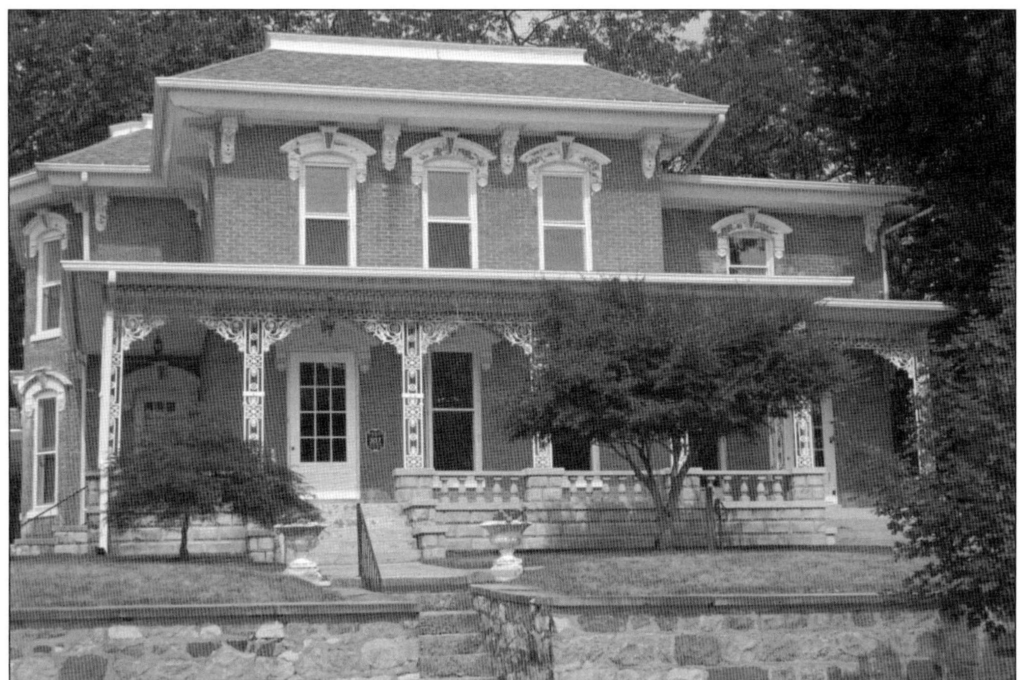

The home of Benjamin F. James at 307 North Church Street is where the normal school commission met to discuss the merits of selecting Bowling Green as the site of a new Northwest Ohio normal school. Built by Norton Reed, the house was at one time the location of the Shakespeare Round Table lending library. Myrtle E. James was the first head of the organization. The lending library holdings were eventually donated to the Bowling Green District Library, now the Wood County District Public Library. The house was donated to the library by Robert and Patricia Maurer in 2006 and named in honor of the former's aunt Martha Maurer Carter. (Courtesy of Marilyn Levinson.)

A parcel of land that included the 11-acre Bowling Green City Park was selected by the normal school commission as the site of the Northwest Ohio normal school. The park had been established by Bowling Green Village Council in 1883 on land that had been purchased from George and Helen Reed Wooster. This photograph shows Wayne Street, which ultimately ran in front of the science, administration, and manual-training school buildings.

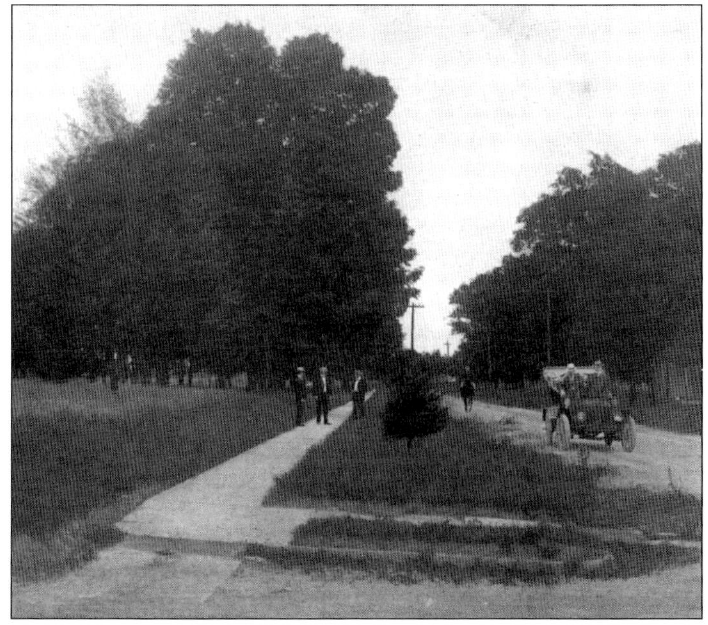

Helen Reed Wooster deeded her farmstead to the college on January 13, 1914. The Wooster house, located at 725 East Wooster Street, served as the first president's home until 1937. Former president emeritus Homer B. Williams and family continued to live in the house until his death in 1943. It later served as the Alpha Chi Omega sorority house and the BGSU Counseling Center. The building was demolished in 1973.

The old Ridge Street School, built in 1888, served as the first elementary training school for Bowling Green State Normal College. Only the first four grades were provided, due to the shortage of free space. Other local schools served as training facilities for the college.

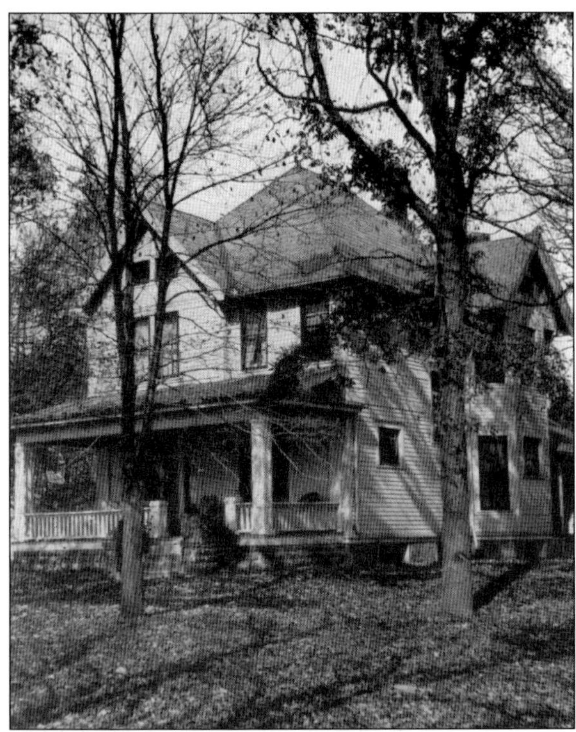

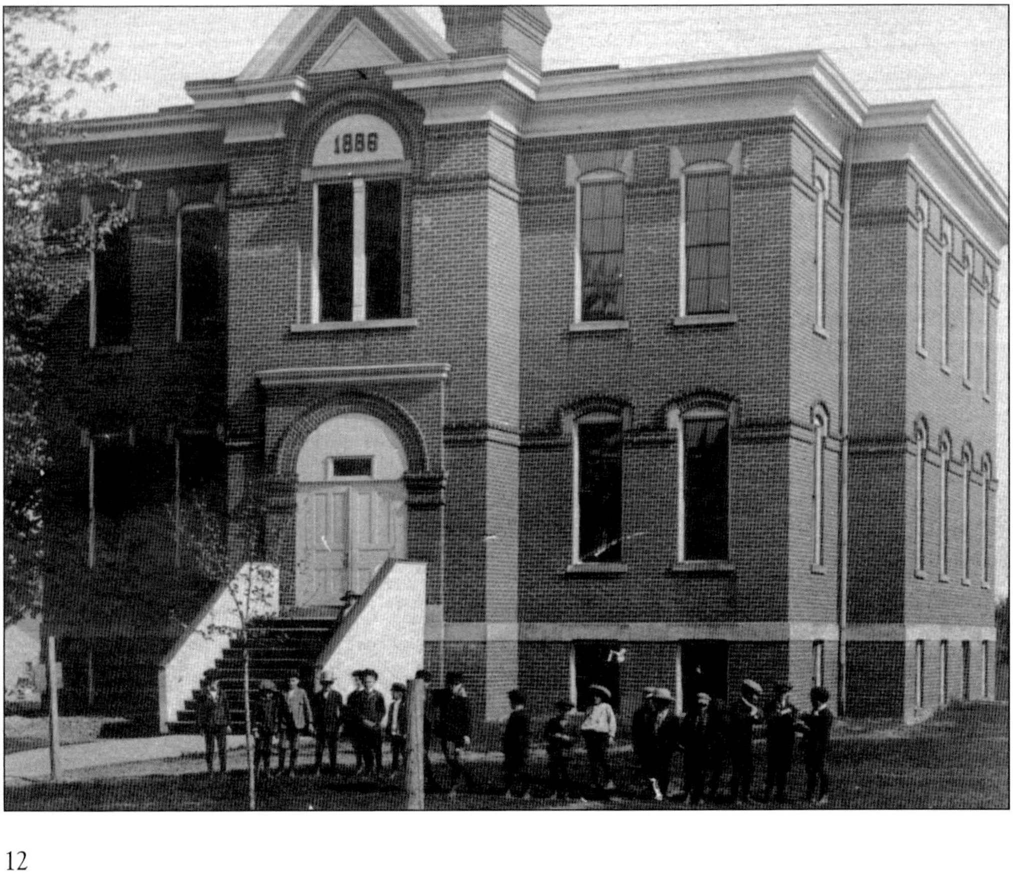

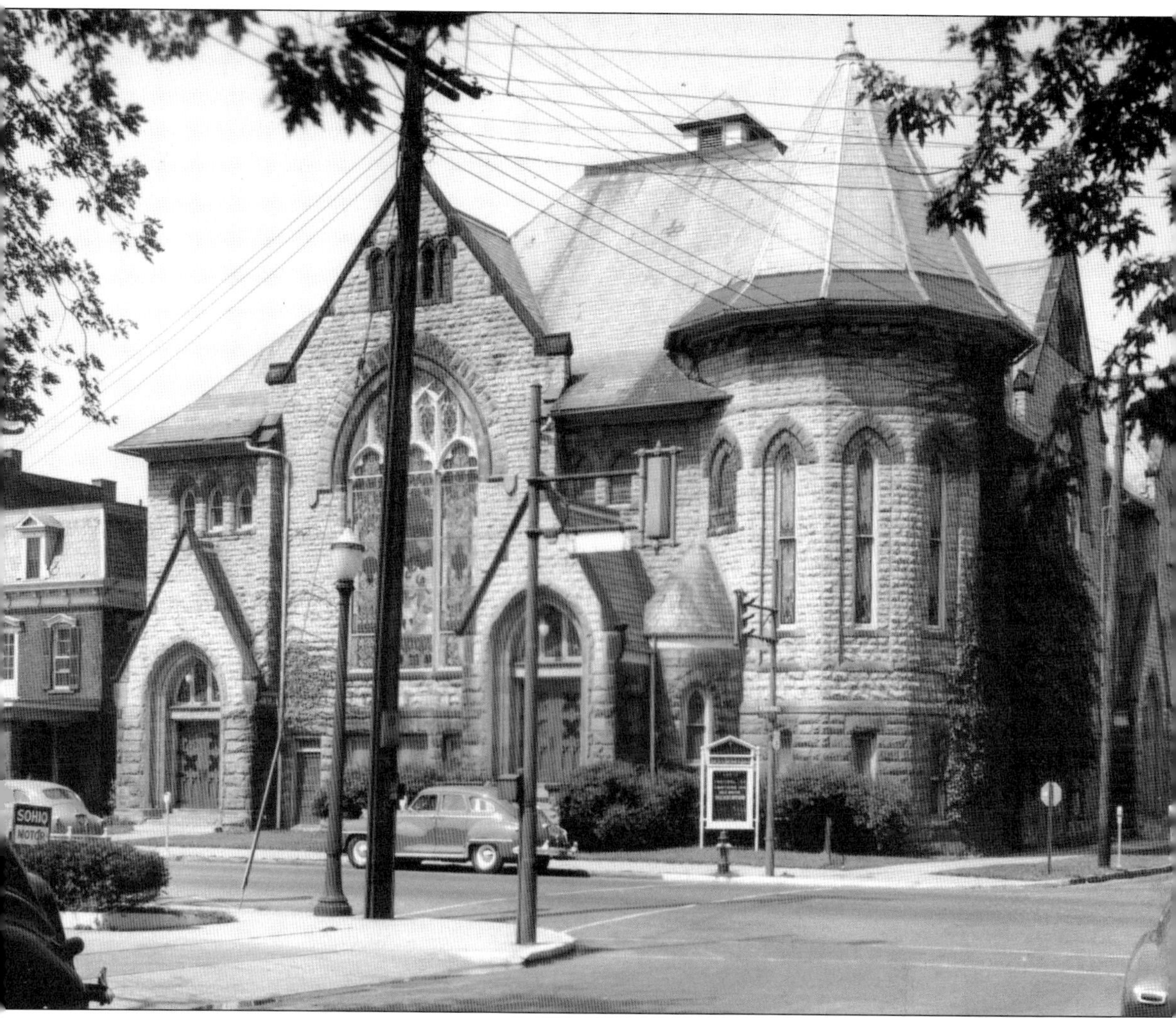

The first Bowling Green State Normal College library was located in the basement of the Methodist Episcopal church at the corner of East Wooster and North Prospect Streets, and James Robert Overman served as the first librarian. The library did not have a reading room, so students had to check out books. Weekly chapel services were conducted at the Church for Normal College students. The church was demolished in the 1960s when the First United Methodist Church was built. Since that time, several convenience stores and gasoline stations have been located on the site.

FIRST ANNUAL
MAY FESTIVAL

ERNEST HESSER, Director

First Methodist Episcopal Church.   *Bowling Green, Ohio.*

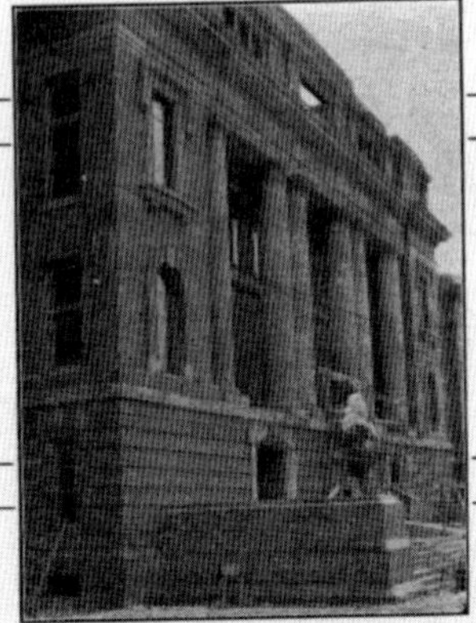

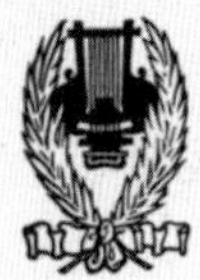

Two Concerts   May 20, 21, 1915

Administration Building, State Normal College

Choral Society composed of the students from the Bowling Green State Normal College and musicians of Bowling Green

Artists

SIBYL SAMMIS-MAC DERMID Soprano	**AGNES KIMBALL-AFFLECK** Soprano
ADA ALLEN Contralto	**FRED NEWELL MORRIS** Basso
HERMAN MILITZER Tenor	**ROSCOE MULHOLLAND** Baritone
PEARL HEISER, Organist	**MARY BEVERSTOCK, Pianist**

Choral Works

"The Holy City," Gaul; "Olaf Trygvason," Greig; "The Heavens Resound," Beethoven; Pilgrims' Chorus, "Tannhauser," Wagner

The annual community college's three-day May Festival, organized by music professor Ernest G. Hesser, was first held at the First Methodist Episcopal Church from May 20 to 21, 1915. Artists from around the country participated in the event. The festival featured a college and community chorus composed of normal college students and local community musicians as well as a children's chorus. Subsequent festivals were held alternately at the church and the Chidester Theatre. A special Victory May Festival was held in 1919 to commemorate a victory and to honor the soldiers who served during World War I. The final May Festival was held in 1921.

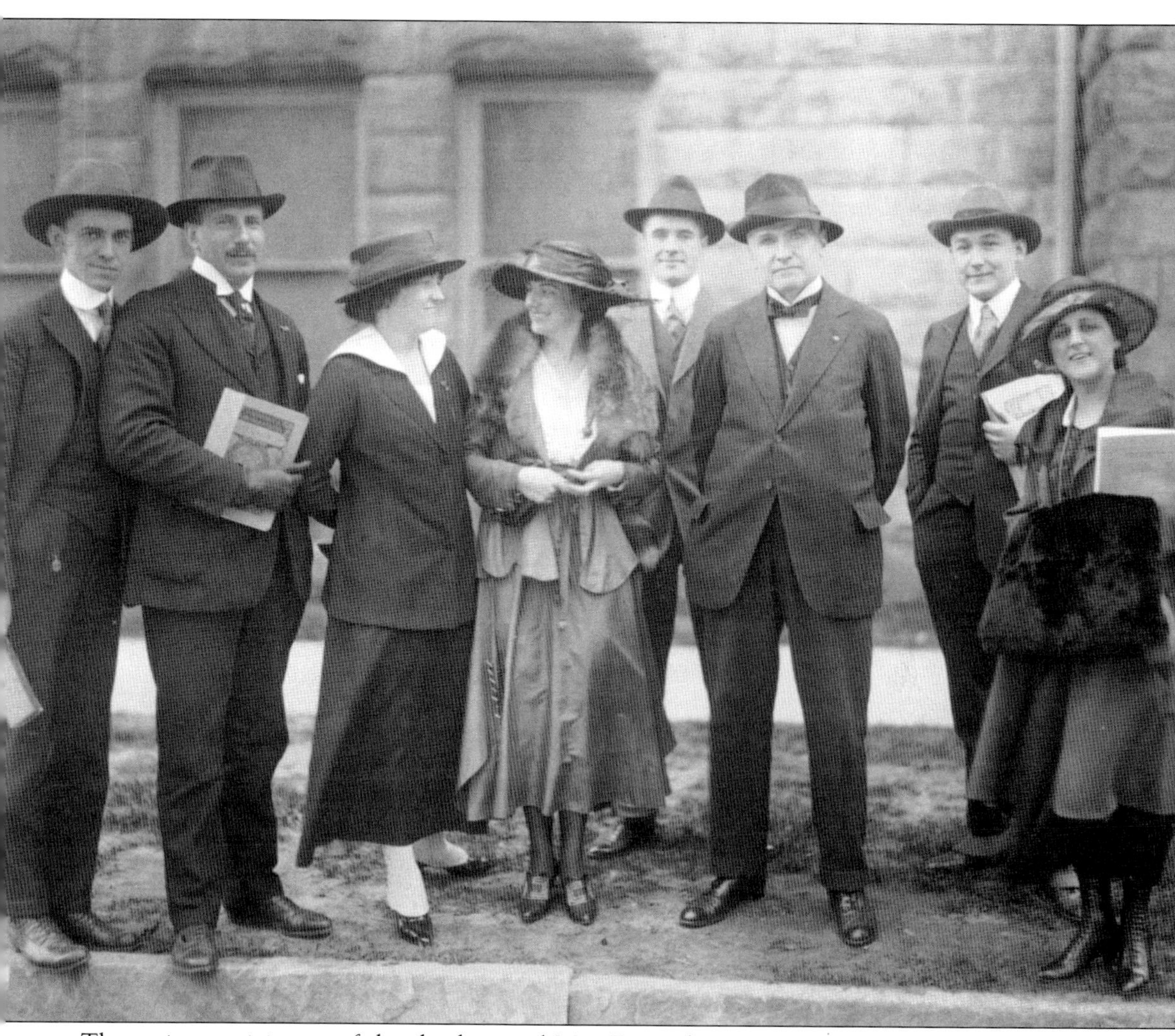

The major participants of the third annual May Festival in 1918 included, from left to right, Ernest G. Hesser (festival director), Charles Tittman (basso), Ruth McConn (accompanist), Merle Alcock (contralto), unidentified, Walter Damrosch (festival conductor and director of the New York Symphony Orchestra), Albert Lindquist (tenor), and Nina Morgana (soprano). The New York Symphony Orchestra and guest speaker Ohio governor James M. Cox were participants.

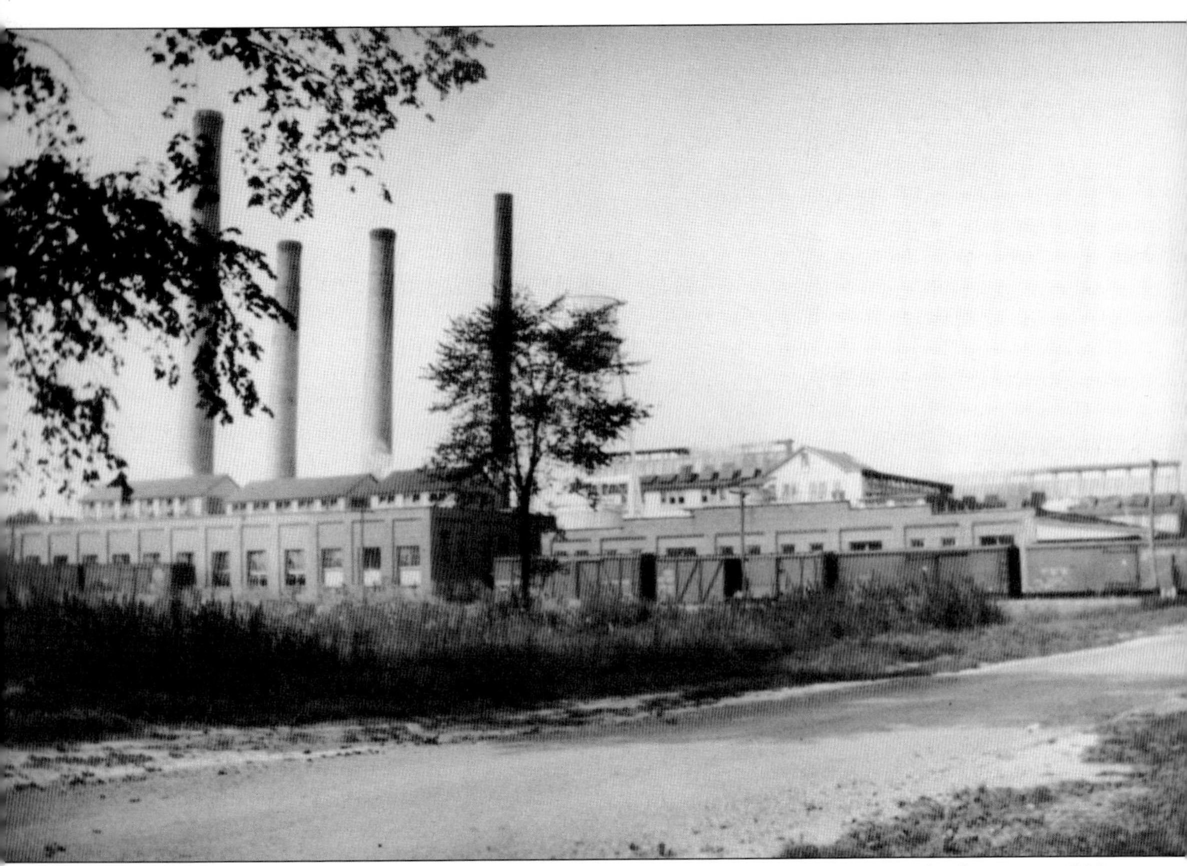

The H.J. Heinz Company of Pittsburgh, Pennsylvania, began construction of a factory at 540 North Enterprise Street in 1914. The advocacy of the Bowling Green Commercial Club and the city council brought the factory to town. Jacob N. Easley helped to secure legal rights to the surrounding streets and alleys from property owners. The factory, which produced ketchup, became a major employer in the community.

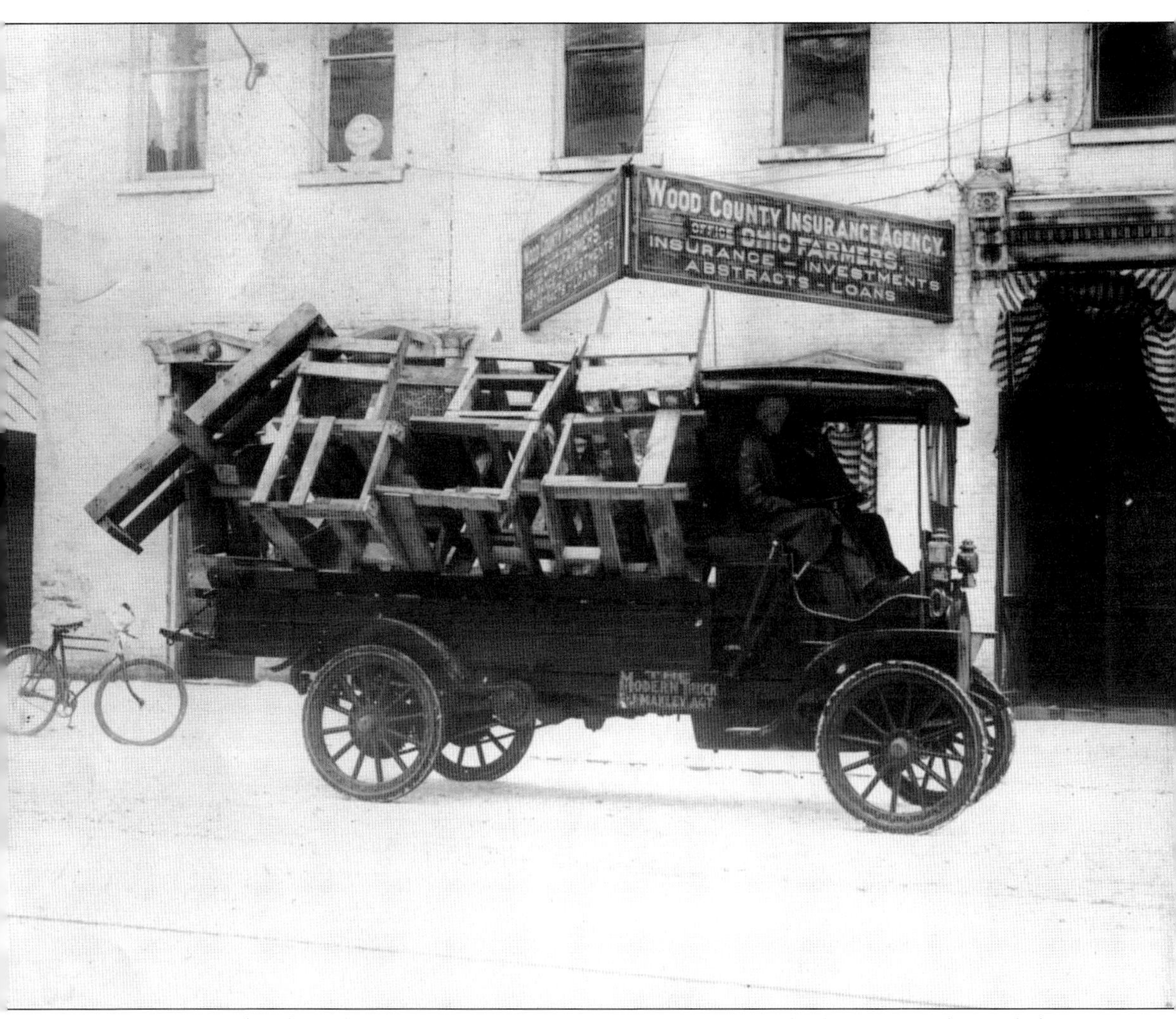

Bowling Green has been home to a diverse group of manufacturing facilities, many located close to the railroad lines. A Modern Truck Company vehicle is shown in front of the Wood County Insurance Agency at 110 West Wooster Street. The company was located at 500 Lehman Avenue. Crystal City Glass, Leonard Range and Stove, the Graham-Logan Motor Car, Bowling Green Motor Car, and the Daybrook Hydraulic Corporation had been located at the same site.

First Annual Commencement

Bowling Green State Normal College

Thursday, July 29, 1915, 10:30 A. M.

Chidester Theatre

The first annual commencement of the Bowling Green State Normal College was held on July 29, 1915, in the Chidester Theatre. That day, 35 women received their two-year diplomas. Music was furnished by Prof. Ernest G. Hesser and his recently organized philharmonic club. The commencement speaker was Dr. Charles Judd, director of the school of education at the University of Chicago.

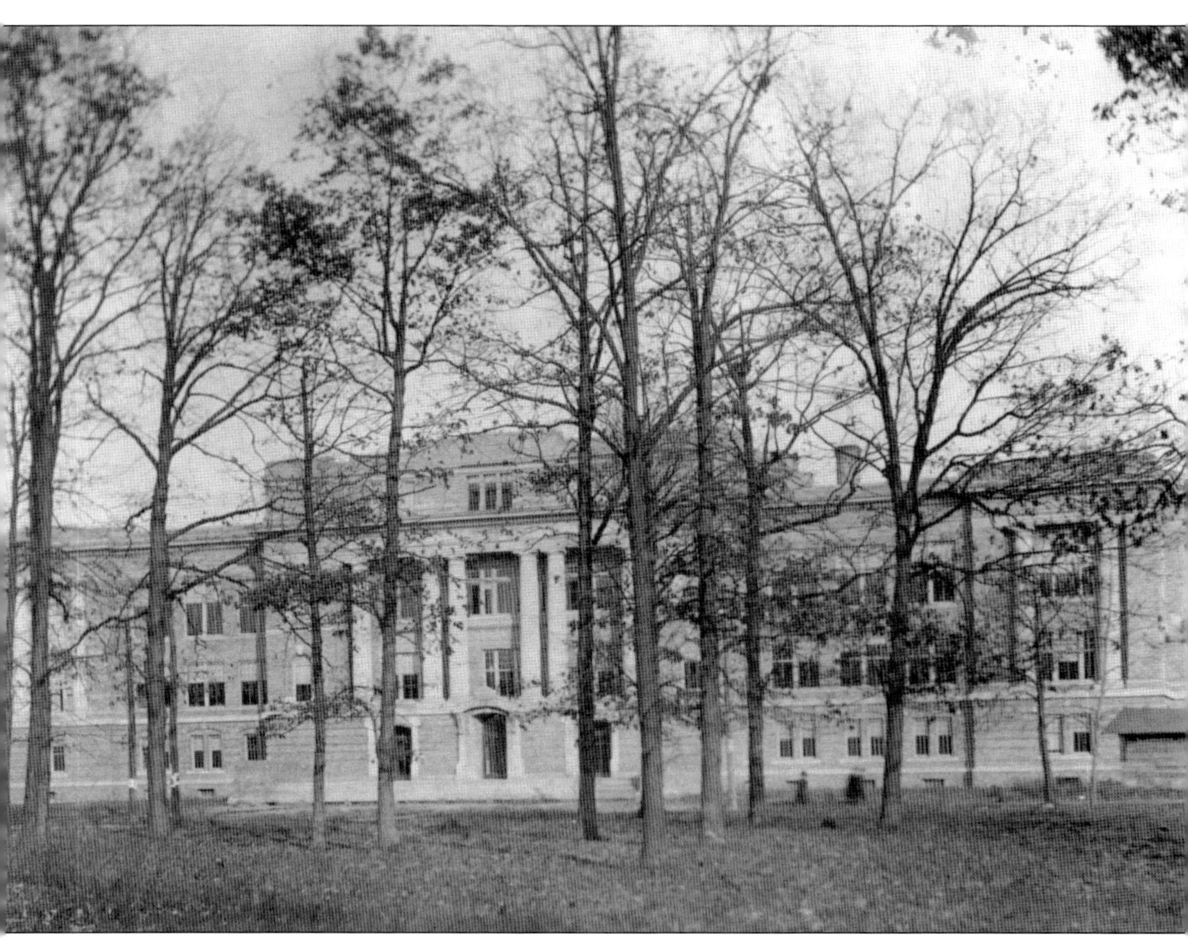

Construction of the administration building was completed in the fall of 1915. The building housed an auditorium, gymnasium, library, classrooms, and offices in addition to an elementary training school comprised of six grades of Bowling Green children. The first college bookstore was later housed in the building.

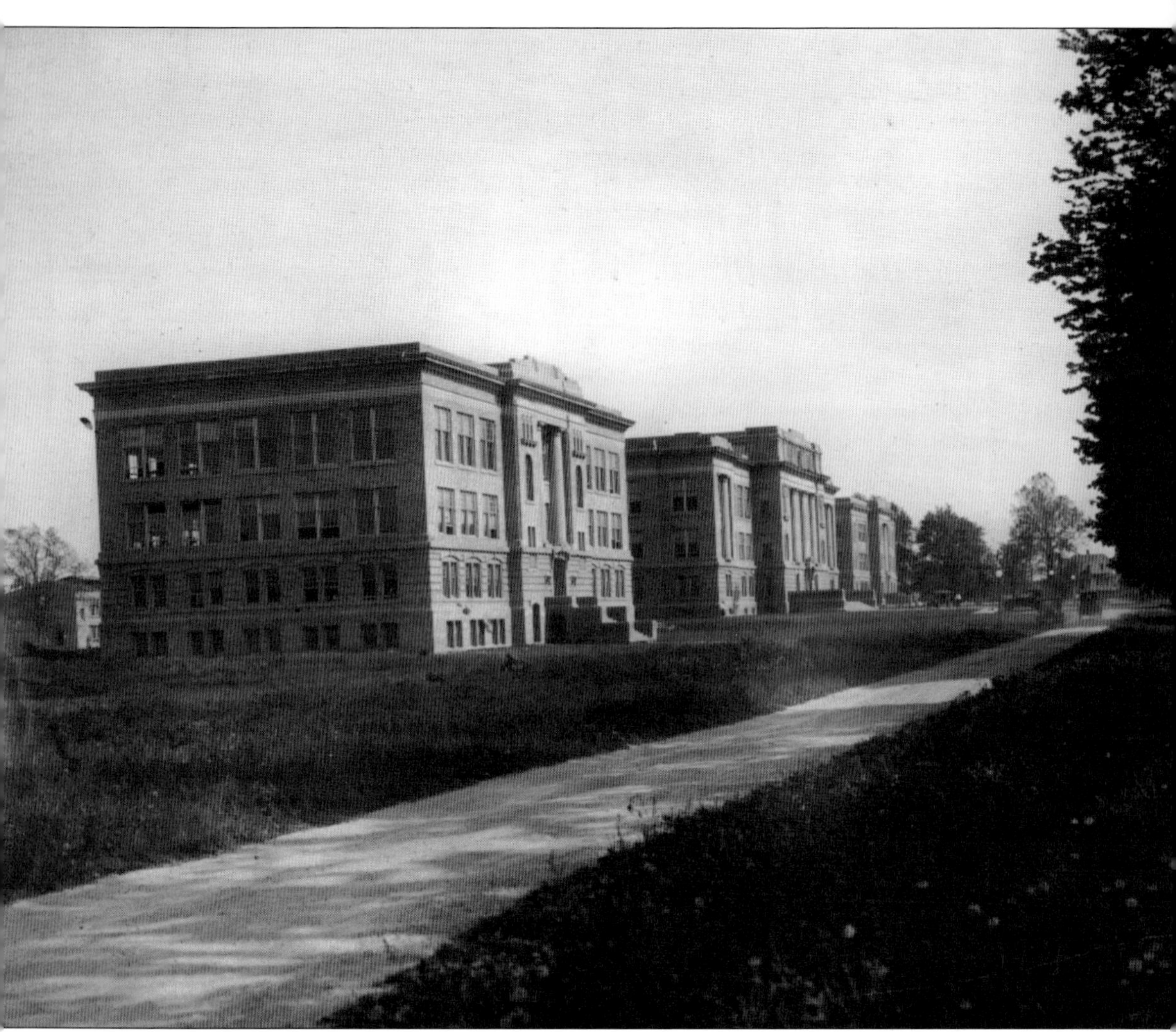

The science (and agriculture) building, pictured in the foreground, was completed in early 1916. It became the home of the agriculture, science, and industrial-arts programs. Grades three through six of the elementary training school were transferred to the new building, which was later named Moseley Hall in honor of the first science faculty member, Dr. Edwin L. Moseley.

A contract for the construction of the manual-training school building was signed in 1916, but due to the shortage of building materials during World War I and major financial problems, construction was not completed until November 1921. It served as an elementary school for local community children from 1922 until 1959. The building was named Hanna Hall in 1959, in honor of Myrna Reece Hanna.

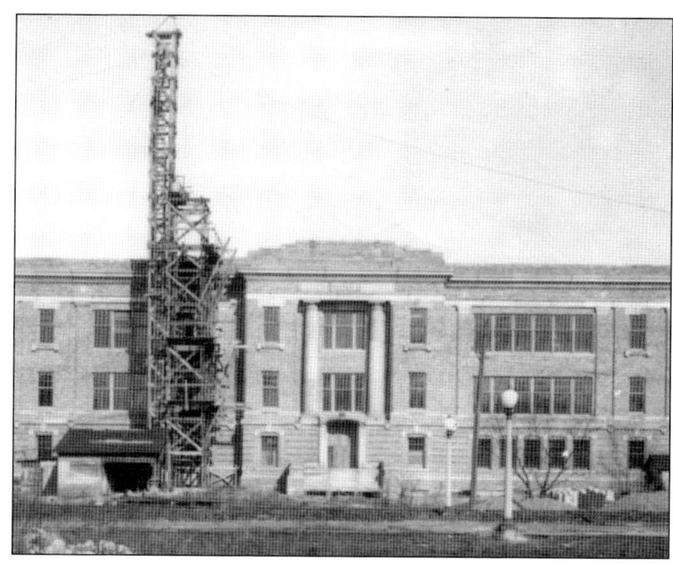

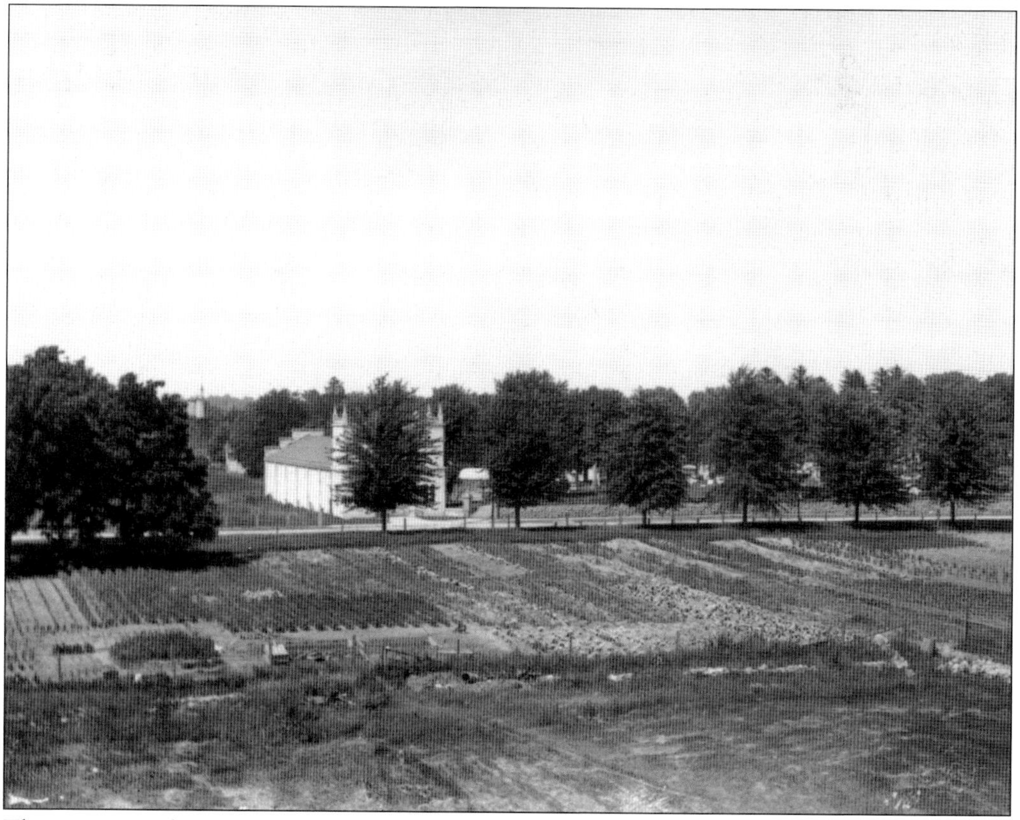

The victory gardens of elementary children attending the manual-training school provided them with an opportunity to raise their own vegetables and support the war effort. The victory garden (or war garden) campaign was first instituted in the United States by the National War Garden Commission during World War I as an effort to reduce increasing pressure on public food supplies. The governments of some European countries also encouraged their citizens to plant gardens. Oak Grove Cemetery can be seen in the background.

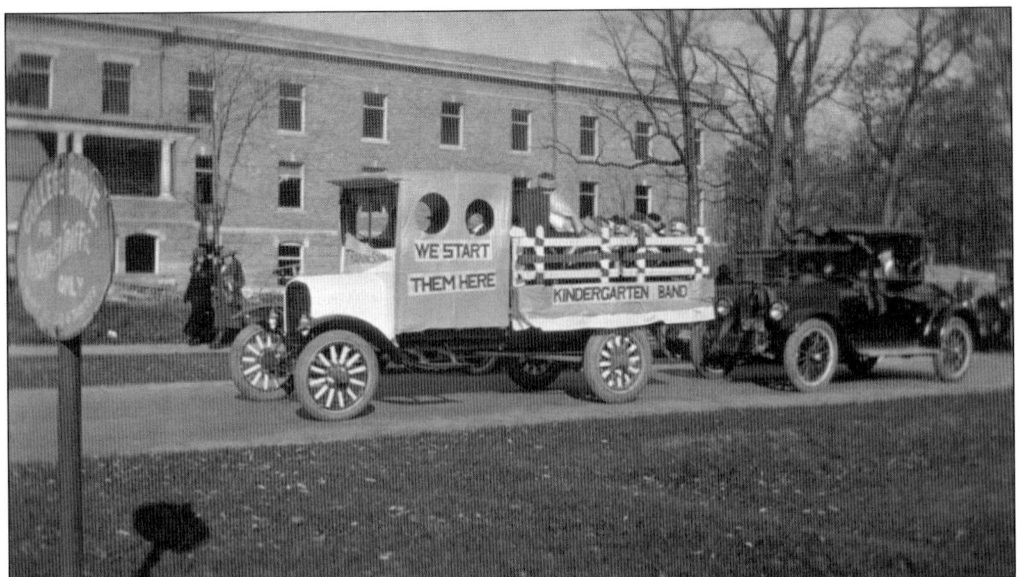

The second annual homecoming parade took place on November 10, 1923. It included floats from various college organizations and automobiles decorated by the townspeople. The parade featured a manual-training school float that showcased a kindergarten band of local children (above). The kindergarten was first opened in September 1922, and the curriculum included music (below), rhythm, language, literature, games, fine and industrial arts, history, nature study, and arithmetic.

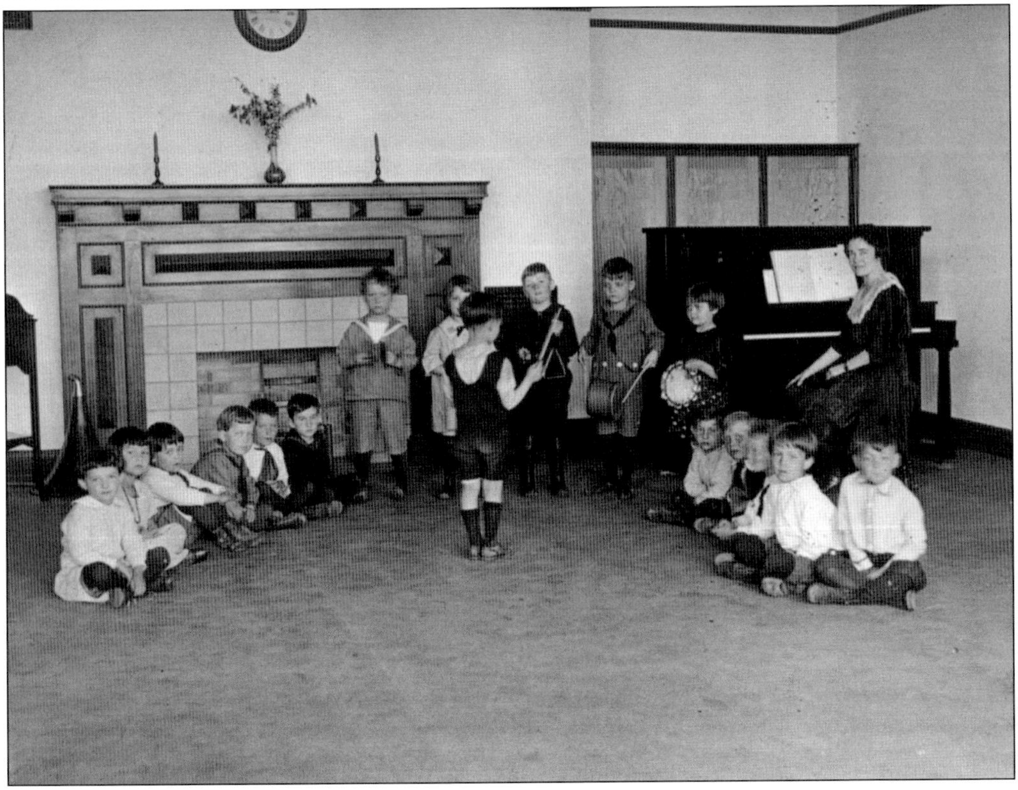

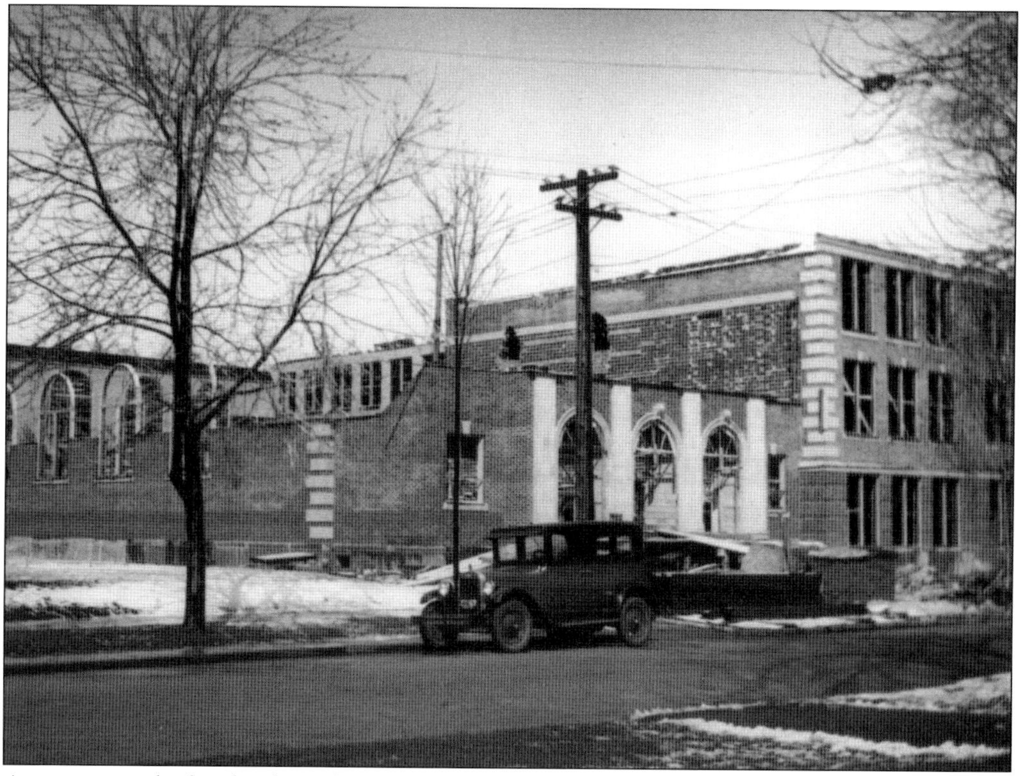

A new senior high school, at the corner of West Wooster and Church Streets, was opened to accommodate an increased enrollment due to a consolidation of rural schools into the Bowling Green City School District. The new high school auditorium is shown under construction. The existing senior high school on Grove Street, which was built in 1914, became the junior high school. When a new senior high school was constructed on Poe Road in 1964, the junior high moved into the building. The Bowling Green Senior and Junior High Schools have served as teacher-training facilities for Bowling Green State University students since its founding.

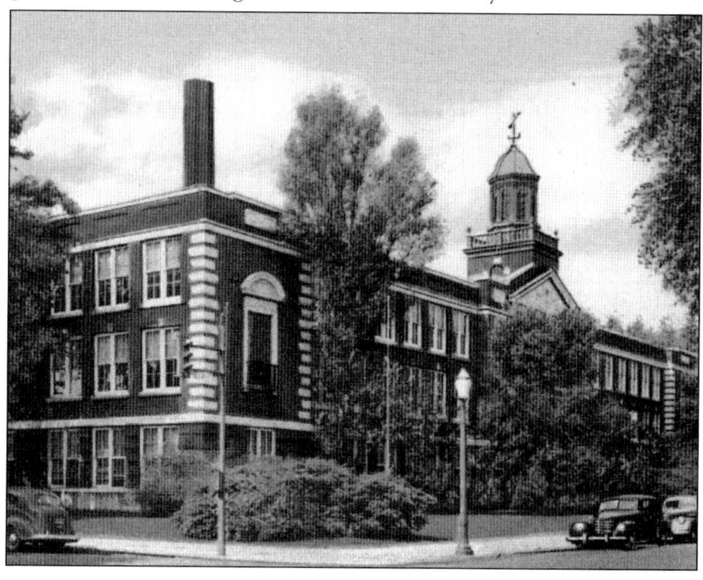

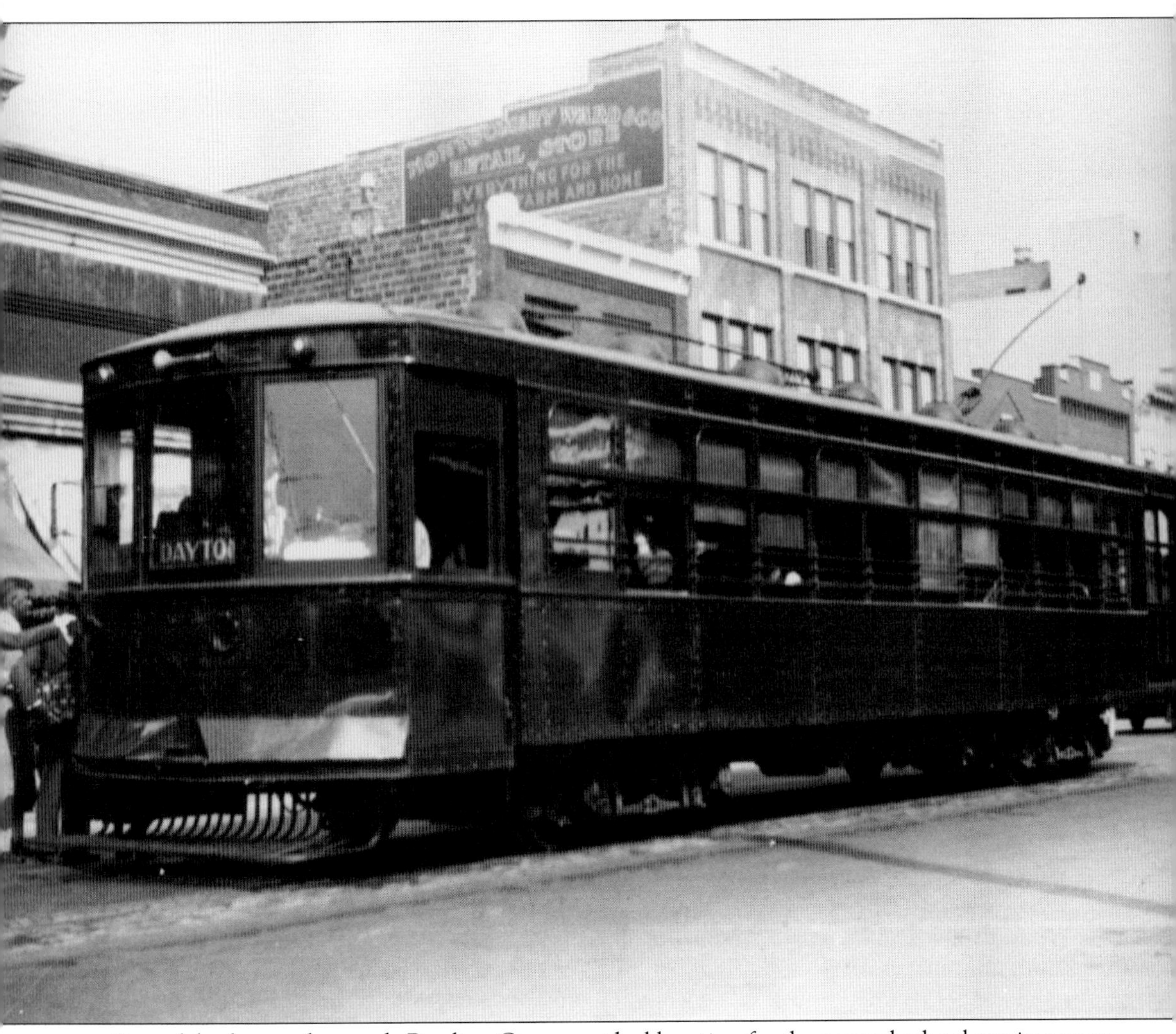

One of the factors that made Bowling Green an ideal location for the normal school was its access to transportation facilities. Several railways traversed the city, including the New York Central and the Toledo, Bowling Green & Southern Traction Company (TBG&S). One of TBG&S Company cars loads passengers in front of Hales News Stand at 170 South Main Street. Hales News Stand was a station until the company closed in 1930.

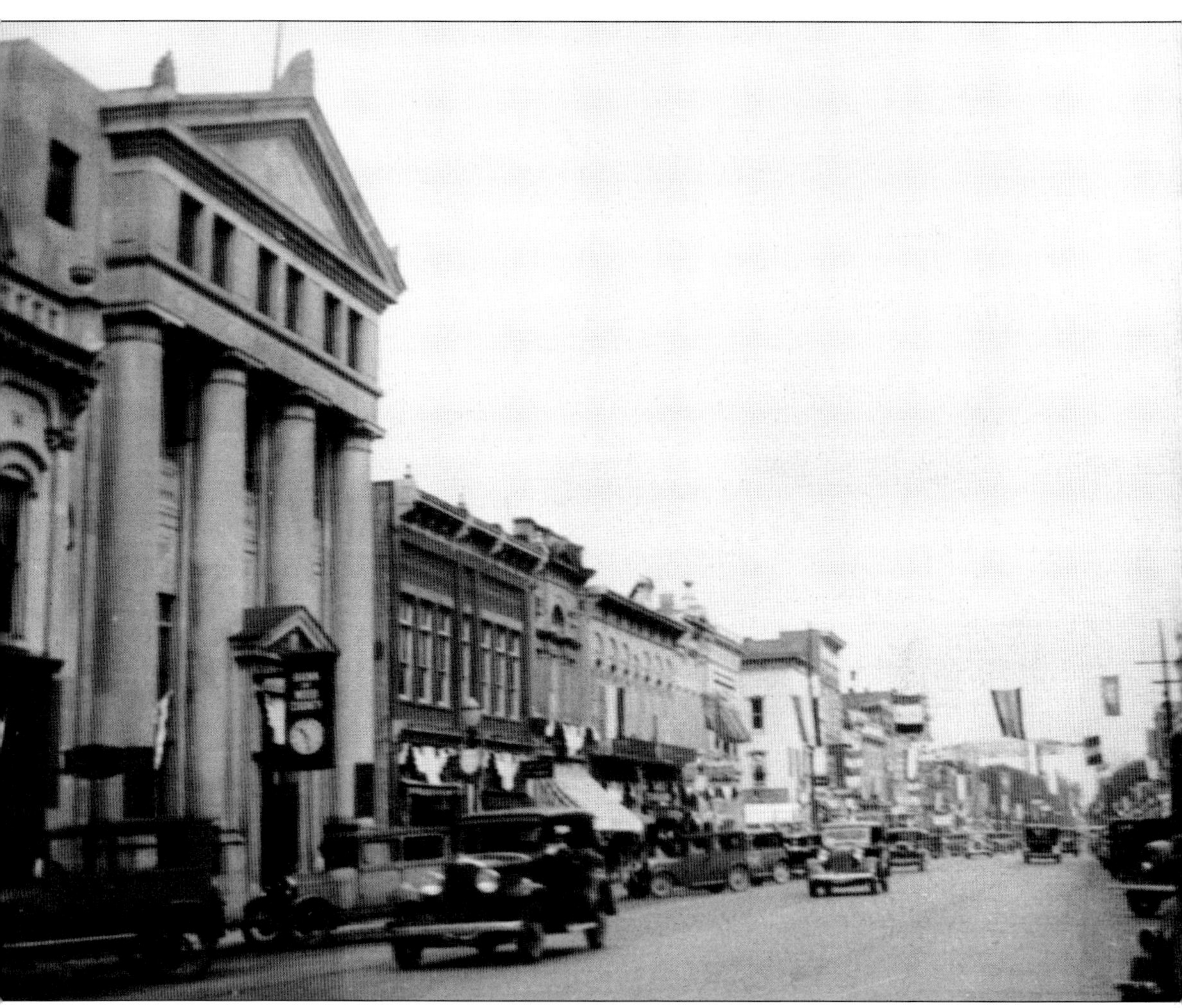

This view of South Main Street looking north prominently features the Bank of Wood County (foreground). The Commercial Bank and Savings Company erected a new building at 130 South Main Street but closed in 1929. The Bank of Wood County opened in the vacated building on November 16, 1931, in the midst of the Great Depression. The Bank of Wood County became Huntington National Bank in 1980.

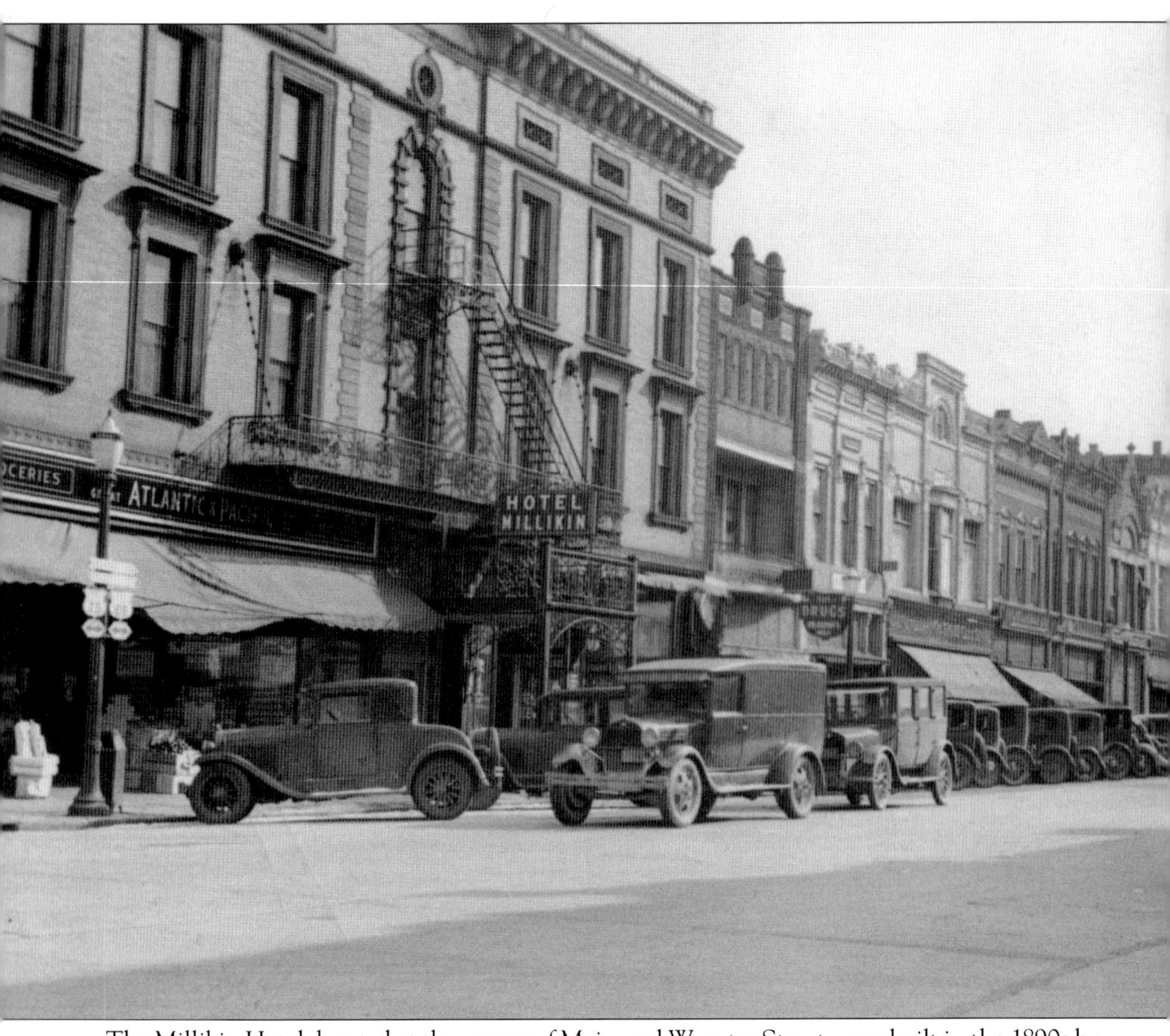

The Millikin Hotel, located at the corner of Main and Wooster Streets, was built in the 1890s by William H. Millikin and operated until the late 1950s. Several businesses have occupied the first floor of the hotel, including the A&P Store, which opened on February 24, 1933. Jed's Barbecue & Brew is located in the space today, while the Millikin Apartments are located in the refurbished hotel space on the second and third floors.

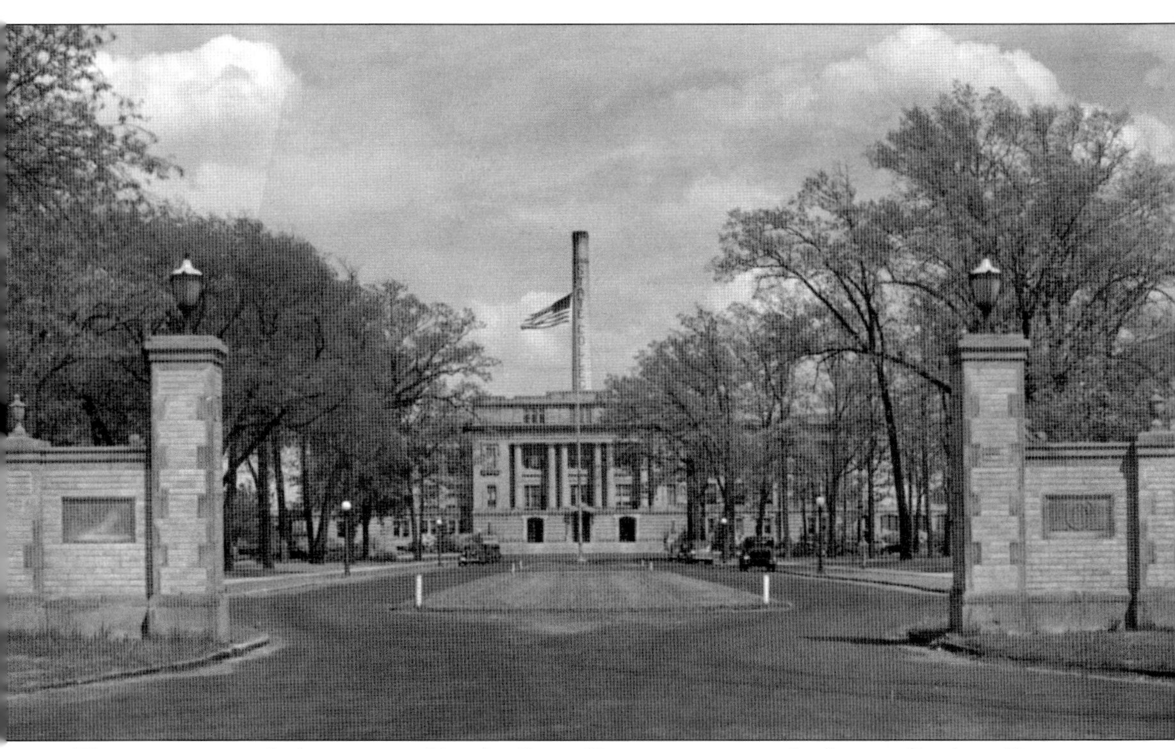

The economic turbulence caused by the Great Depression cast a shadow on Bowling Green State College when the state threatened to close it and convert it into a mental hospital in 1933. Local citizens, in the form of the Northwestern Ohio Educational Protective Agency, came to the rescue. Their vigorous campaign created such a public uproar that a majority of Senate Finance Committee members voted against the proposal. The college persevered through yet another trial with the advocacy of the community.

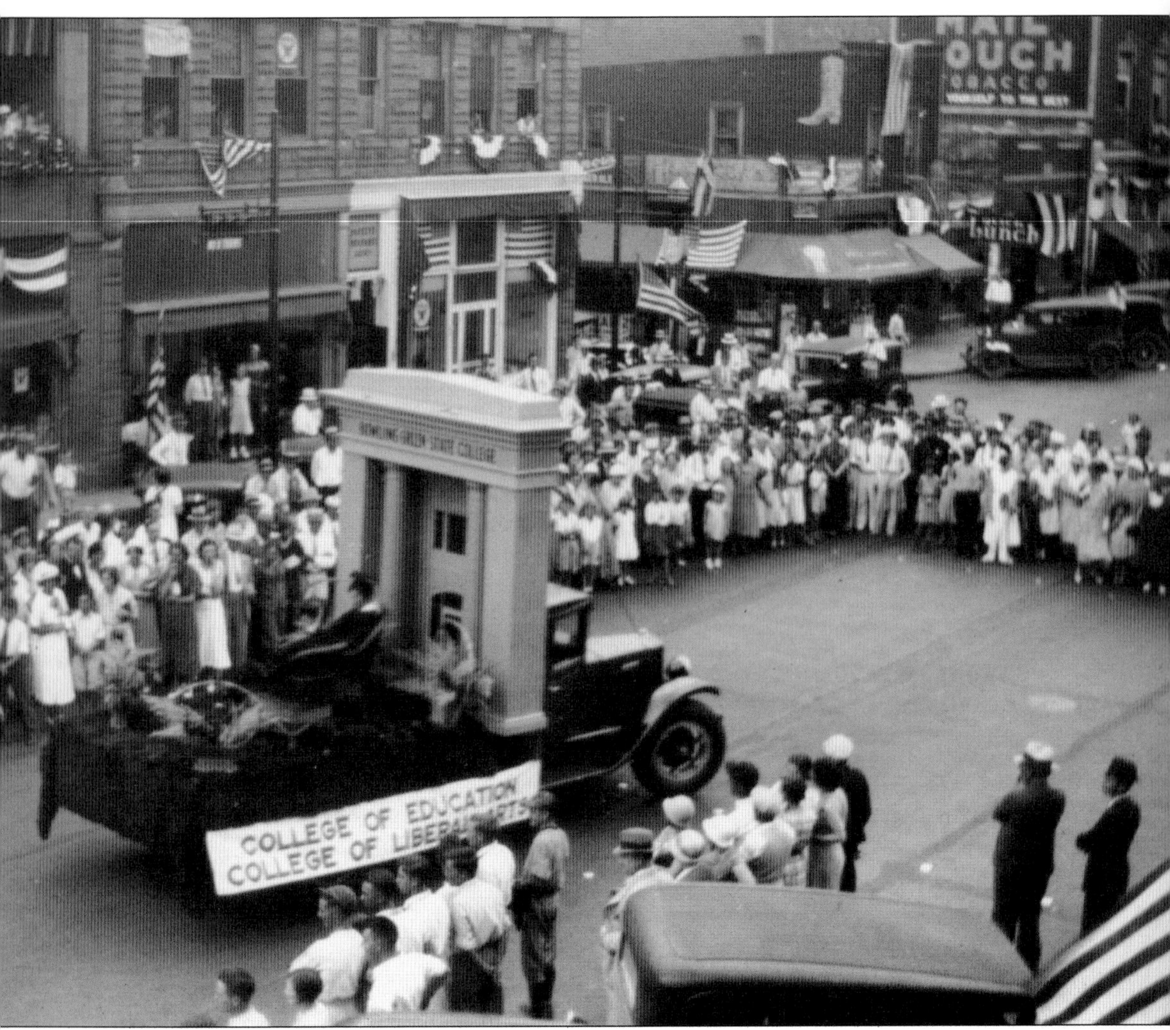

The Bowling Green centennial celebration, which began on August 31, 1933, included a variety of events that were held in the community and at the college. The festivities included an air show, church services, fireworks, a historical pageant, music, a parade, and speeches. A queen was selected to reign over the events. The parade traveled down Main Street to Court Street; pictured here is the Bowling Green State College float.

The second president's residence, located at 838 East Wooster Street, was purchased in 1937 and used for that purpose until 1963. A Montgomery Ward catalog company home, it was built by Virgil H. Taylor in 1932. It was later the home of the alumni center, the popular culture center, and the popular culture department. The house was demolished to make way for the new Falcon Health Center.

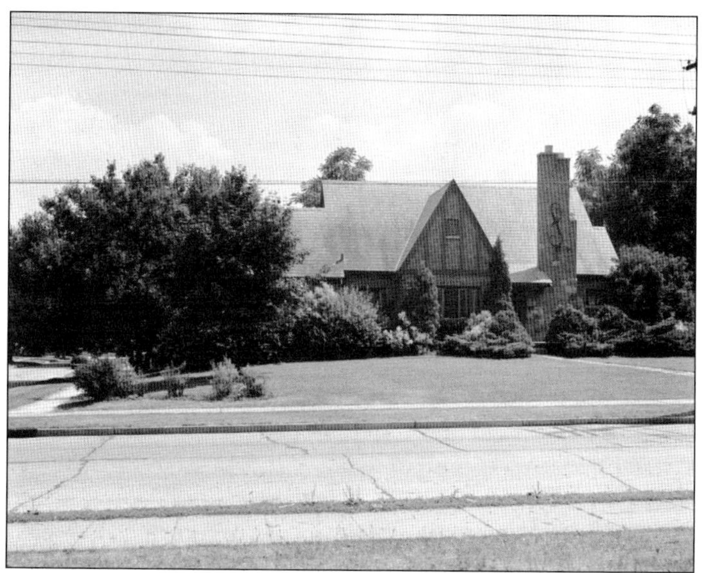

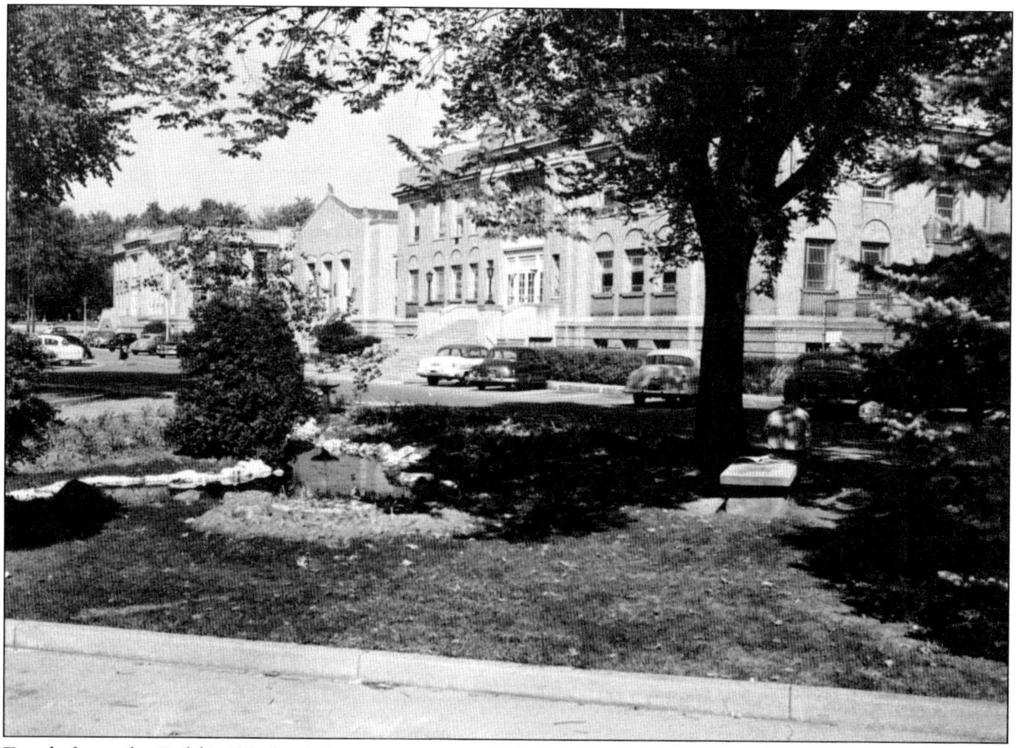

Funds from the Public Works Administration and the Works Progress Administration supplemented local and state money to finance the construction of the women's physical education building (background) in 1938 and the natatorium (middle) in 1939. The men's physical education building (foreground) was constructed in 1927. The natatorium housed a swimming pool that played host to swim meets, physical-education classes, the Swan Club, and community swimming classes. The natatorium was demolished in 1978 during the construction of the Gertrude Eppler Health and Physical Education Complex. The men's and women's gymnasiums have played host to the many intercollegiate and local athletic events.

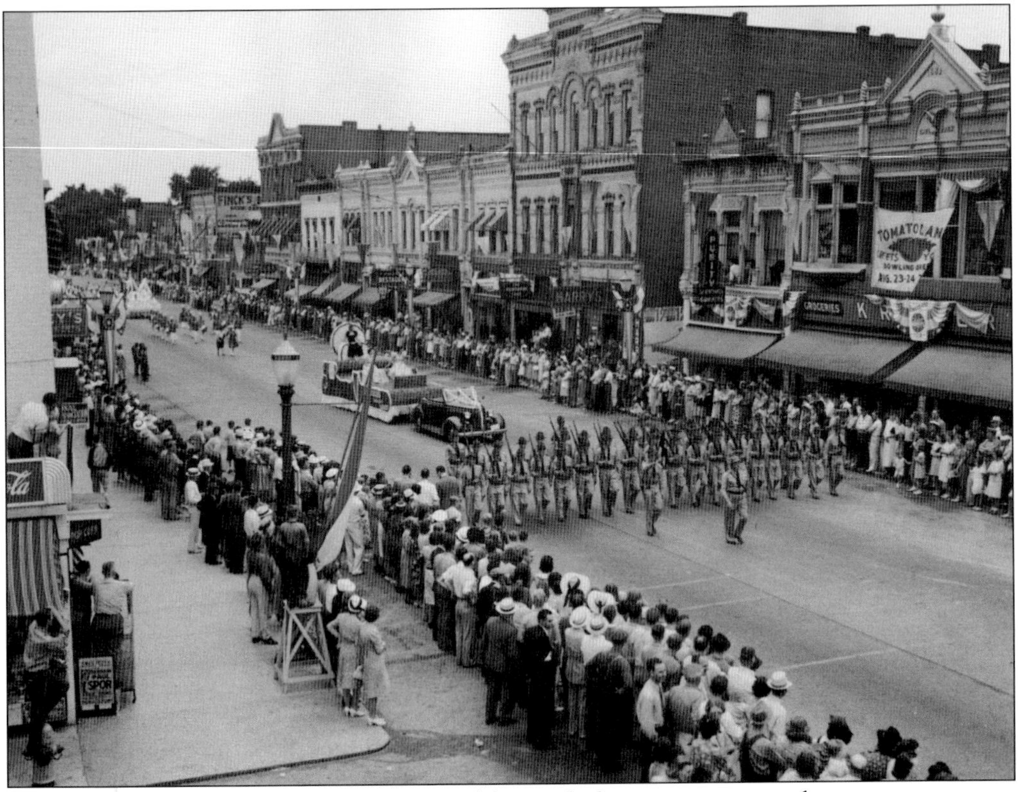

The first tomato festival was held in 1938 and featured a beauty contest to select a tomato queen; entertainment was comprised of community and university talent and a parade. The event was sponsored by the H.J. Heinz Company, local businesses, and Bowling Green State University. The 1939 parade is pictured on North Main Street near the intersection of Wooster Street.

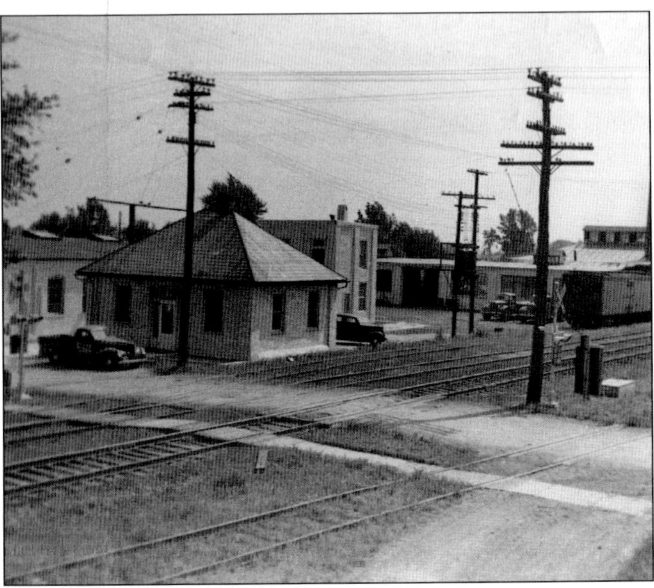

Daybrook Hydraulic Corporation was established in 1939 by Herbert O. Day and Andrew F. Brooker. Located at the site of the former Gramm-Logan Motor Car Company at 500 Lehman Avenue, Daybrook manufactured hydraulic cylinders for truck equipment. During World War II, the company manufactured steel treadway bridge builders, or "monster trucks," with hydraulic cranes, which were used to position military pontoon bridges by the Army. The plant was awarded the Army-Navy E Award in 1945 for production excellence.

Two

AIRPORT, K-RATIONS, AND POSTWAR EXPANSION

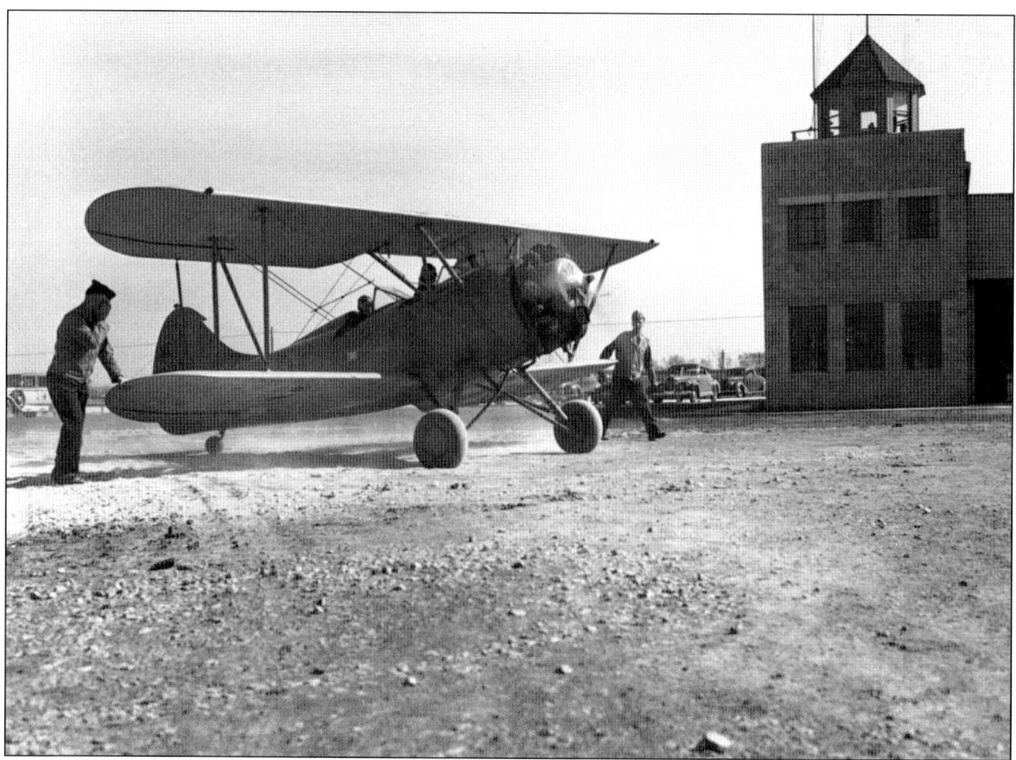

The entrance of the United States into World War II adversely affected Bowling Green State University. Shrinking enrollments from young men being called to serve their country and the ensuing revenue reduction created a challenge. Securing the V-5 and V-12 naval training programs provided a solution. Land for an airport was purchased by the university, and an abandoned hangar was transferred to the site. The programs were discontinued in 1945. The wartime prosperity of town and gown continued after the war with the influx of veterans who took advantage of the GI Bill's educational benefits.

The Electrical Dealers of Bowling Green

And

The Ohio Northern Public Service Co.

Present

'Alice In Electric Wonderland'

With a Cast of Bowling Green State University Players

Thursday, Dec. 19   **8:15 P.M.**

Senior High School Auditorium

CAST

Alice	Mary Lou Shelton
Rabbit	Lois Mayfield
Queen of Hearts	Eulalah Moellman
Queen of Spades	Jean Anne Goodnight
Queen of Diamonds	Virginia Zeigler
Queen of Clubs	Marian Andrews
Mrs. Everywoman	Elizabeth Hamlin
Home Economist	Mary Neighbor

STAGED BY UPTON PALMER
EDWARD CHRISTIAN, Assistant Director
HILDRETH SLATER, Stage Manager

Gifts of Electric Appliances Courtesy of the following
Bowling Green Electrical Dealers

BILL'S HOME APPLIANCE SHOP
W. J. GILLESPIE
LION STORE
RAPPAPORT'S
WIGGINS SUPPLY CO.

Food Used in Demonstration Courtesy of
ENGLISH FOOD MARKET

The Northeastern Public Service Corporation of New York was a public utilities–management company for electricity and water. Its Western Division district office was located at 109 South Main Street. Bowling Green was the largest electric and water company in the district. The company sponsored cooking demonstrations promoting the use of electric appliances, and in Bowling Green, the demonstrations were held in the Cla-Zel Theatre and the high school auditorium. A unique way of promoting the use of electric appliances was the presentation of a play, *Alice in Electric Wonderland*, starring a cast of Bowling Green State University students. The play was presented locally and in Brookville, Indiana.

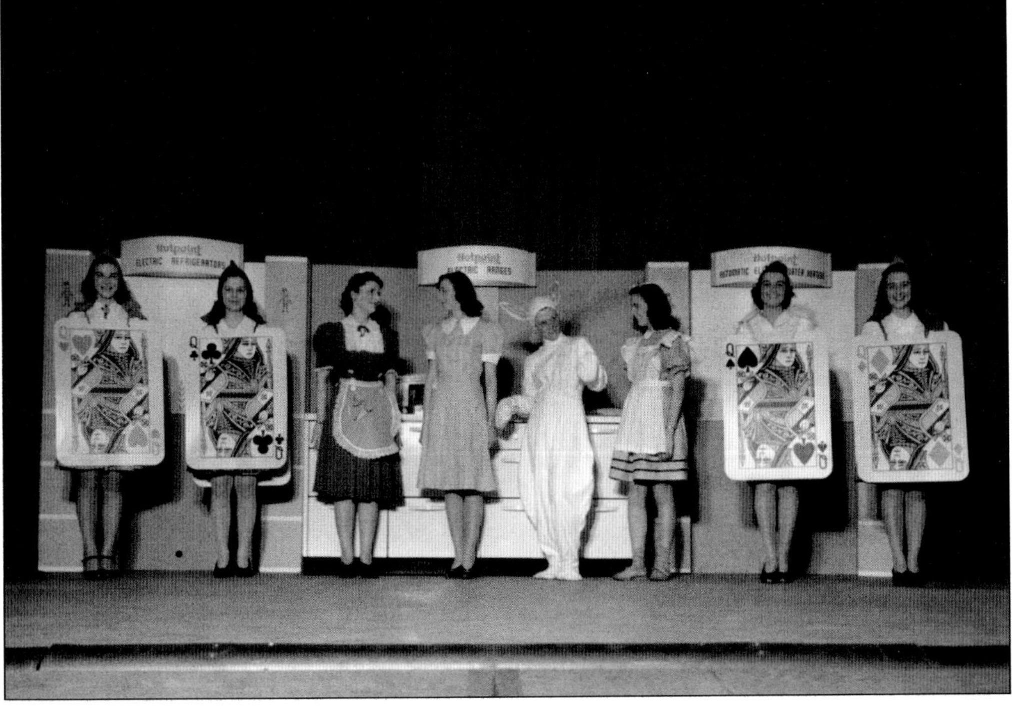

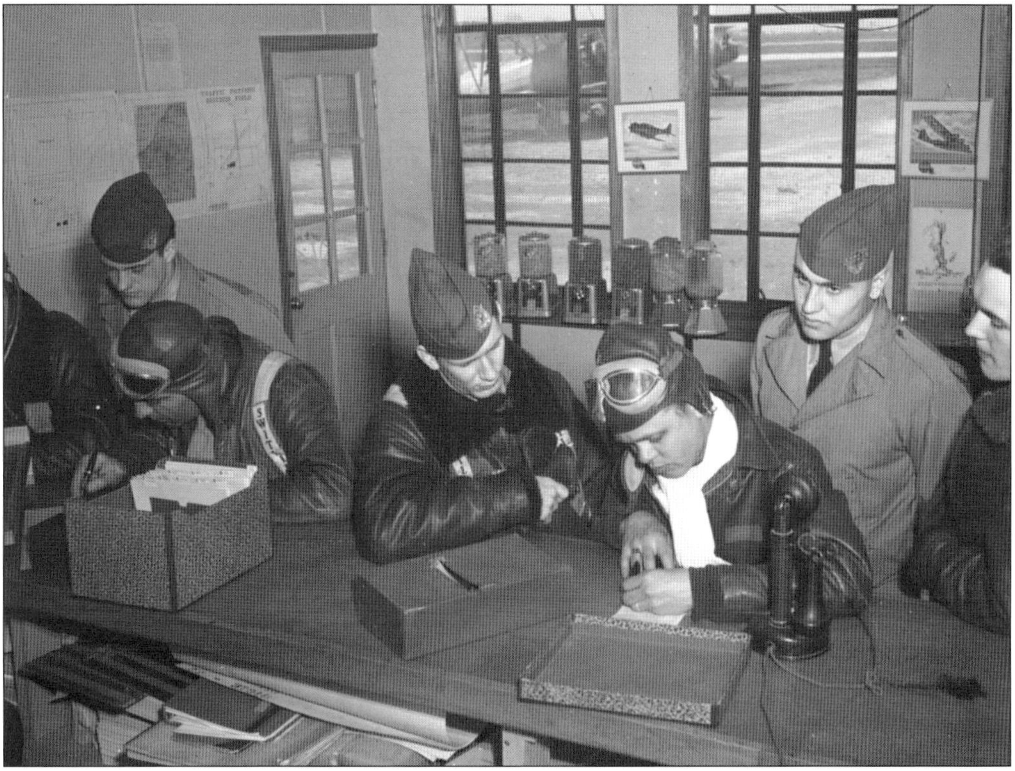

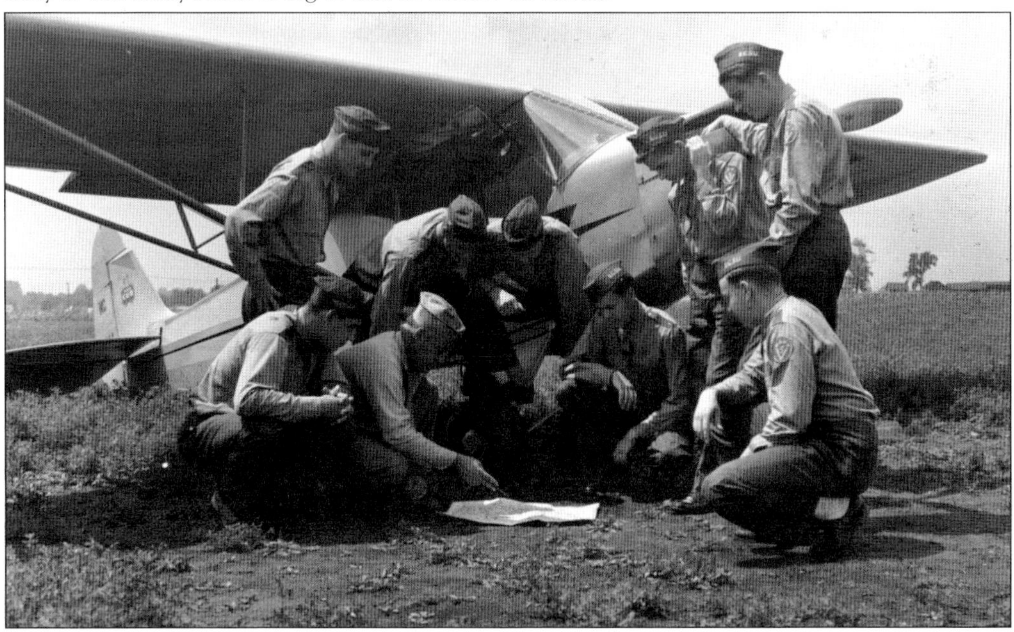

Bowling Green was selected as a site for the Civilian Pilot Training Program in 1939. Sponsored by the Civilian Aeronautics Authority, the program was administered by a faculty member. Flight training was given in nearby Findlay. The program was replaced by the Navy's V-5 program. The first group of V-5 cadets to be trained was instructed by Bucky Swander, and the cadets reported daily to the ready room to log in and to receive direction.

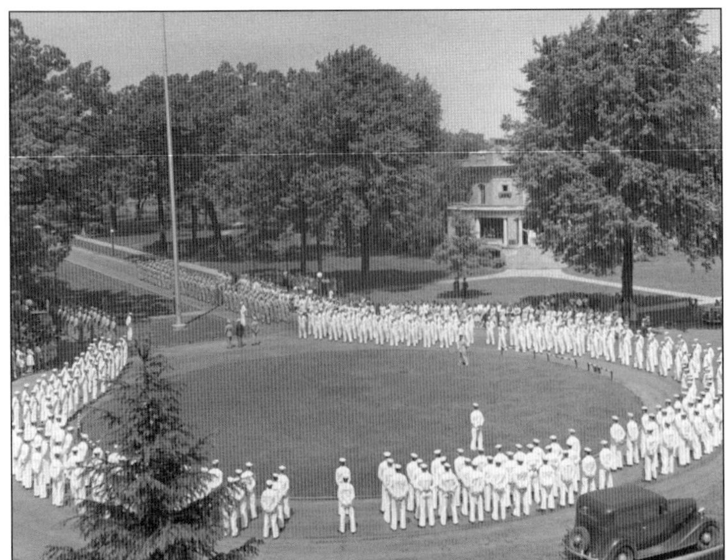

The drills, precision marches, formations, reviews, and daily flag ceremonies by V-5 or V-12 cadets were a common sight from 1942 until 1945. Dress uniforms were required during formal reviews.

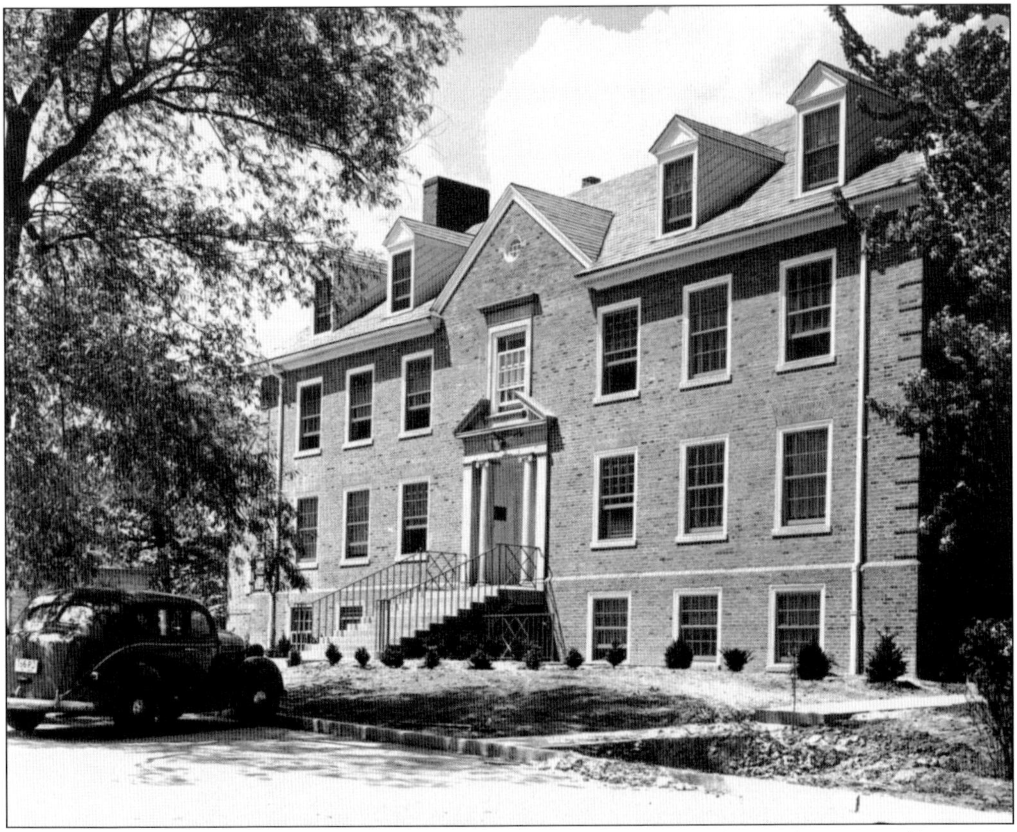

The first student health center, Johnston Health Services Building, later Johnston Hall, was the only building constructed between 1939 and 1945. Completed in 1942 to support the V-5 and V-12 programs, it housed a 36-bed hospital and provided care for students. Limited services were provided to Bowling Green residents. A cerebral palsy center, named Happy Hall, was added to the building in 1950. A child-development center was later housed in the space.

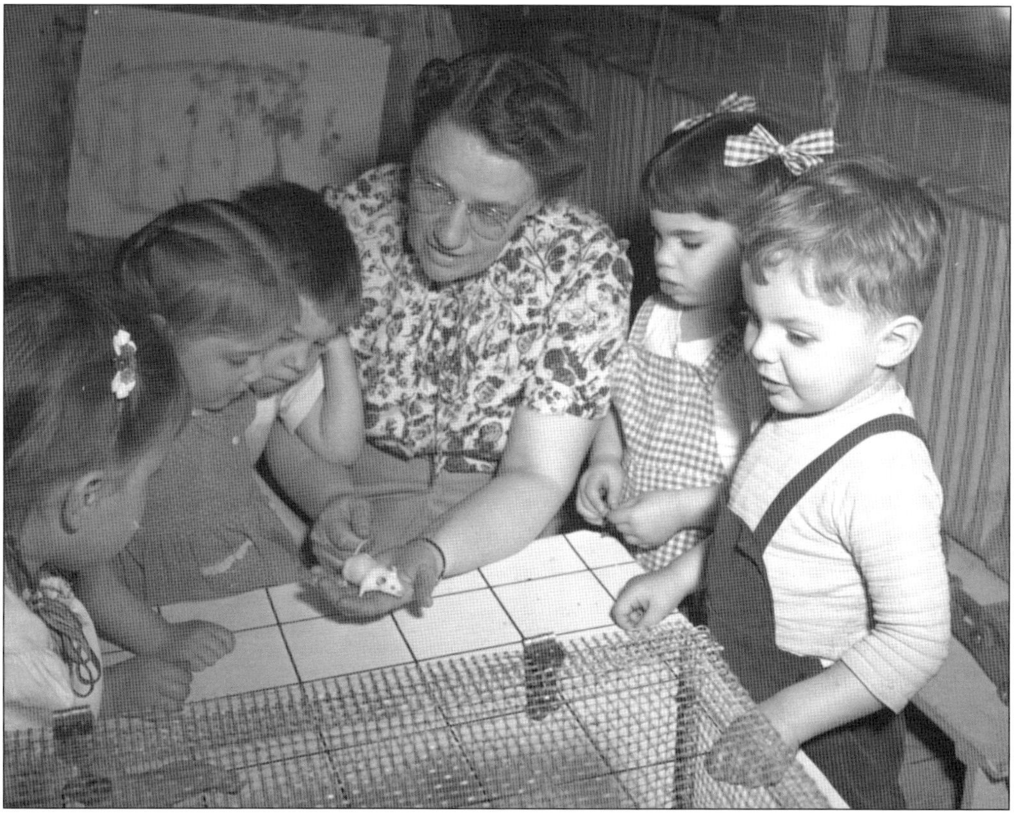

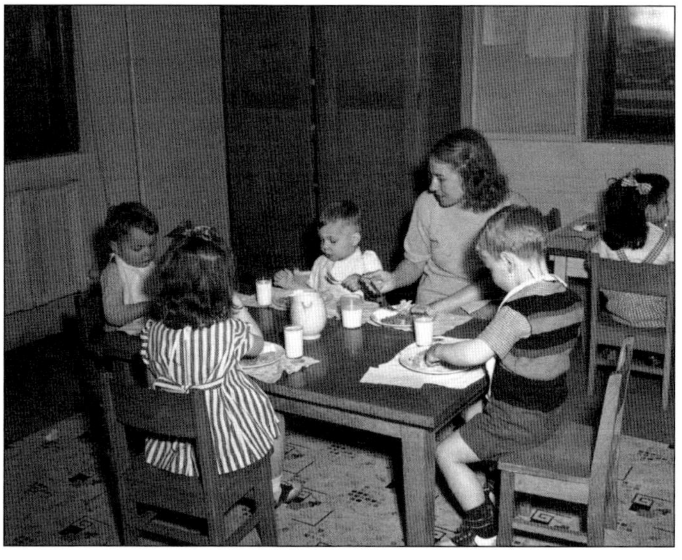

The first local nursery school was opened by the manual-training school in the summer of 1942 to care for the children of local working mothers. Financed under the federal Lanham Act, the school provided educational and recreational activities for children ranging in ages from two to six. It was open from 6:00 a.m. until 5:30 p.m. six days a week. Field trips to the city park and other local sites were taken, and a nutritious lunch was provided for the children. The extended school service provided the same types of programs for older children up to 12 years.

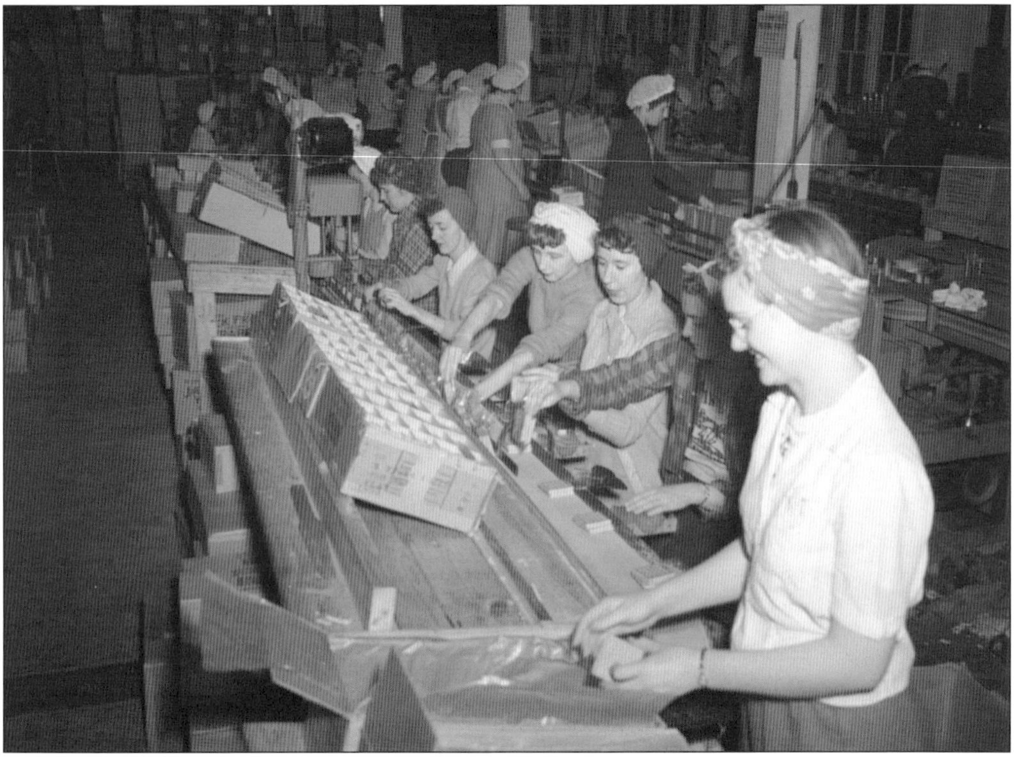

The local H.J. Heinz Company plant was opened in 1914 and closed in 1975. Both community members and BGSU students were employed by the company. During World War II, coeds and local citizens worked together to help the war effort by assembling and packaging K-rations, or care packages, for the troops. In 1944, German and Italian prisoners of war were transported daily from Camp Perry to work in the plant, and the company built a camp to house some of the prisoners of war. A fire destroyed the plant in 1980. A student housing village, the Heinz-site Apartments, has been constructed on the site.

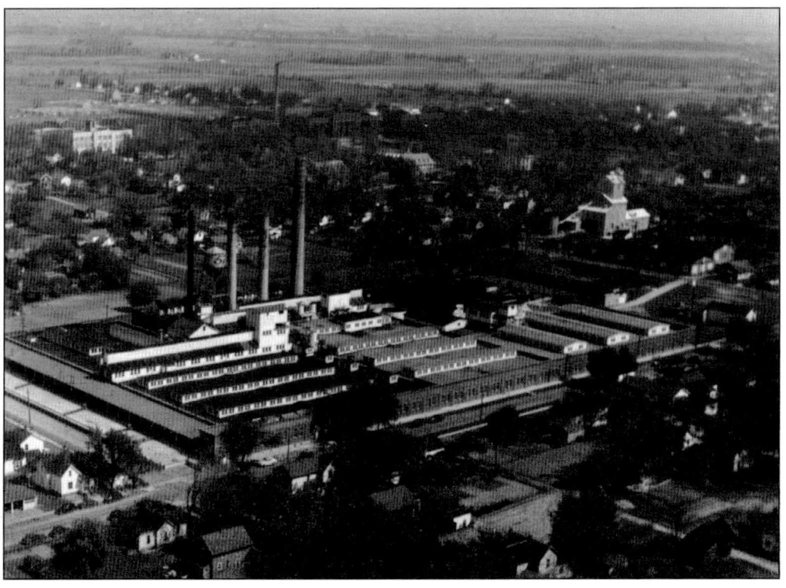

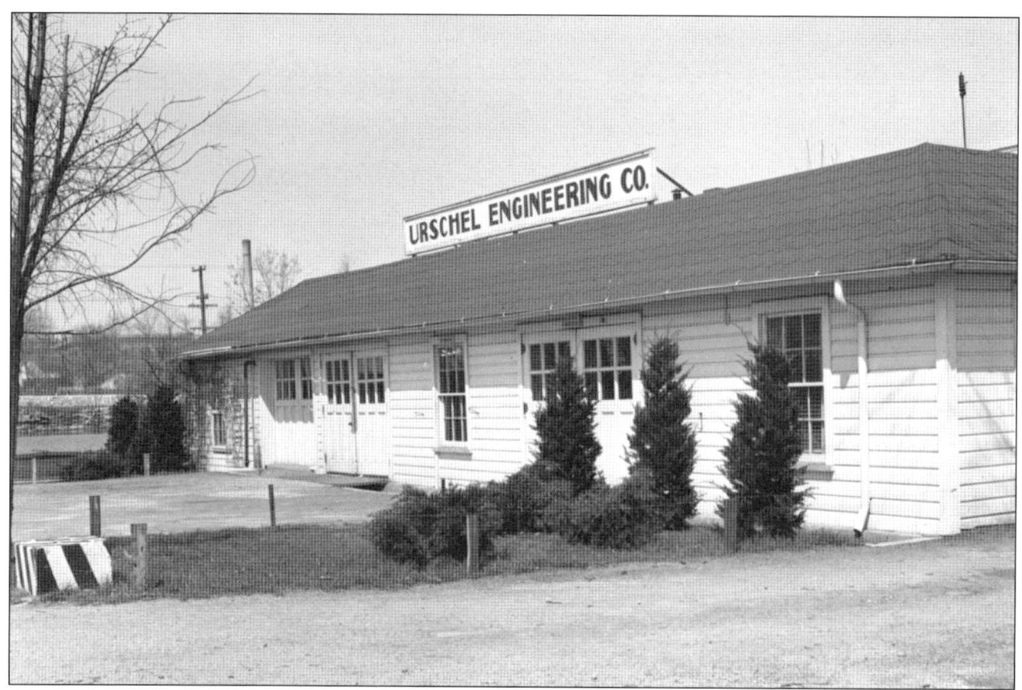

Urschel Engineering, formerly Urschel Machine Company and Urschel Drop Forge Company, was founded by Bertis H. and Jacob W. Urschel in 1914. During World War II, the company fabricated parts for British and US military equipment. The Urschels held a patent for a special universal joint.

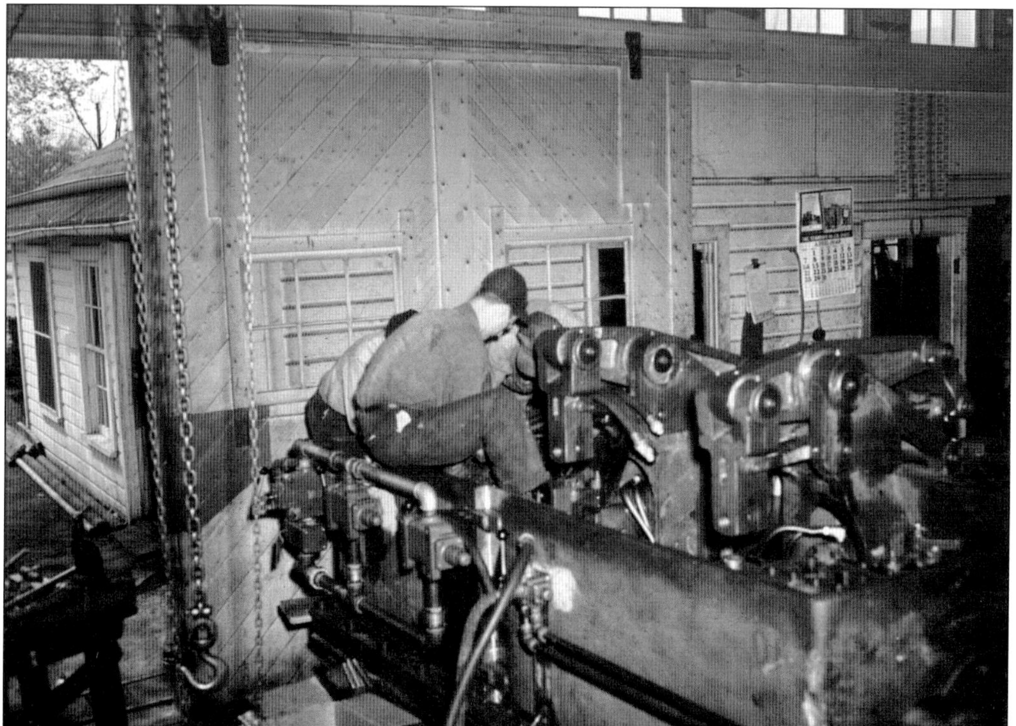

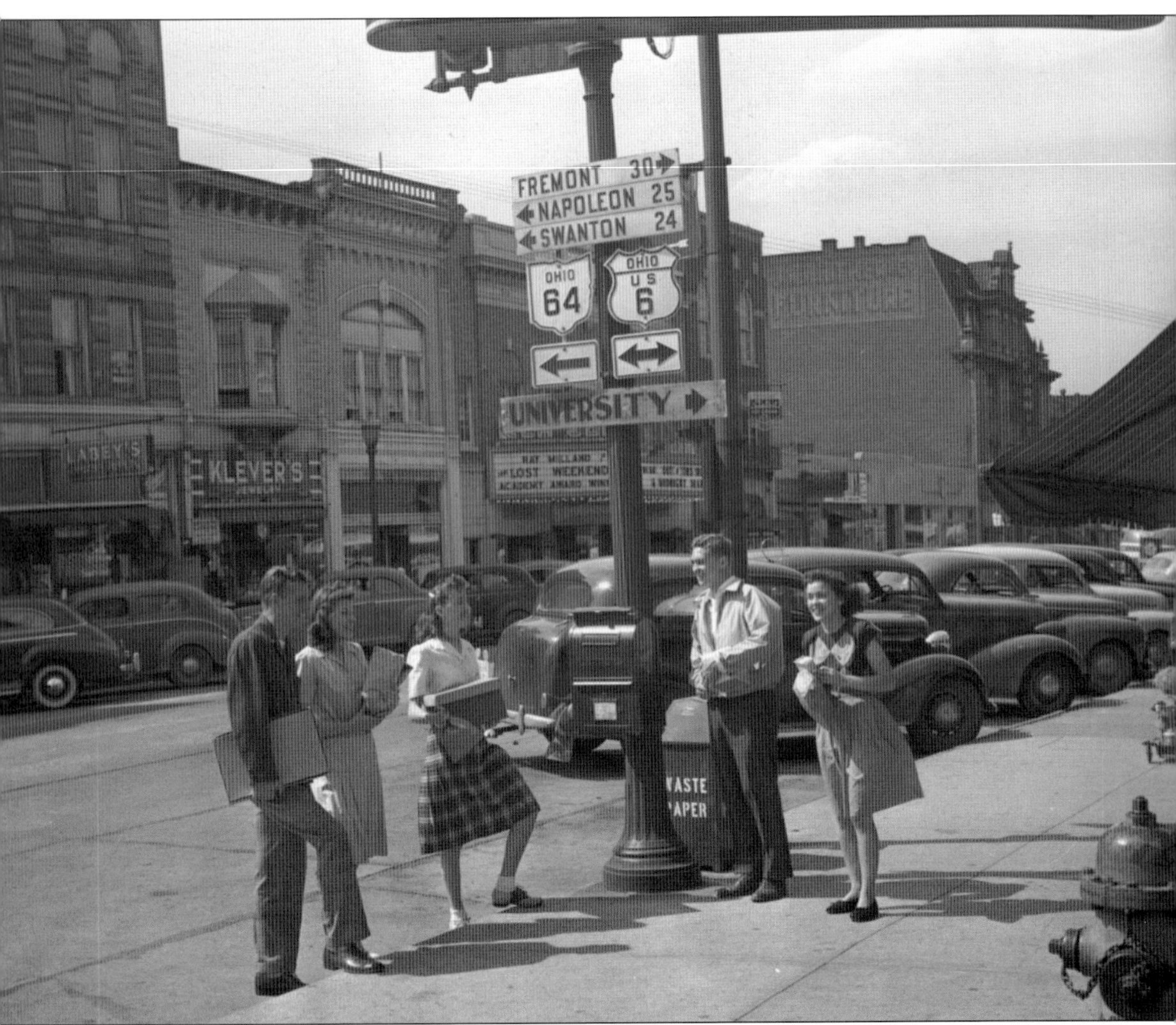

The corner of Main and Wooster Streets (the four corners) has always been congested with shoppers. This photograph, which was taken in front of Lloyd Walgreen Agency (Centre Drugs) at 102 North Main Street, features a group of BGSU students.

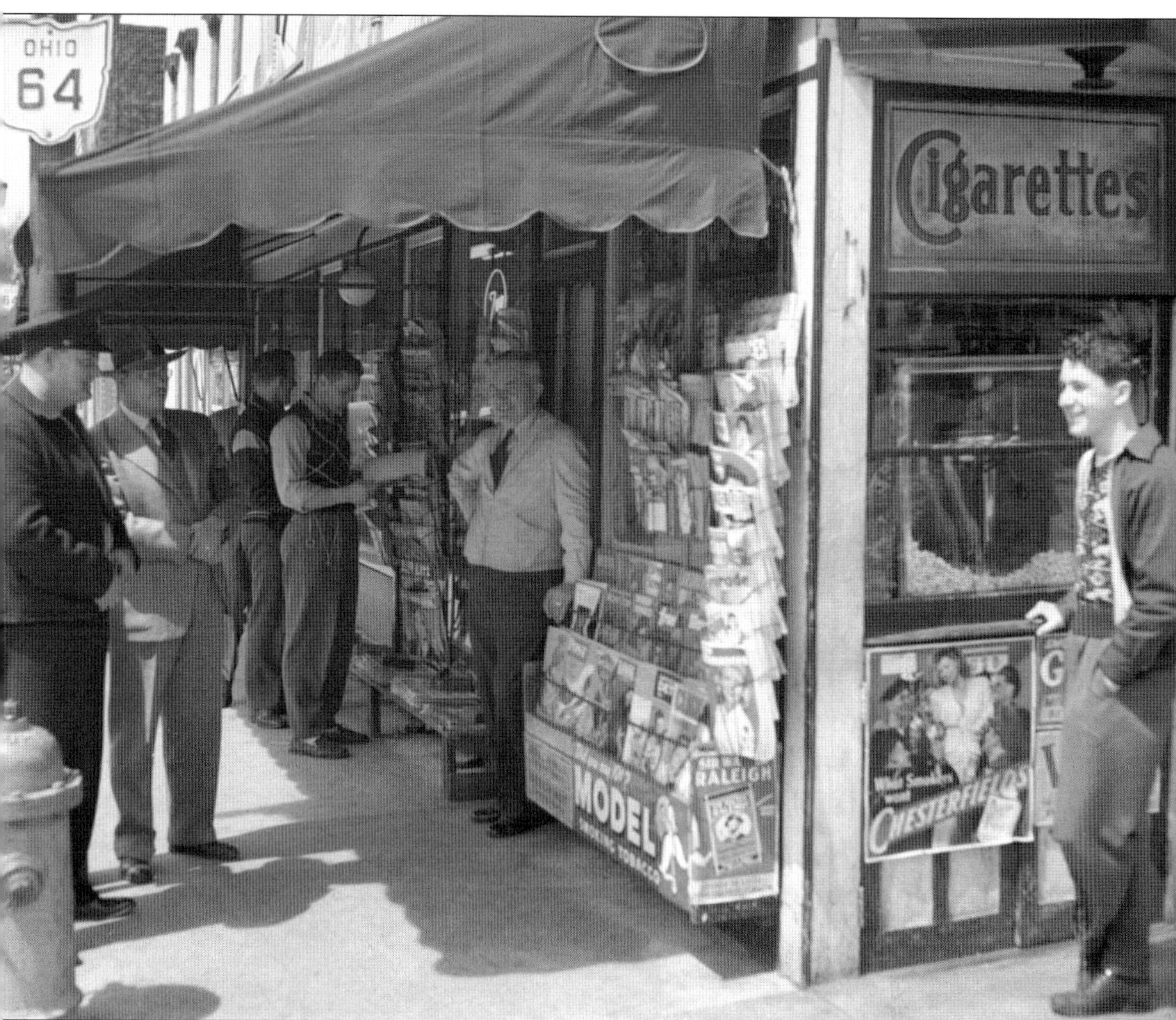

Cook's News Stand was located at the 100 West Wooster at the corner of North Main Street. A popular hangout, residents and student gathered there to browse an array of comic books, magazines, and newspapers. Beverages, snacks, and tobacco products were also sold. The newsstand later moved to 111 East Wooster Street and served as the Greyhound passenger station.

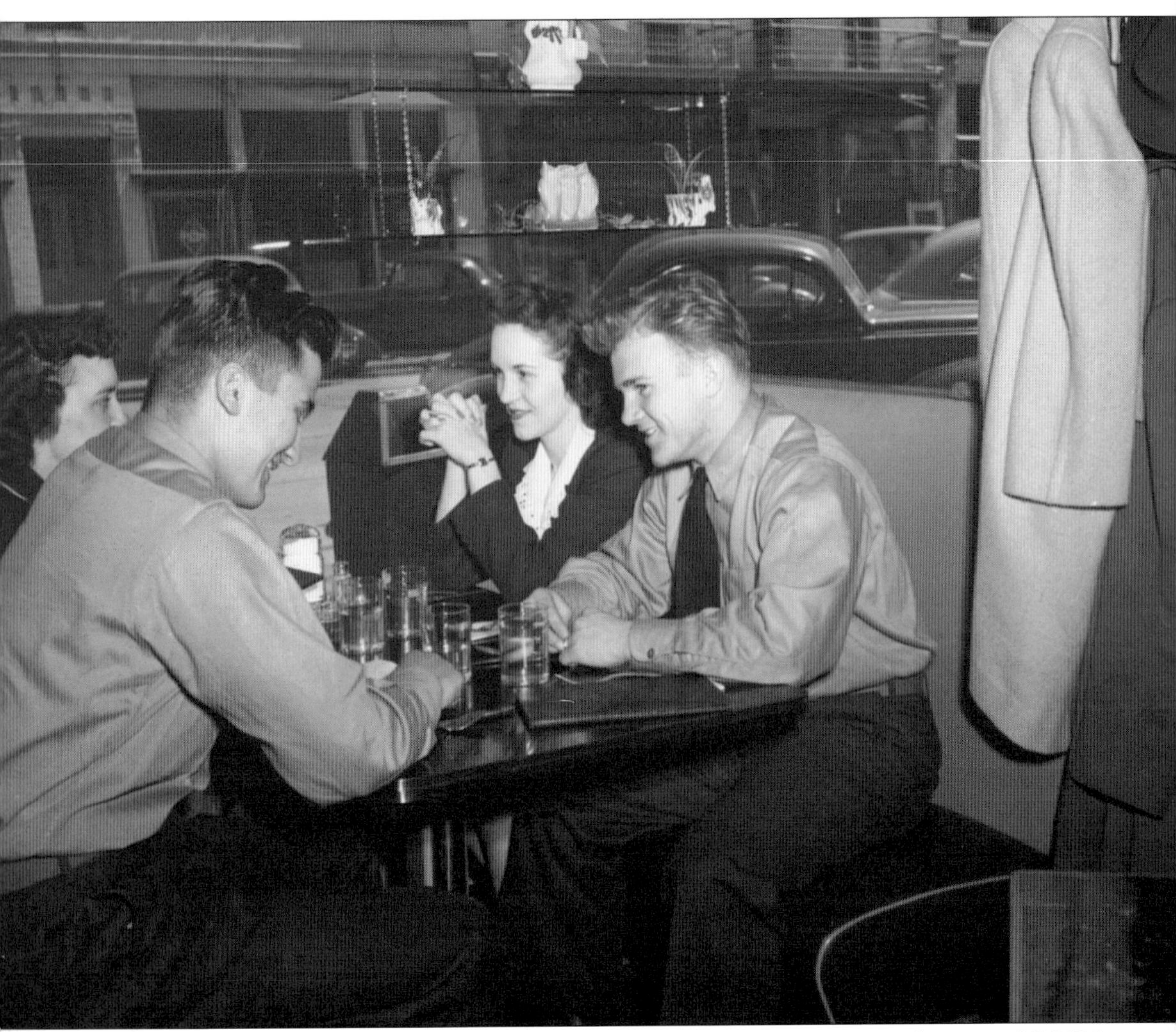

Muir's Restaurant at 163 North Main Street was one of the many restaurants that served BGSU students. The site was later the home of Main Restaurant and the Bowling Green Chamber of Commerce and the Private Industry Council.

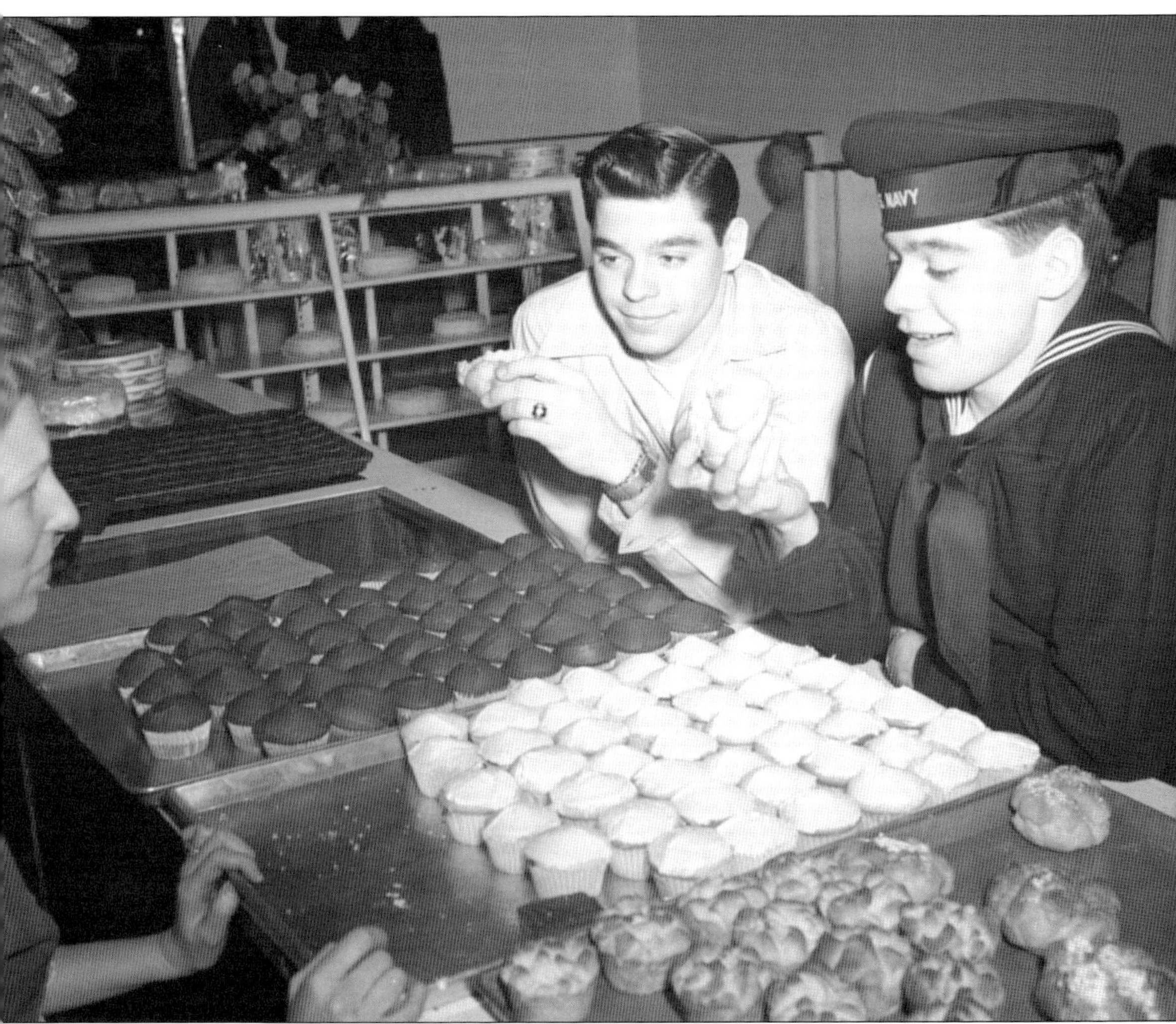

The Ross Bakery was located at 203 North Main Street in the McKenzie-Kabig Building. The bakery featured a variety of homemade bread, rolls, cakes, pies, cupcakes, and cookies. Pisanello's Pizza is currently located at this address. The upper rooms were once the home of the Shakespeare Roundtable Library.

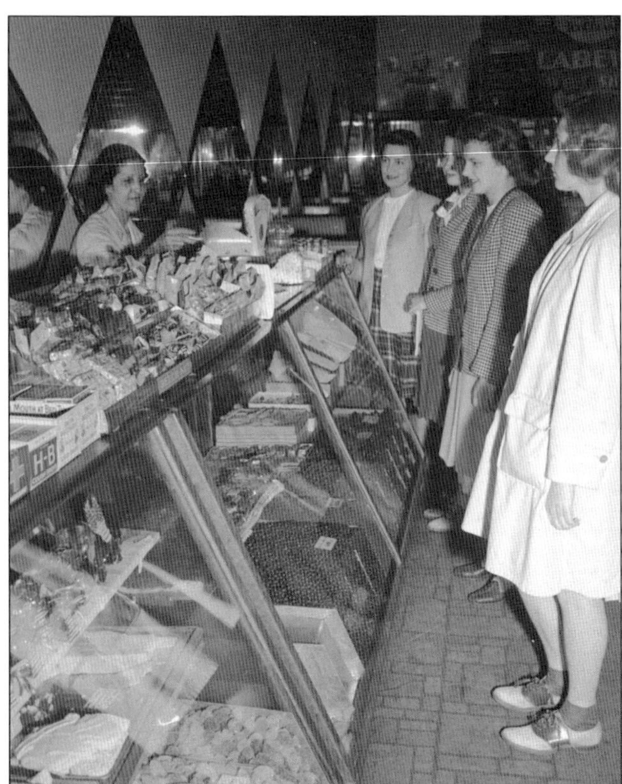

Labey's Confectionery was located at 117 North Main Street. Don & Helen's Cafeteria, Petit's Pizzeria Restaurant, and Petit's Alpine Restaurant later occupied the site.

Isaly's Dairy (or Isaly's Falcon Dairy Store), home of the giant ice-cream cone, was located at 104 South Main Street. In addition to frozen treats, the store sold dairy products and deli meats, especially their famous chopped ham. Easy Street Café is now located at this site.

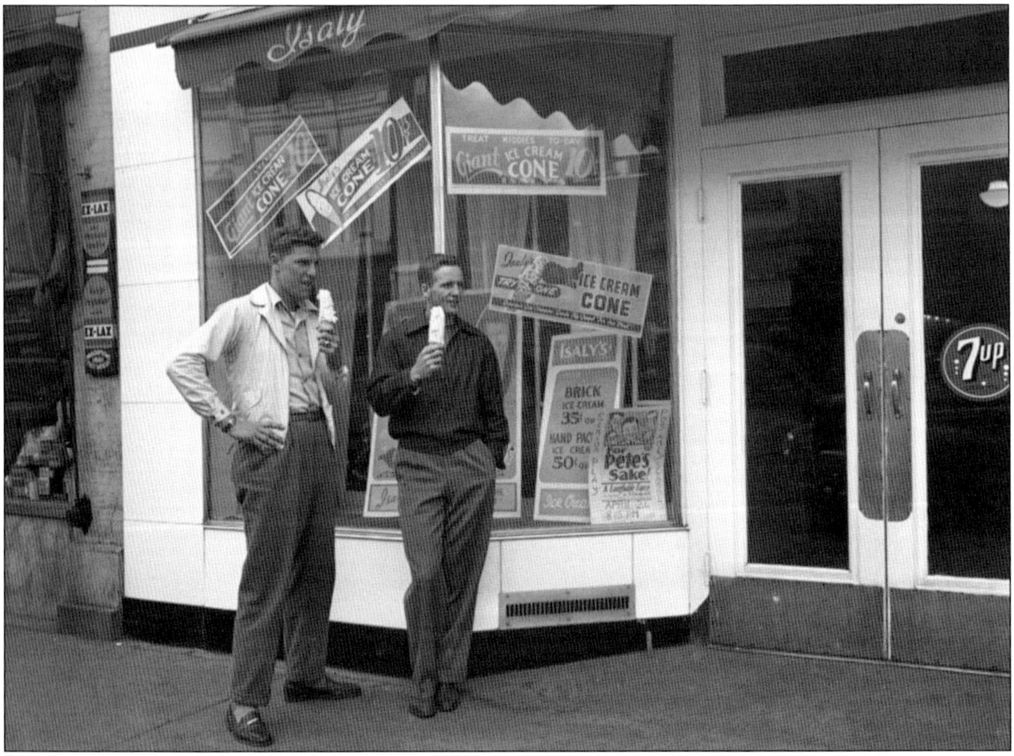

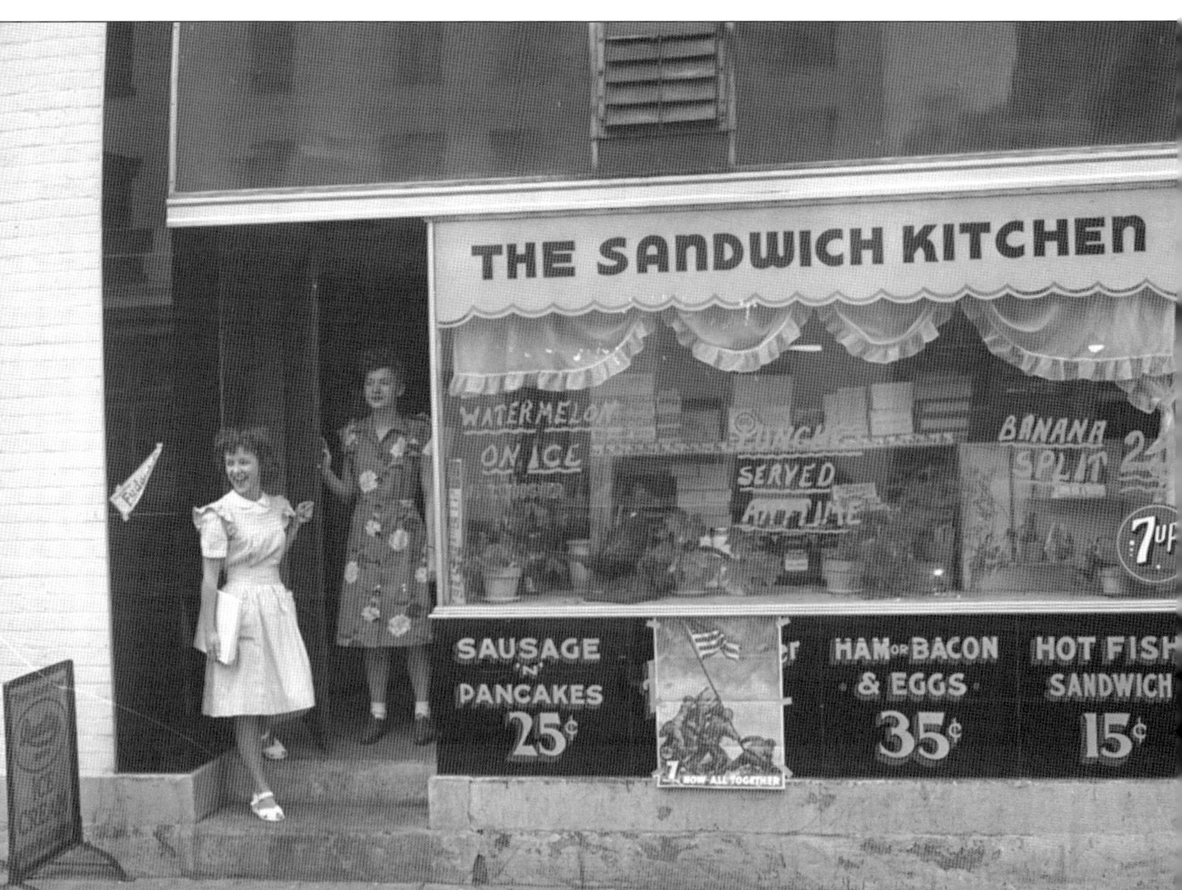

The Sandwich Kitchen was located at 115 West Wooster Street. B.B.Q. Lunch, the Coffee Shop, and Burch's Hat Shop were located at the site. The entrance was later bricked up and incorporated into the building at 100 South Main Street.

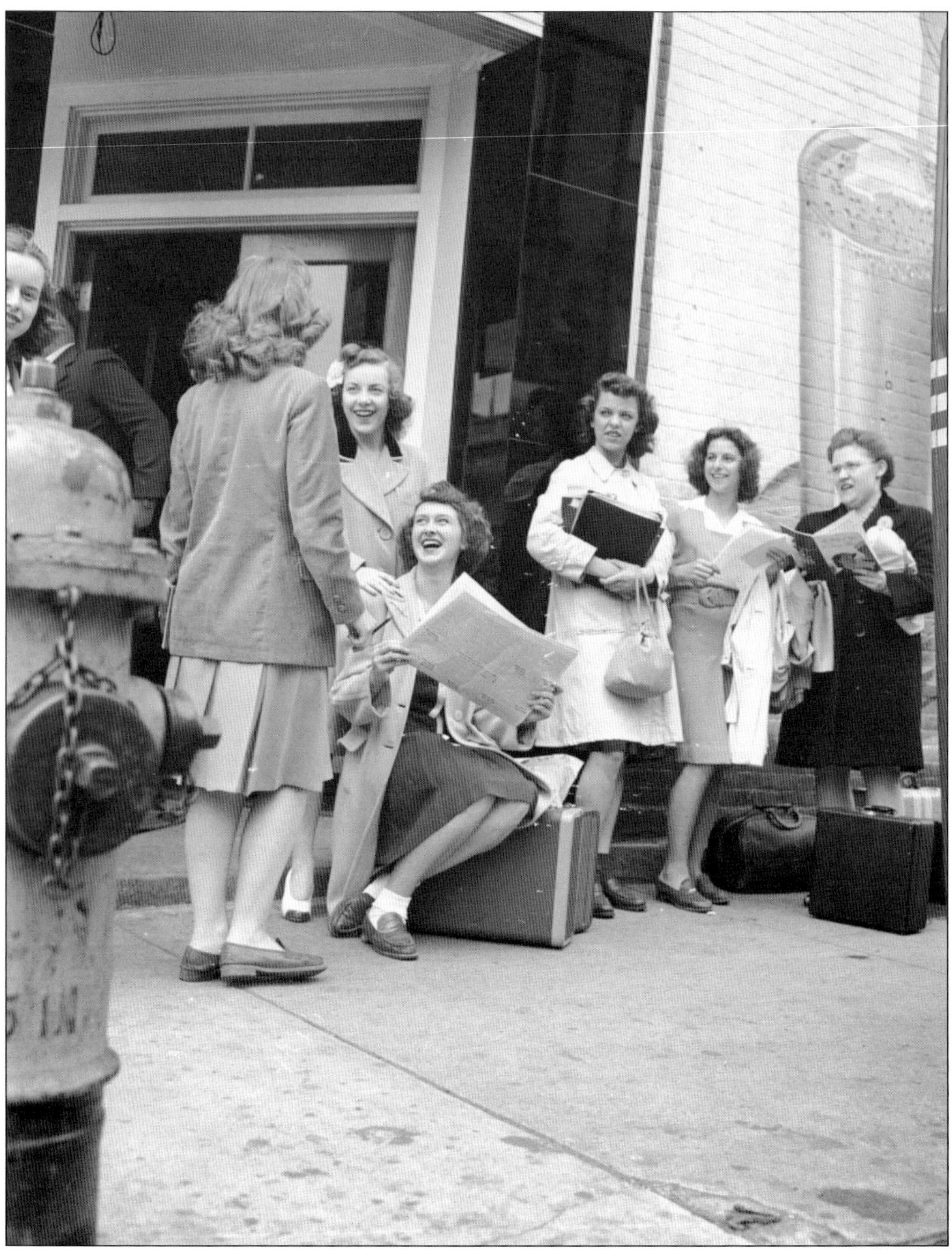

The Greyhound passenger station in Bowling Green was originally located at 111 East Wooster Street at Cook's News Stand, near the corner of North Main Street. Greyhound provided affordable reliable transportation for BGSU students, local residents, and visitors. Service to Bowling Green was discontinued in the late 1990s.

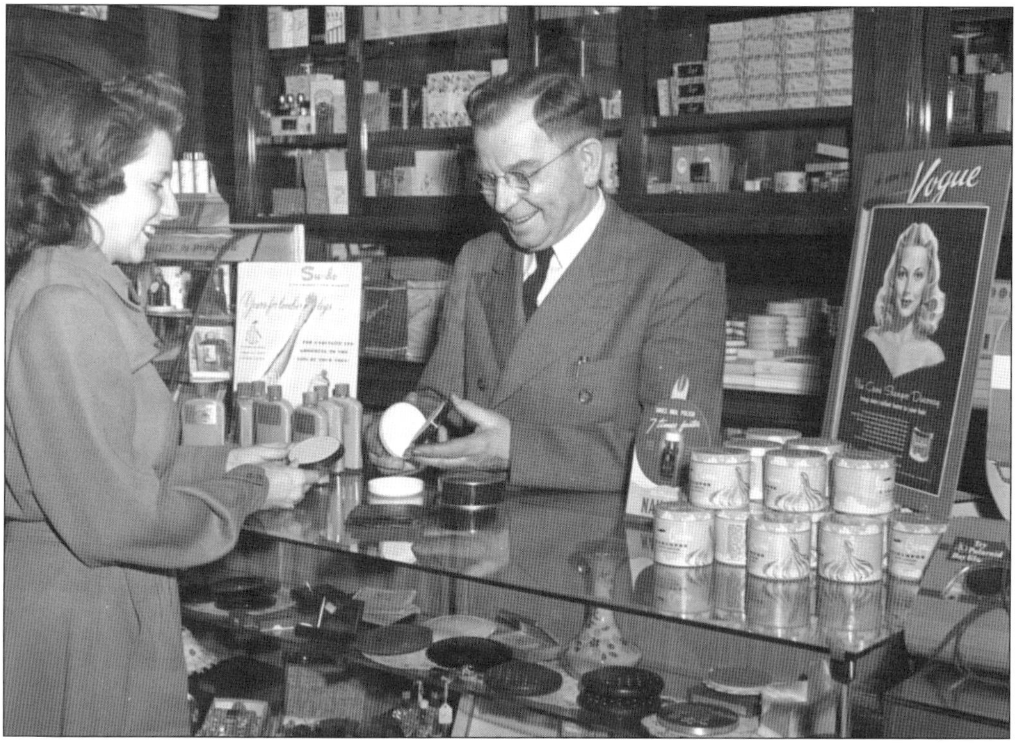

The first drugstore in Bowling Green, Roger's Brothers Drugs, was located at 135 North Main Street. Founded in 1864 as Rogers Drugs, the store carried general merchandise, toiletries, medicines, prescription drugs, and photography equipment. Rogers also featured a soda fountain.

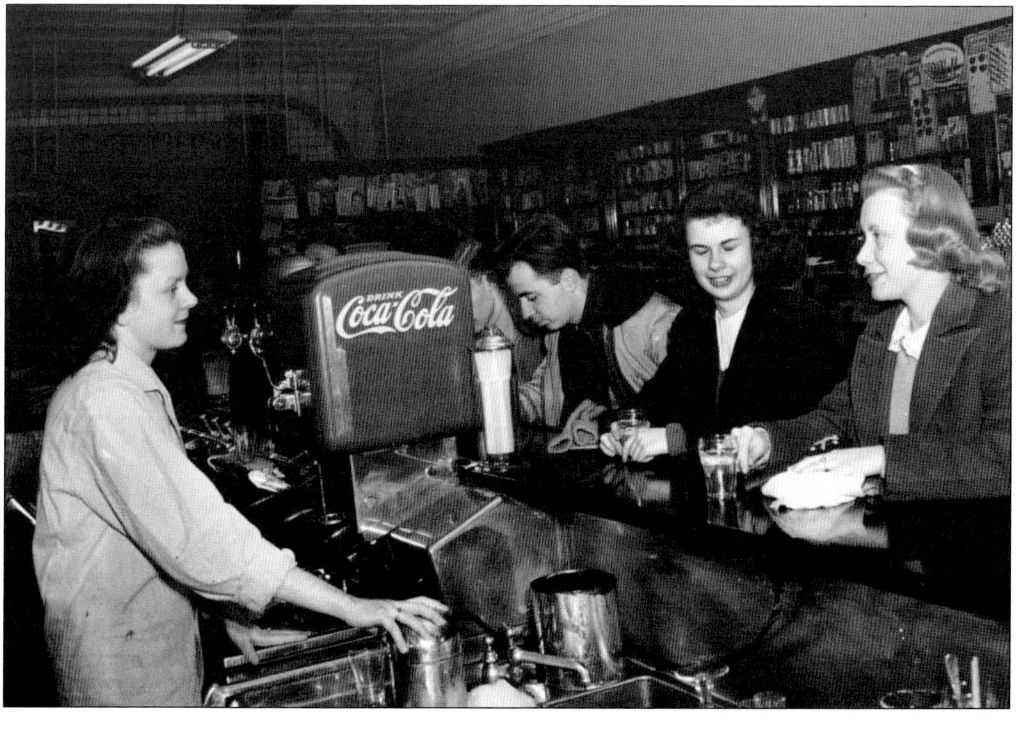

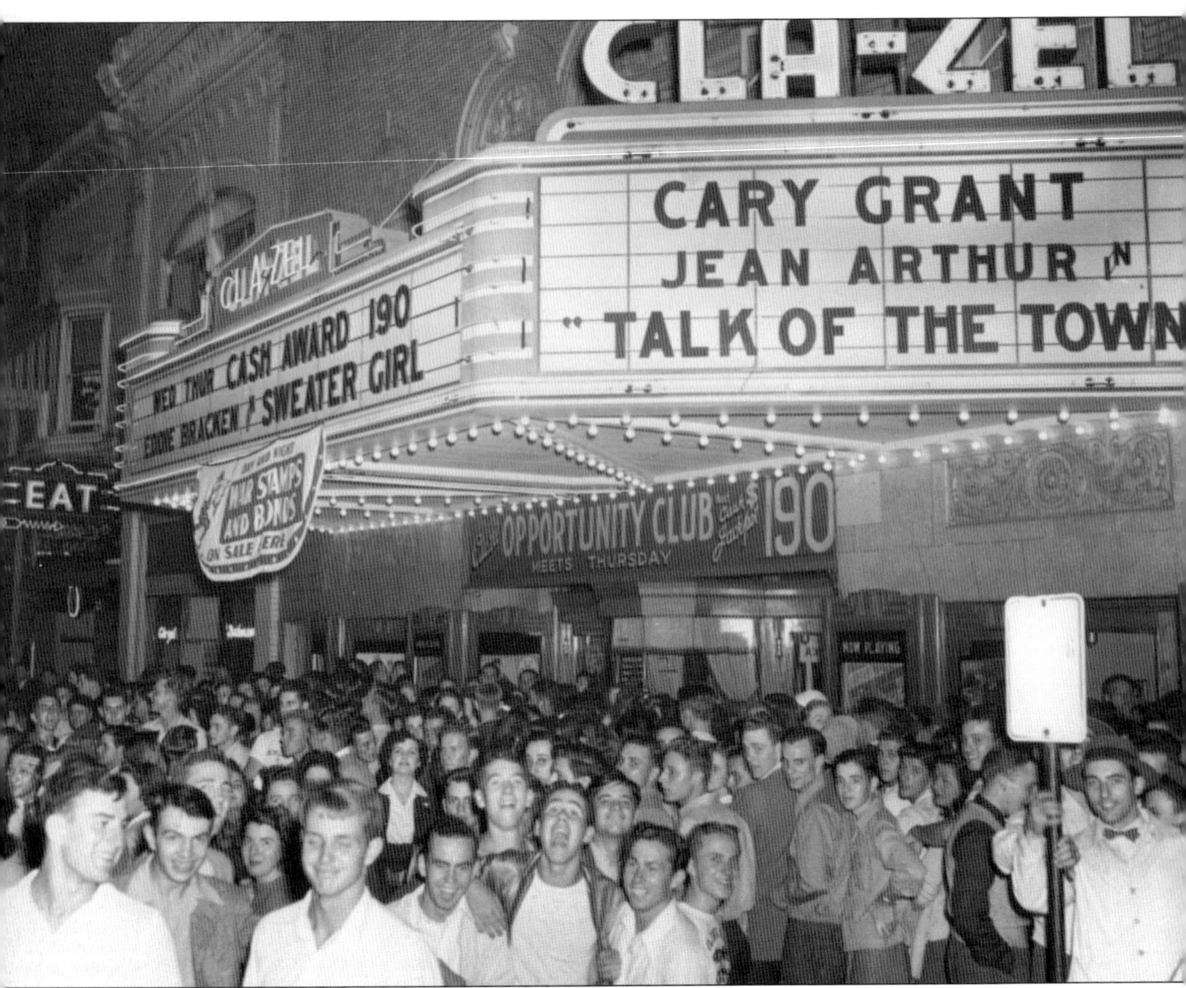

The Cla-Zel Theatre, located at 129–131 North Main Street, was built in 1926 by Clark and Hazel Young. The building has been restored and now serves as an entertainment venue. Featuring a spacious dance floor and two full-service bars, the Clazel Theatre can be booked for wedding receptions and other special events.

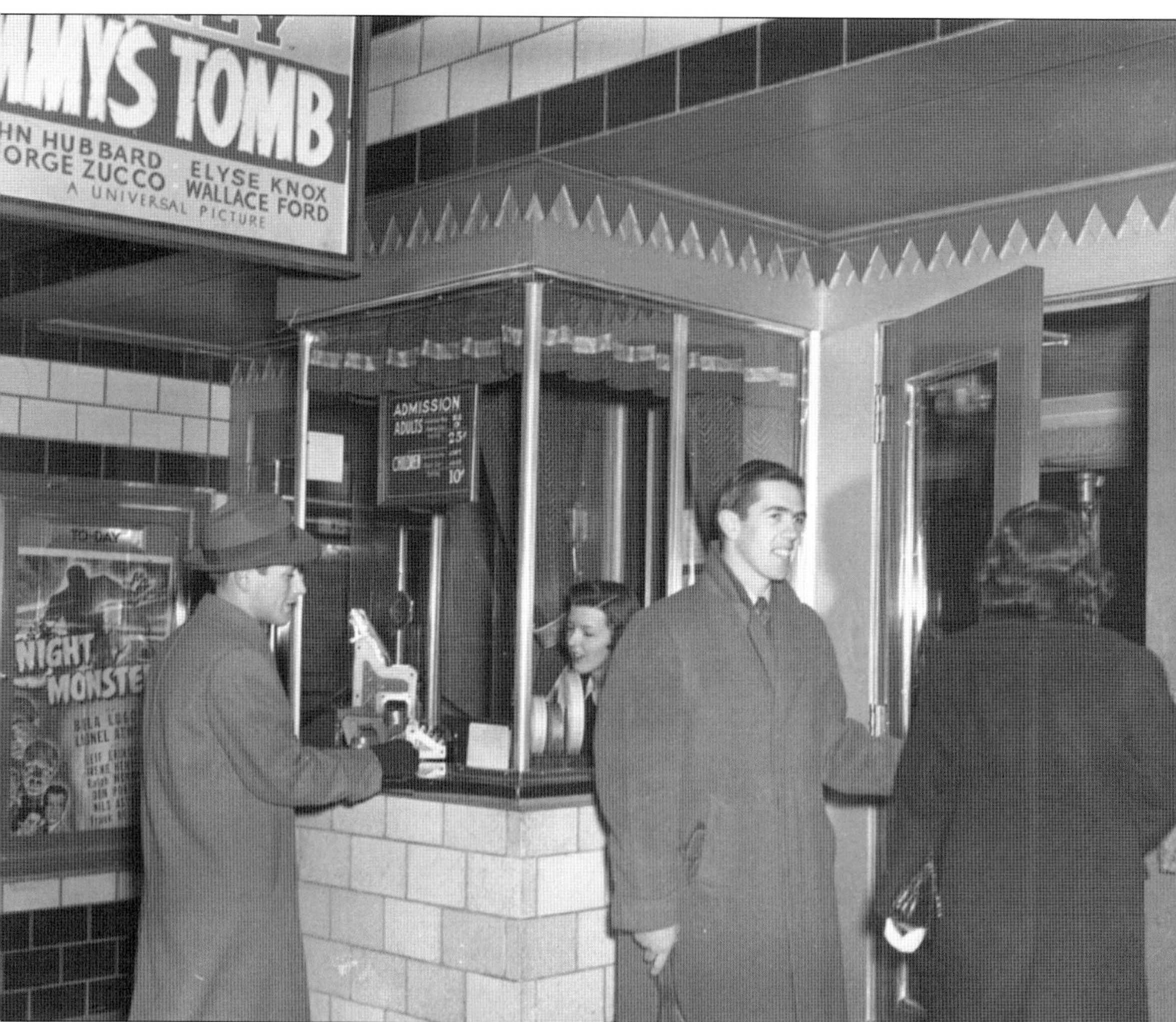

The new Lyric Theatre was located at 143 East Wooster Street and built in 1935 by Clark and Hazel Young. The Bowling Green Chamber of Commerce and Madhatter Music Company later occupied the site, which is now Insomnia Cookies.

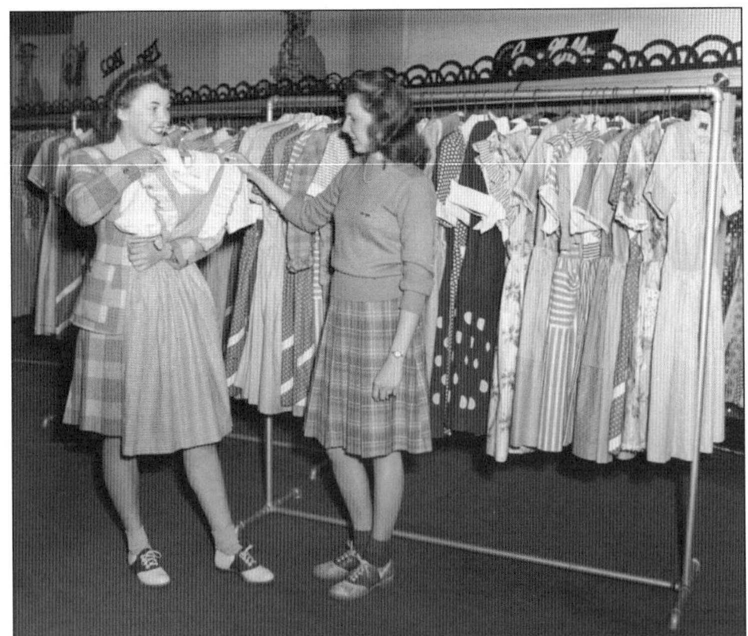

The A. Froney Company Department Store, founded as a dry-goods store in 1889 by Albert Froney, was originally located at located 139–145 South Main Street. The store later moved to 133 North Main Street and carried a full line of women's clothing.

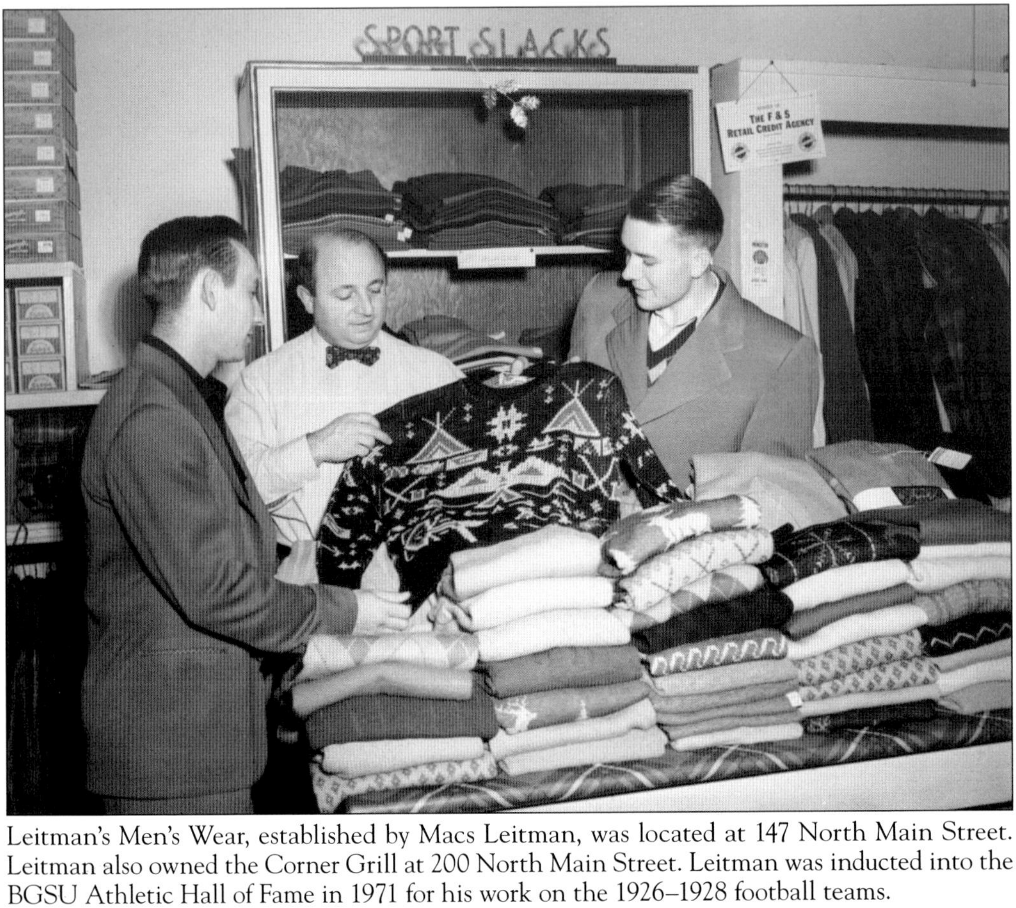

Leitman's Men's Wear, established by Macs Leitman, was located at 147 North Main Street. Leitman also owned the Corner Grill at 200 North Main Street. Leitman was inducted into the BGSU Athletic Hall of Fame in 1971 for his work on the 1926–1928 football teams.

O.S. Carr & Son Grocery was located at 428 East Wooster Street, formerly the site of John J. Maas Grocery. The Flowerhouse later occupied the site.

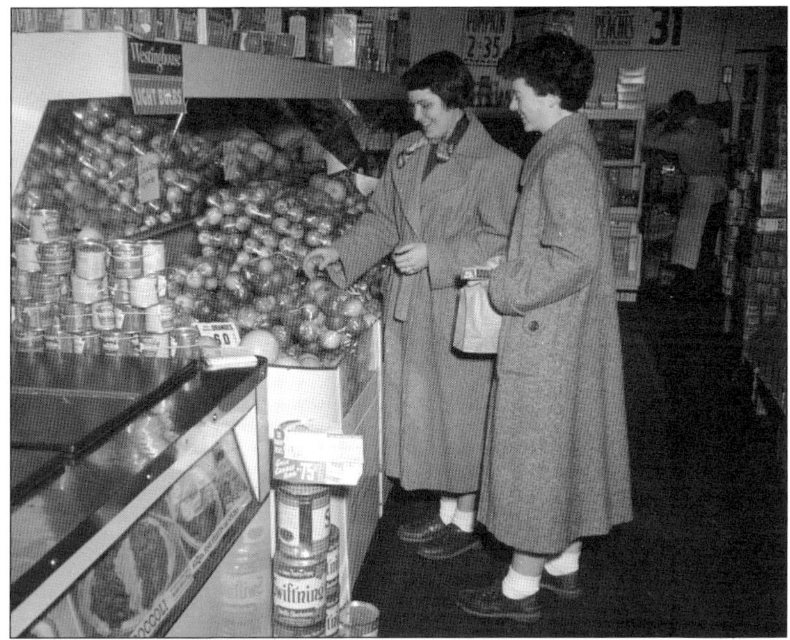

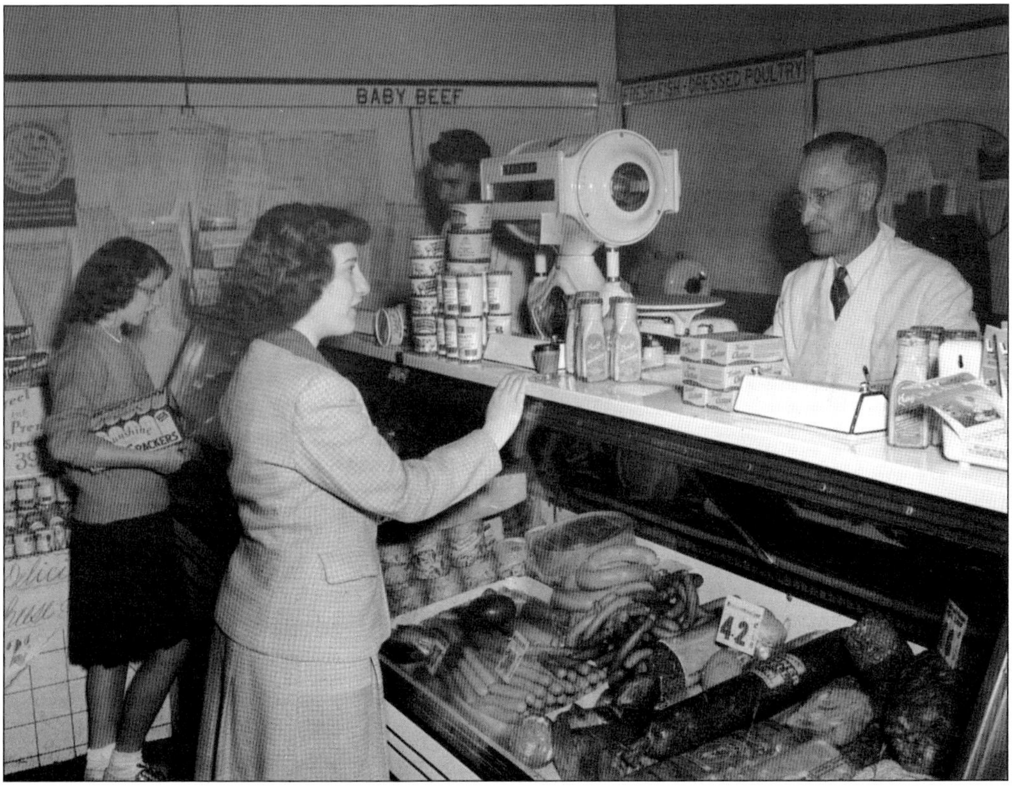

English Food Market was located 139–141 West Wooster Street. Established by Virgil R. English, the grocery was originally located at 104 South Main Street. Leimgruber's Floor Coverings & Electrical Appliances, A Cut Above Beauty Salon, and the Archive Company are among the businesses that later occupied this site.

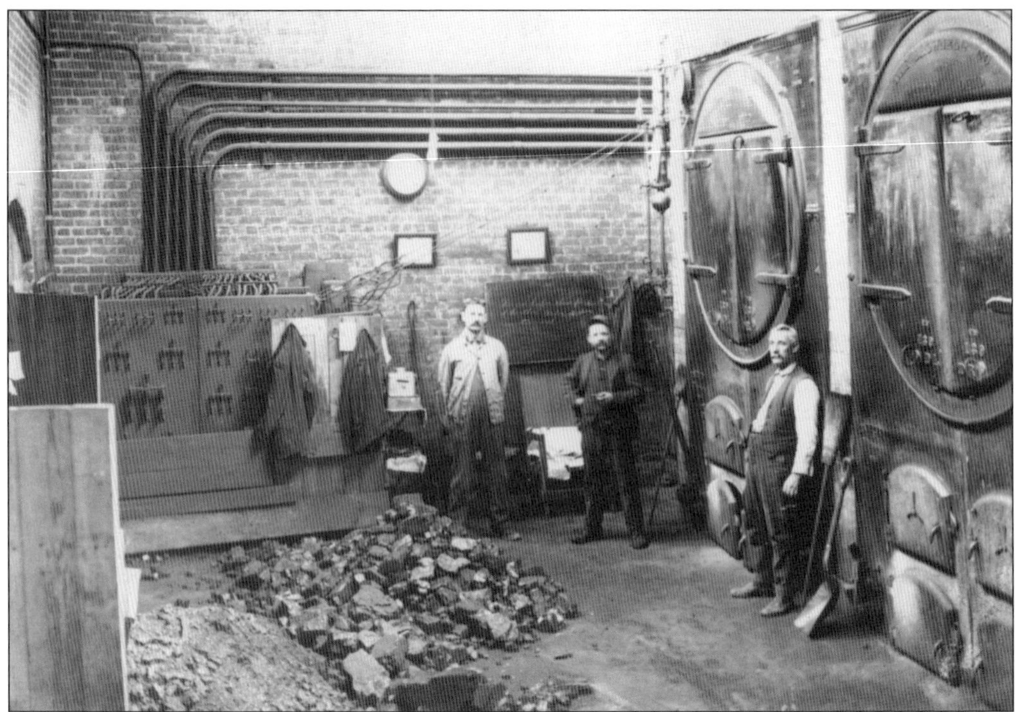

The university has provided employment for local residents in a variety of occupations, including carpenters, cashiers, cooks, custodians, electricians, groundskeepers, locksmiths, maintenance workers, mechanics, nurses, plumbers, police officers, secretaries, administrators, and faculty.

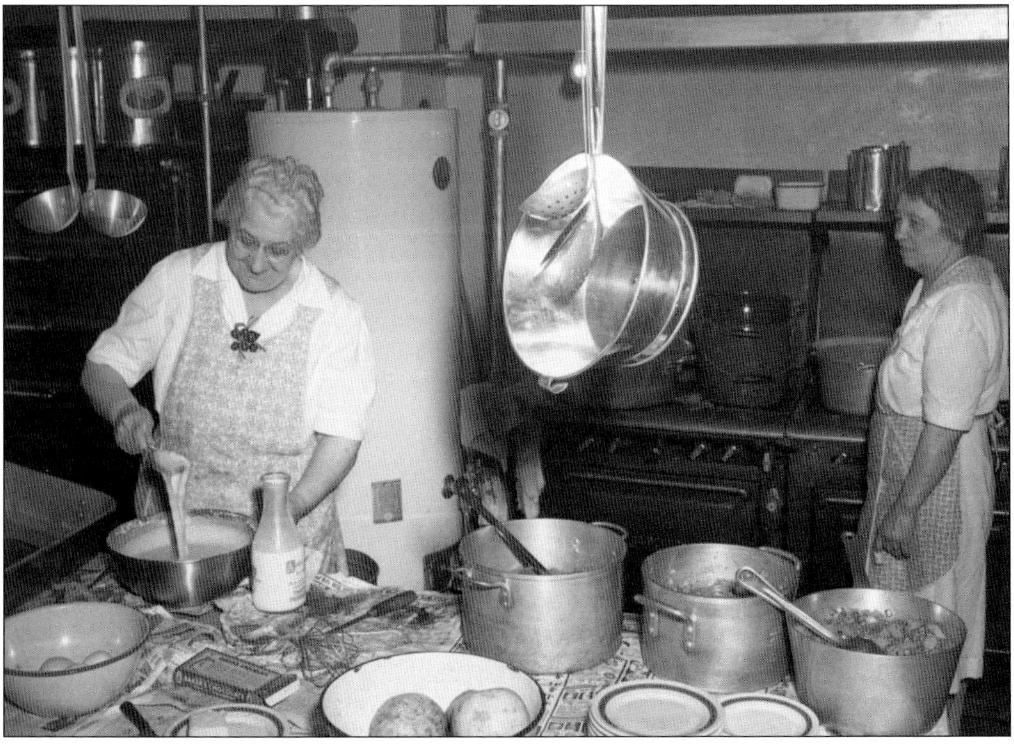

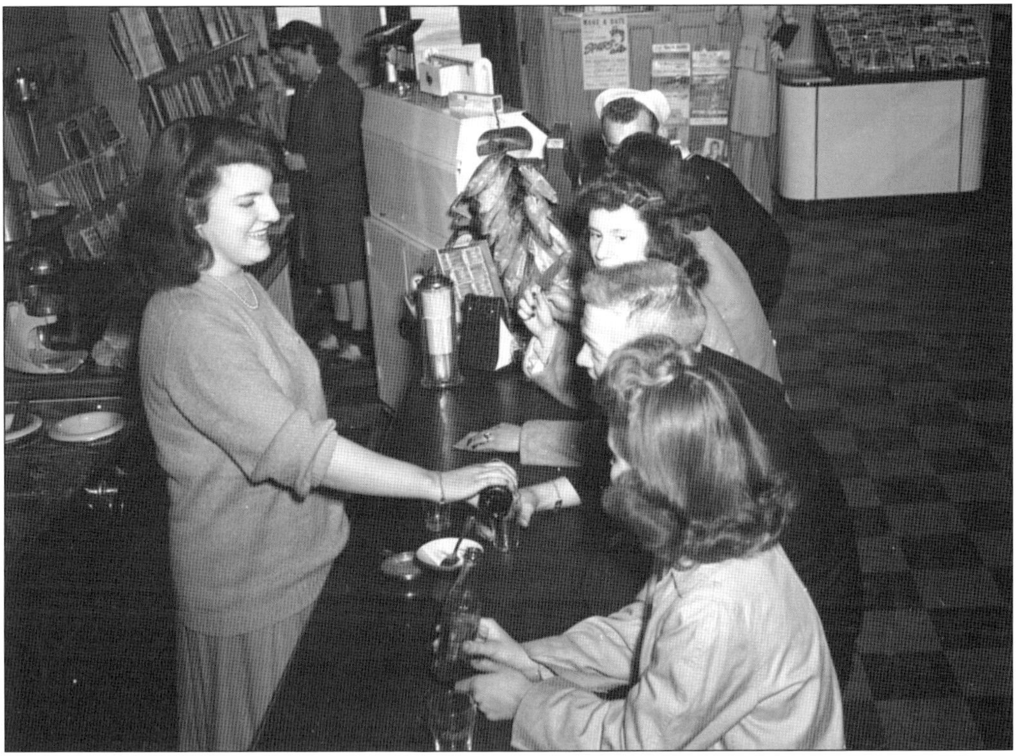

Centre Drug, formerly the Lloyd Walgreen Agency Drug and the Lincoln & Dirlam Drug Store, was located at 102 North Main Street. The store featured a snack counter and soda fountain. Cameras and photography equipment were sold in addition to prescription drugs and a variety of miscellaneous merchandise.

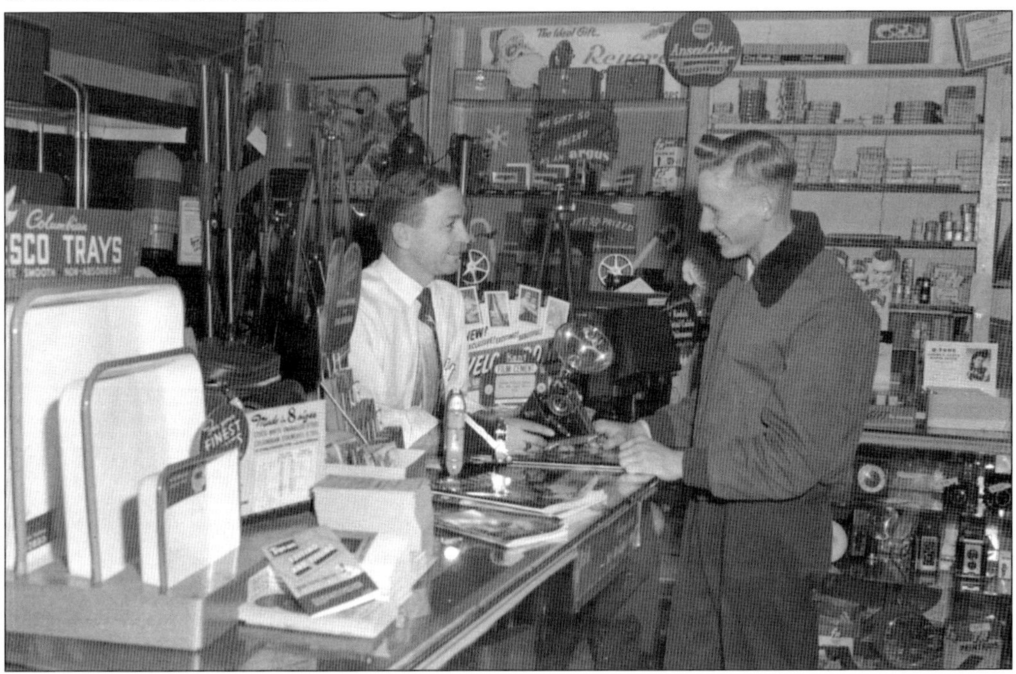

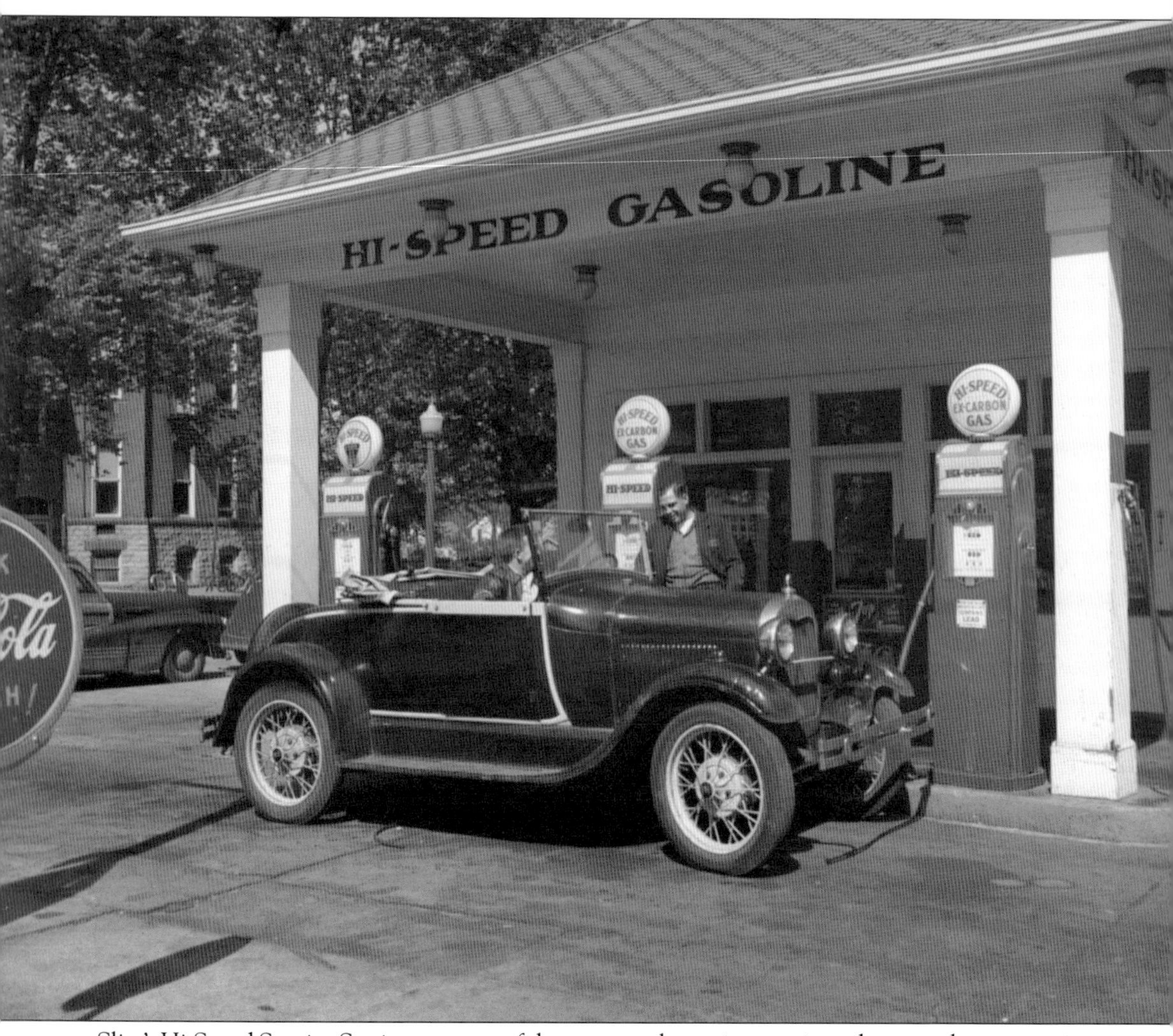

Slim's Hi-Speed Service Station was one of the many early services stations that met the automotive fuel and repair needs of Bowling Green residents and BGSU students. The station was located at 455 South Main Street. South Main Elementary School can be seen in the background.

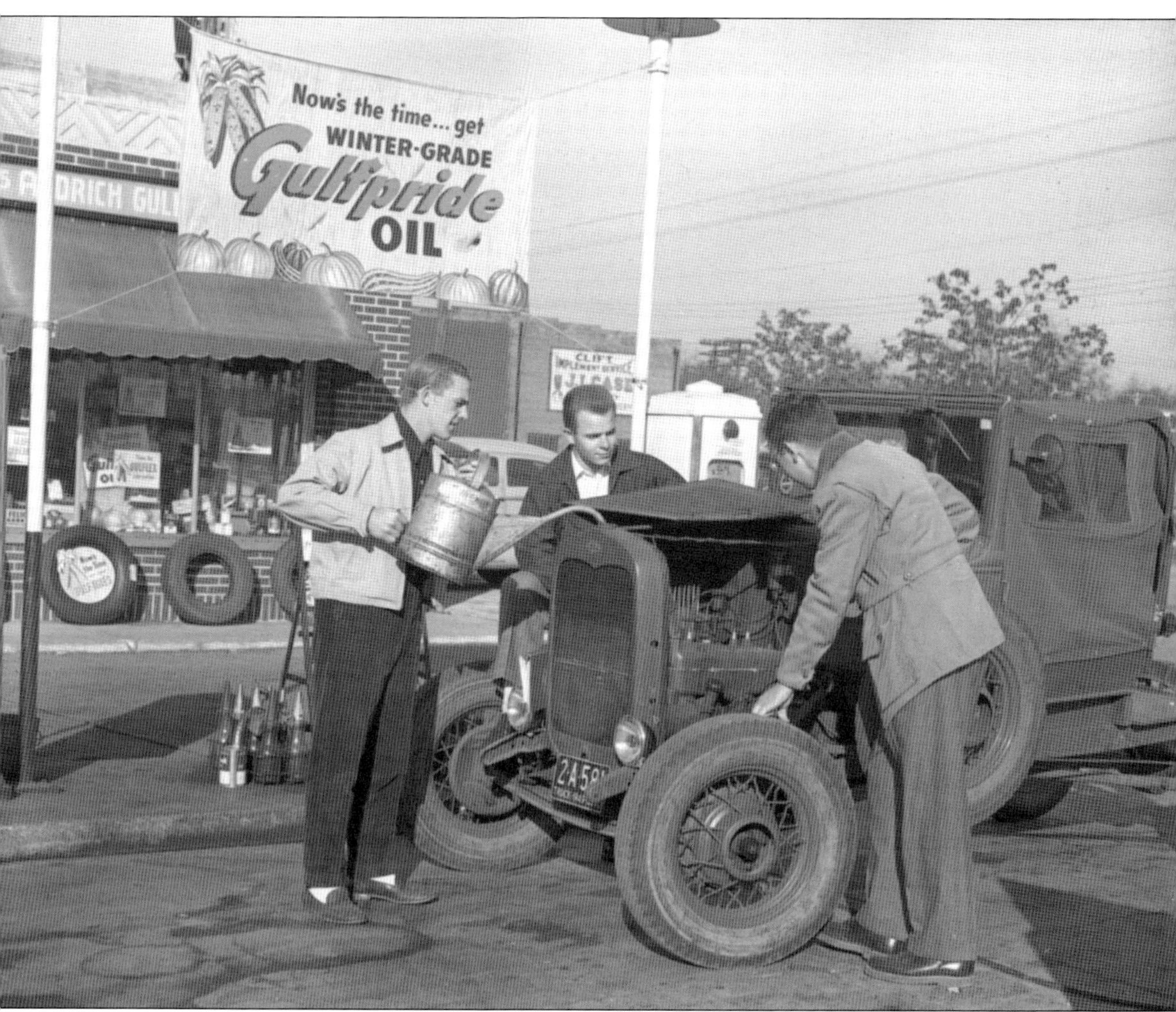

Aldrich Gulf Service Station was located in close proximity to the BGSU campus, at 435 East Wooster. The station provided automotive repairs, parts, and gasoline. Mason Gulf Service & U-Haul, and later Mason's BG Care, were located at this site.

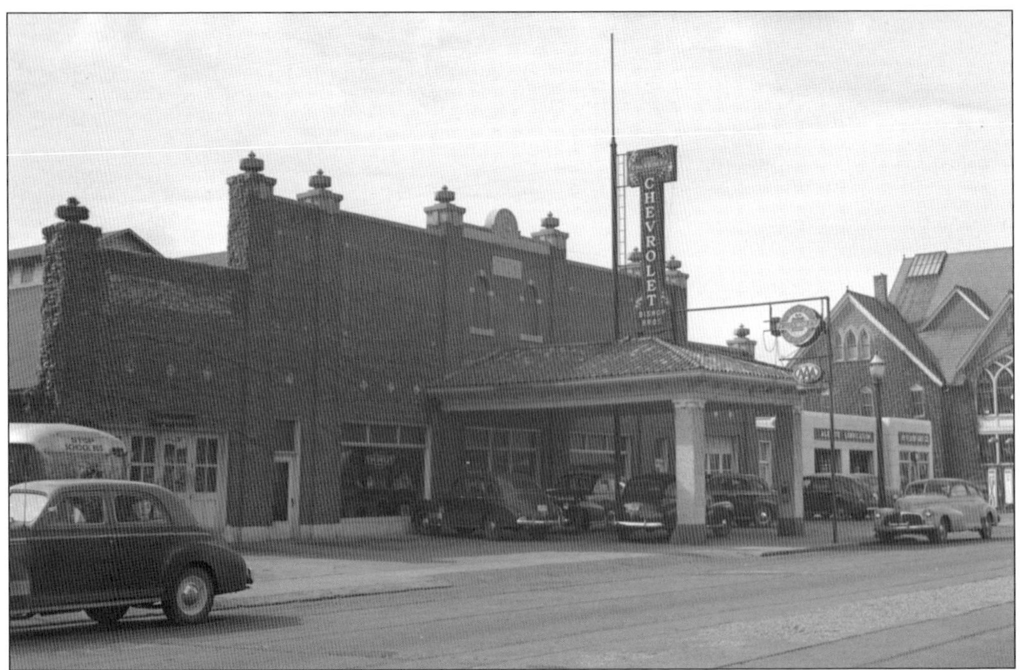

Bishop Brothers Chevrolet, formerly Bishop's Blacksmith Shop and Garage, was located at 280 South Main Street. Ralph Thayer Chevrolet later became the authorized dealer and occupied the building. The federal building, including the post office, is currently located at the site.

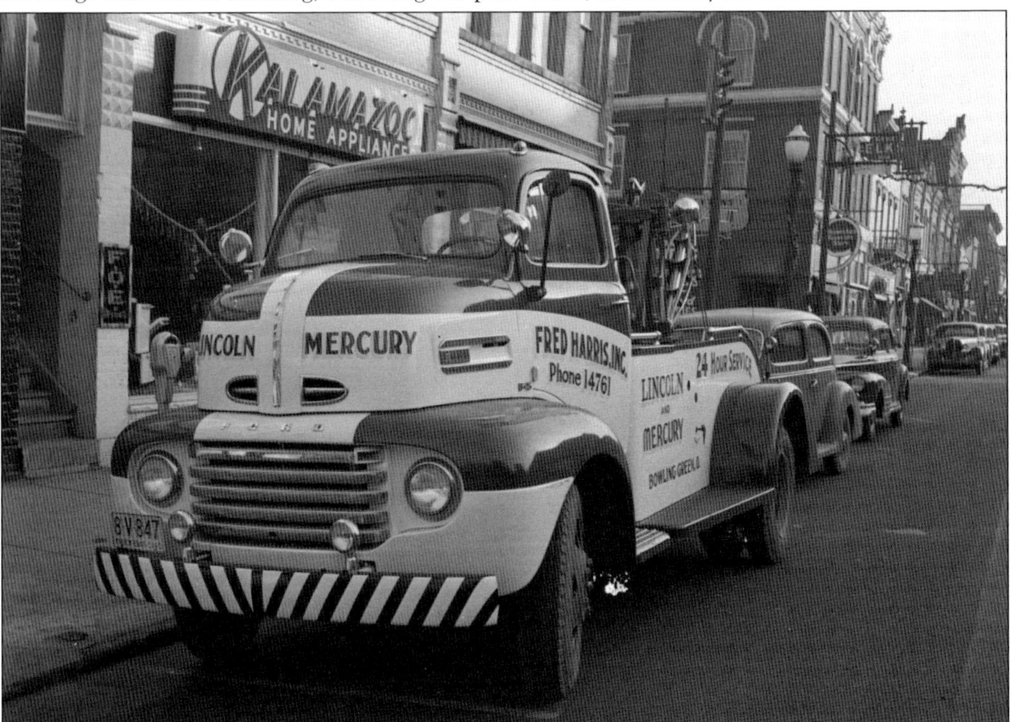

Fred Harris Lincoln-Mercury was located at 222 North Main Street and provided service for all makes of vehicles.

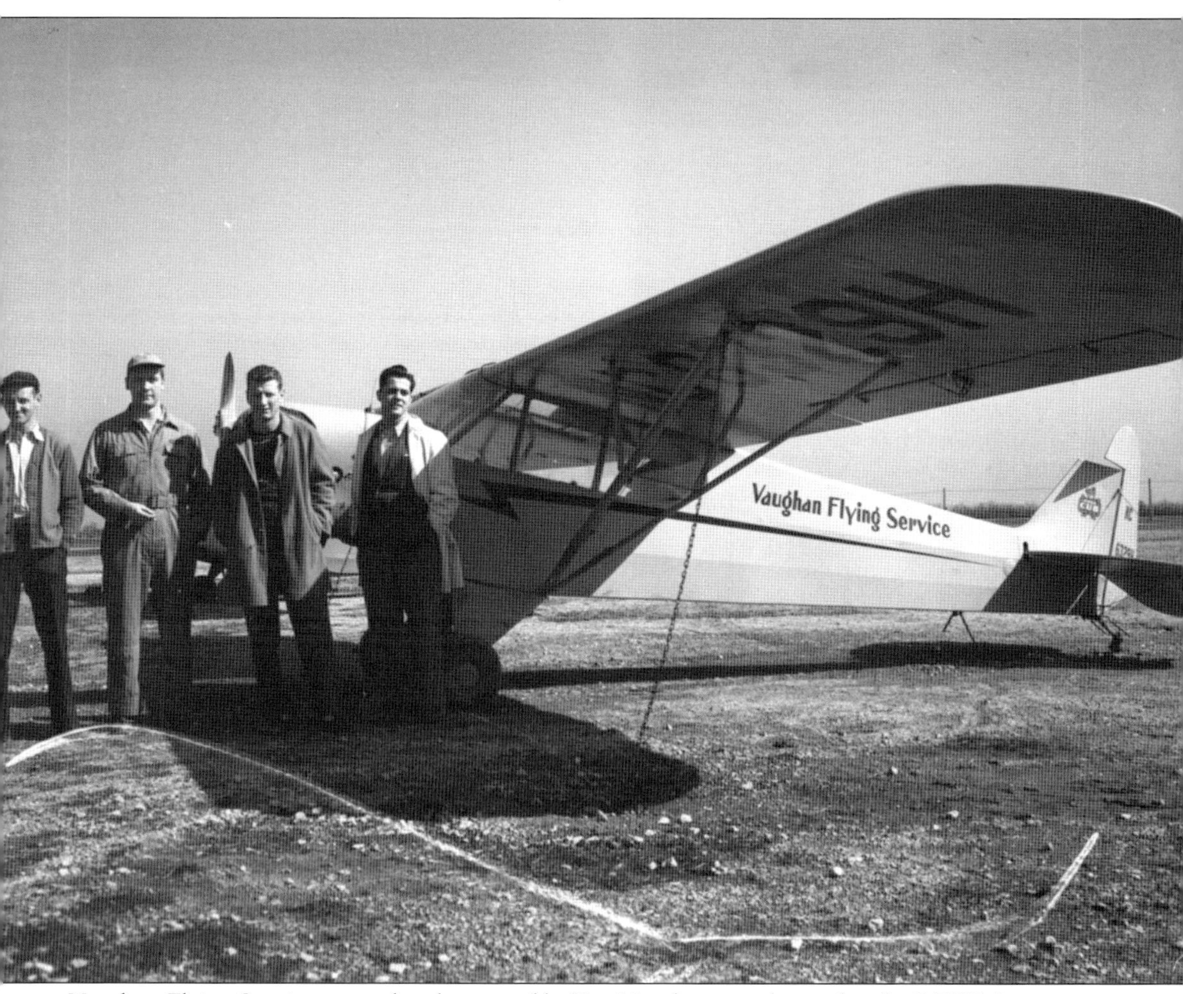

Vaughan Flying Service, owned and operated by Ray Vaughan, was located at the BGSU Airport.
Vaughan offered charter flights and individual flight instruction, and as the manager of the airport
he was involved in the Civilian Pilot Program.

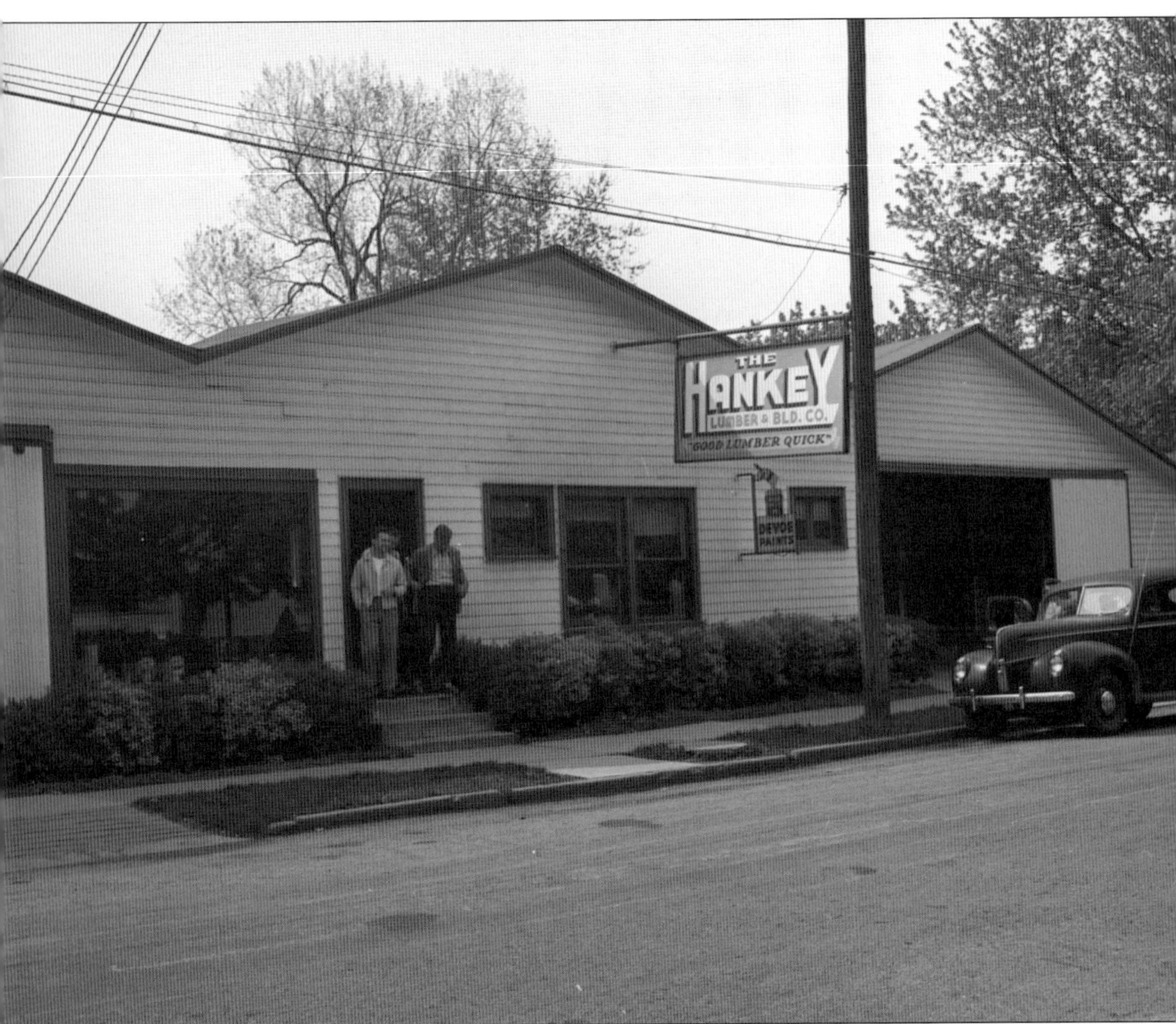

The Hankey Lumber & Building Company, located at 212 South Prospect, was founded by John R. Hankey as the Hankey Lumber Company. The lumber used in the construction of many local and university building projects came from Hankey Lumber & Building Company.

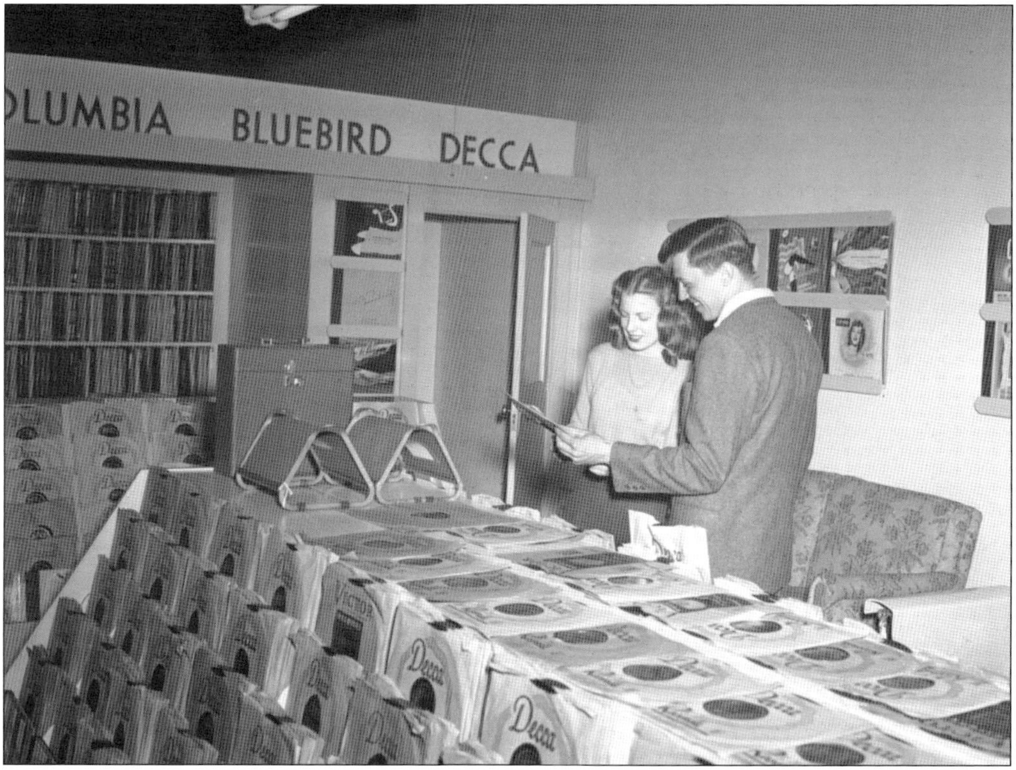

The Lion Store Appliance Shop
was located at 145 North Main
Street and carried records from a
wide variety of labels in addition to
a diverse selection of appliances.

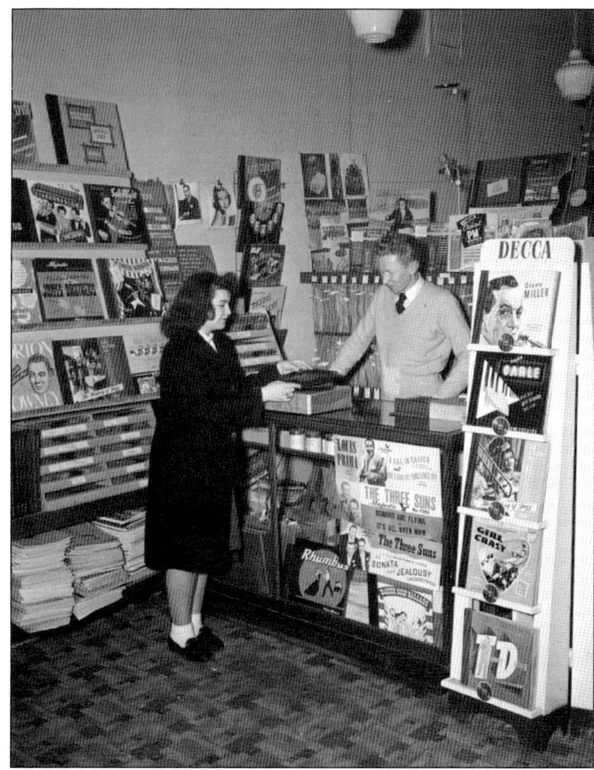

Bigelow Music Shoppe, located
at 126 East Wooster Street, sold
records and sheet music. The store
was owned by Jack Bigelow, a former
member of the Bigelow Family Band.

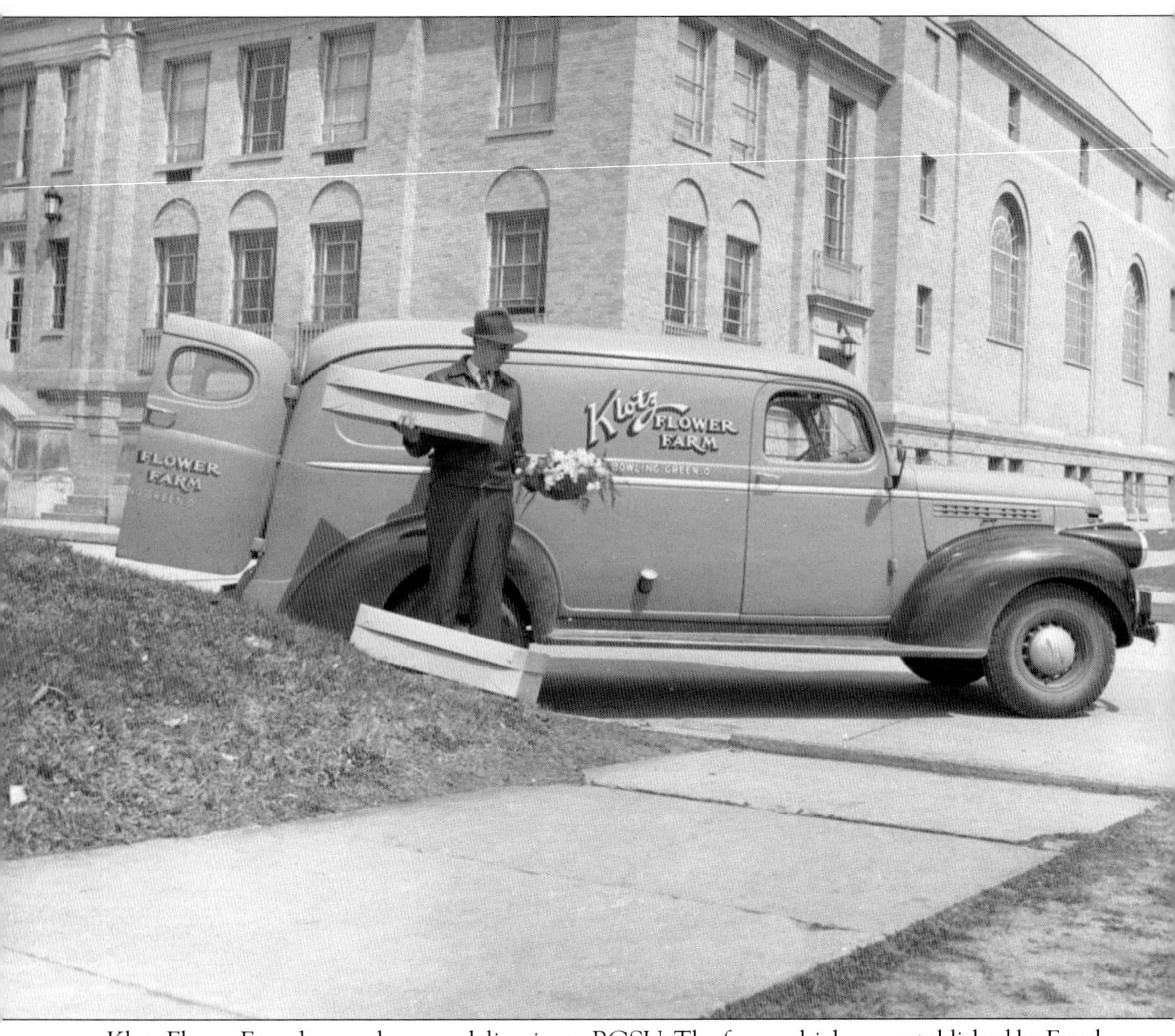

Klotz Flower Farm has made many deliveries to BGSU. The farm, which was established by Frank J. Klotz, is still family owned and located on Napoleon Road.

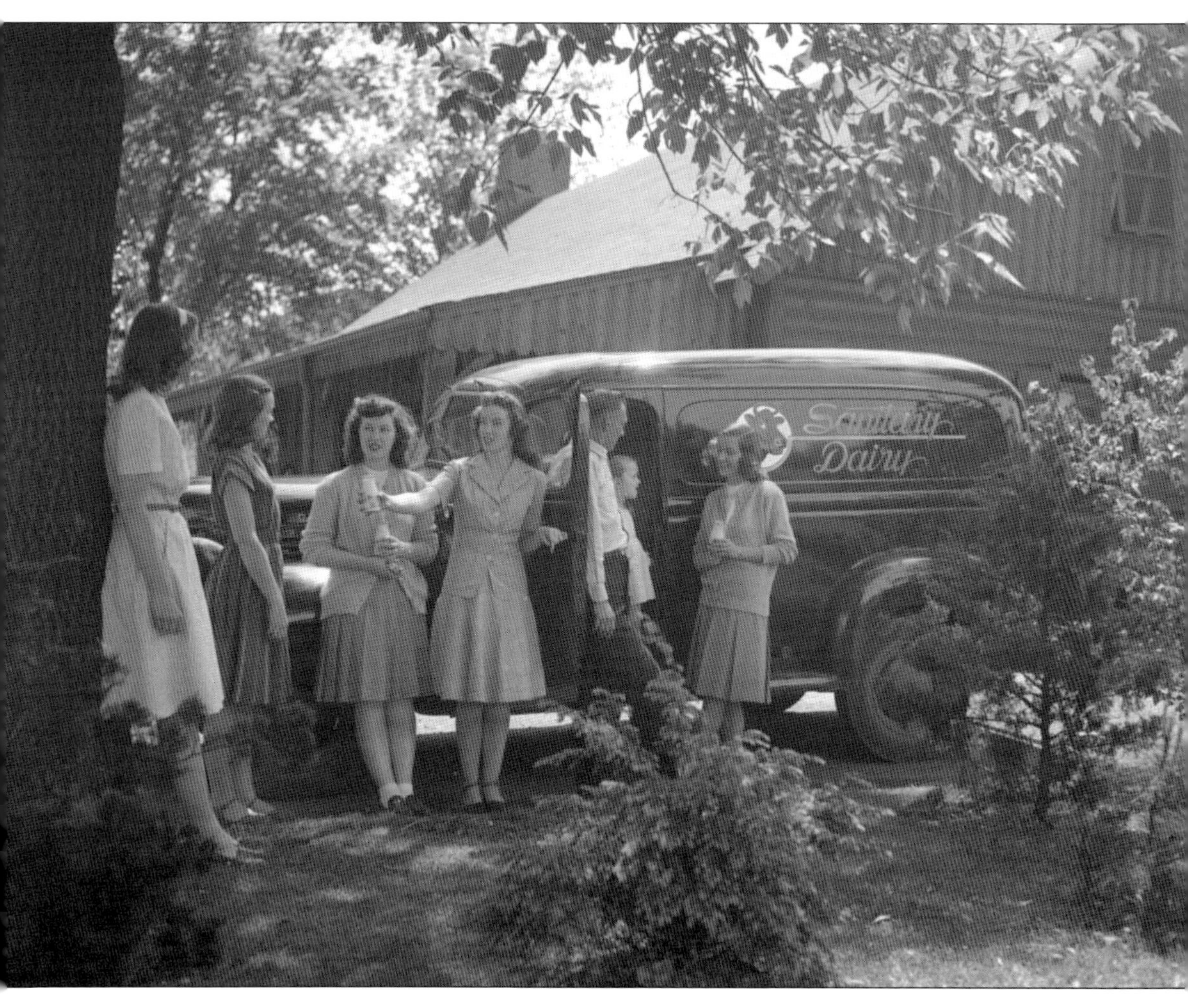

Sanitary Dairy, located on West Wooster Street near what is now Wintergarden Road, made regular deliveries to the BGSU campus. Owned and operated by the Keep family, the dairy originally delivered milk in a horse-drawn wagon.

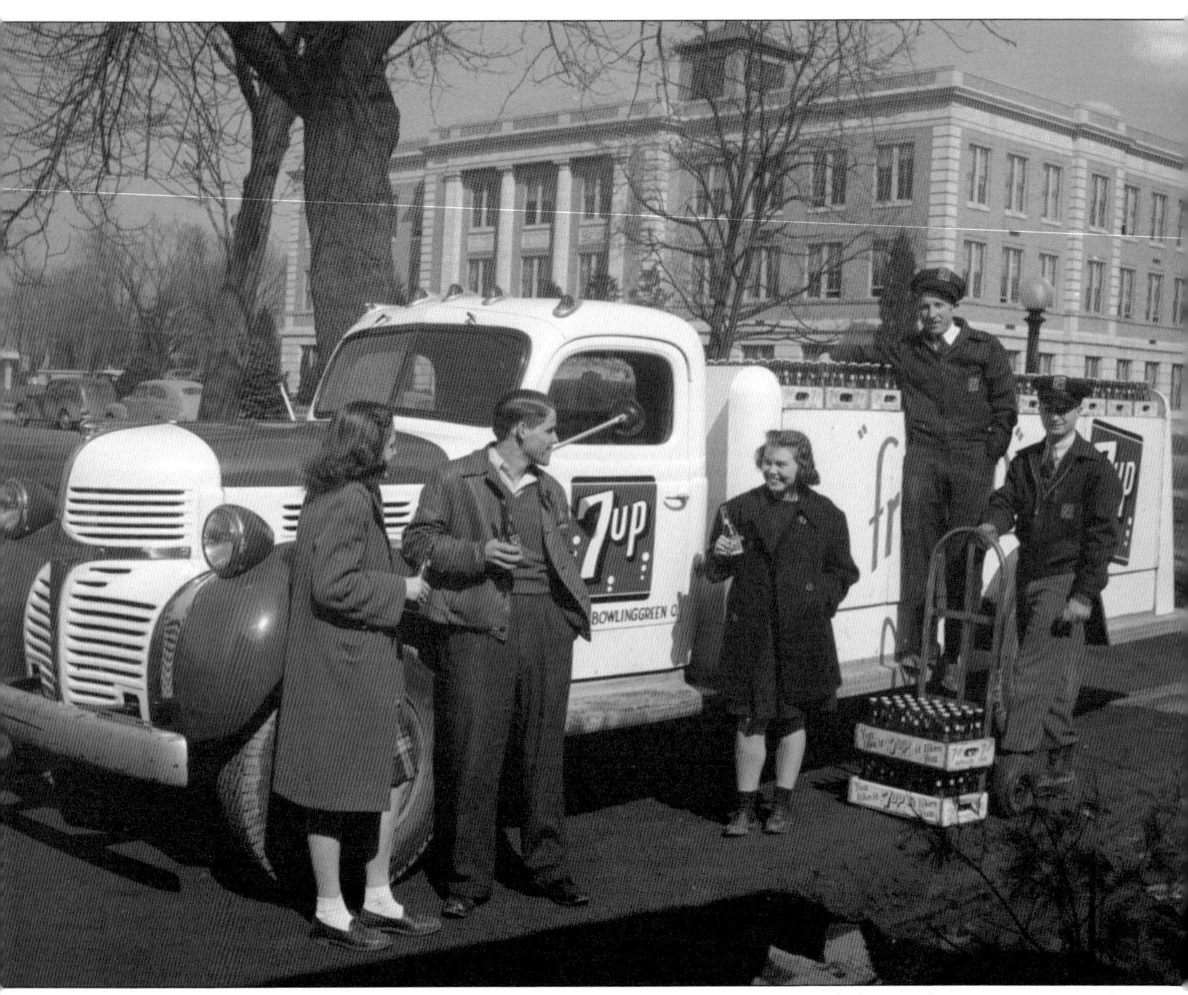

The Seven-Up Bottling Company at 347 North Maple Street delivered to campus and local homes.

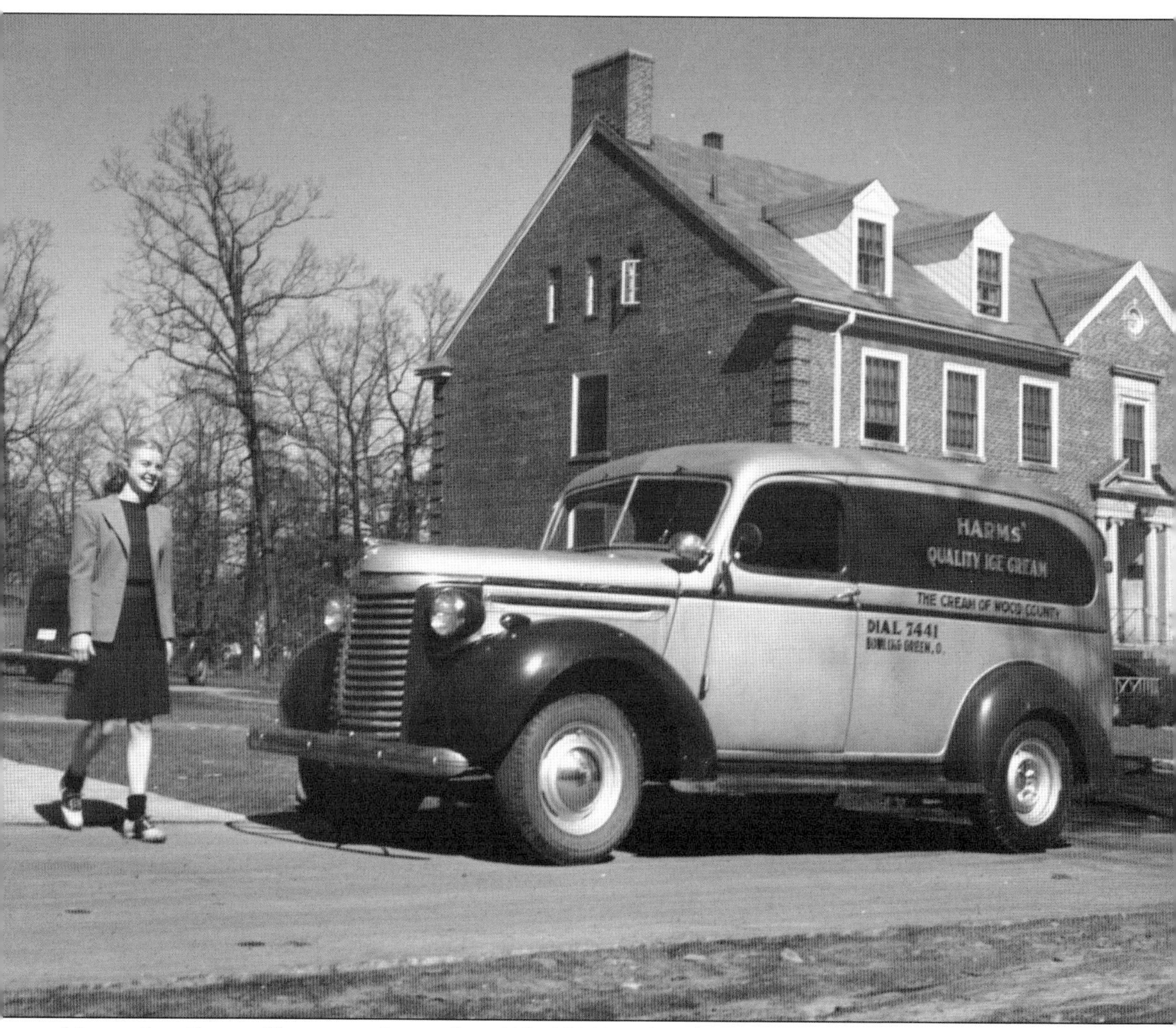

Harms Ice Cream Company, located at 112–124 East Washington Street, provided fresh ice cream to many of the local eateries. The company regularly delivered to campus buildings, including fraternity and sorority houses and dining facilities. Harms Dairy Store was located at the same address.

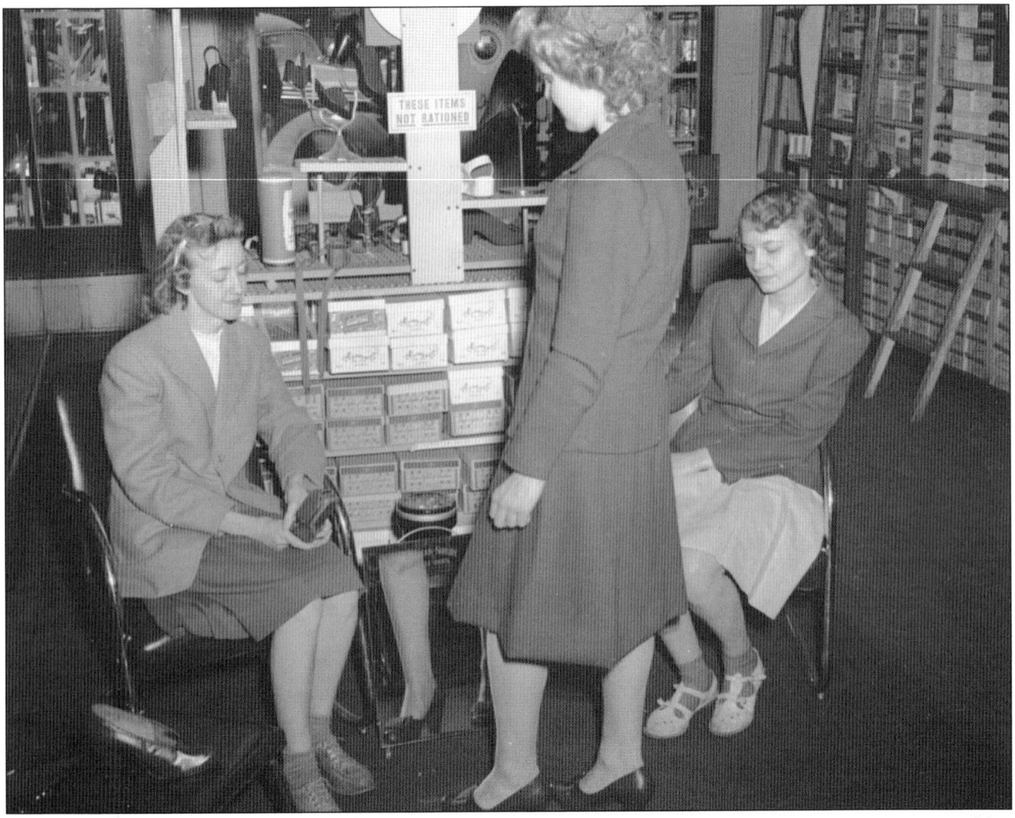

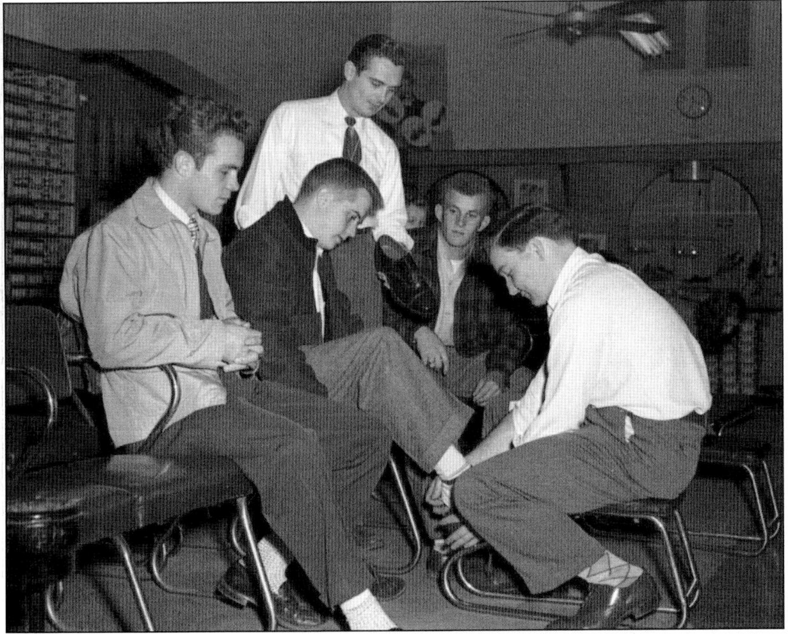

Uhlman's Shoes was originally located at 128 North Main Street. The business was owned by Frederick W. Uhlman and sold men's and women's shoes. The shoe store later moved to 124 North Main Street. Finders Records now occupies the original Uhlman's building.

Uhlman's Clothing, which was located at 128 North Main Street, featured a full line of men's and women's clothing and accessories. The Frederick W. Uhlman & Company later operated Uhlman's Fine Ladies Apparel at 101 South Main Street in the Milliken Hotel and Uhlman's Department Store and Hair Salon at 139 South Main Street.

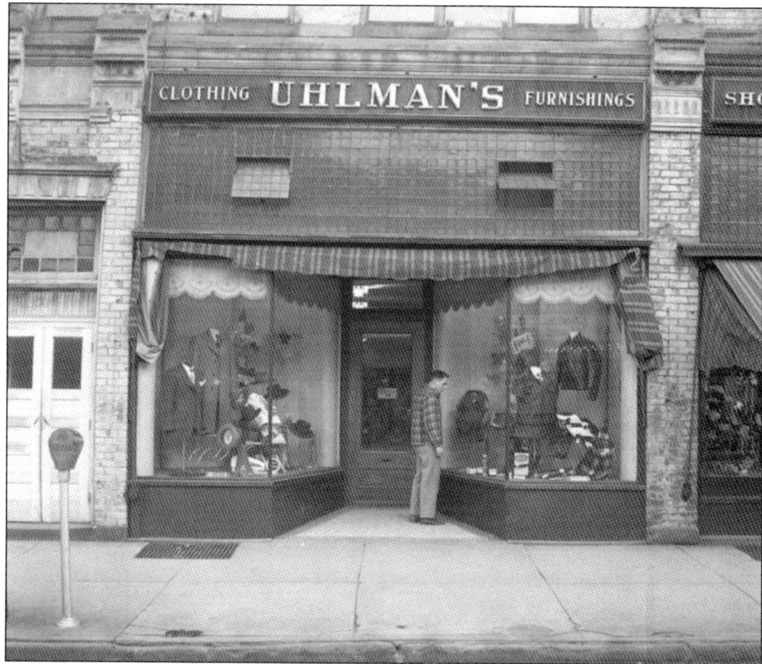

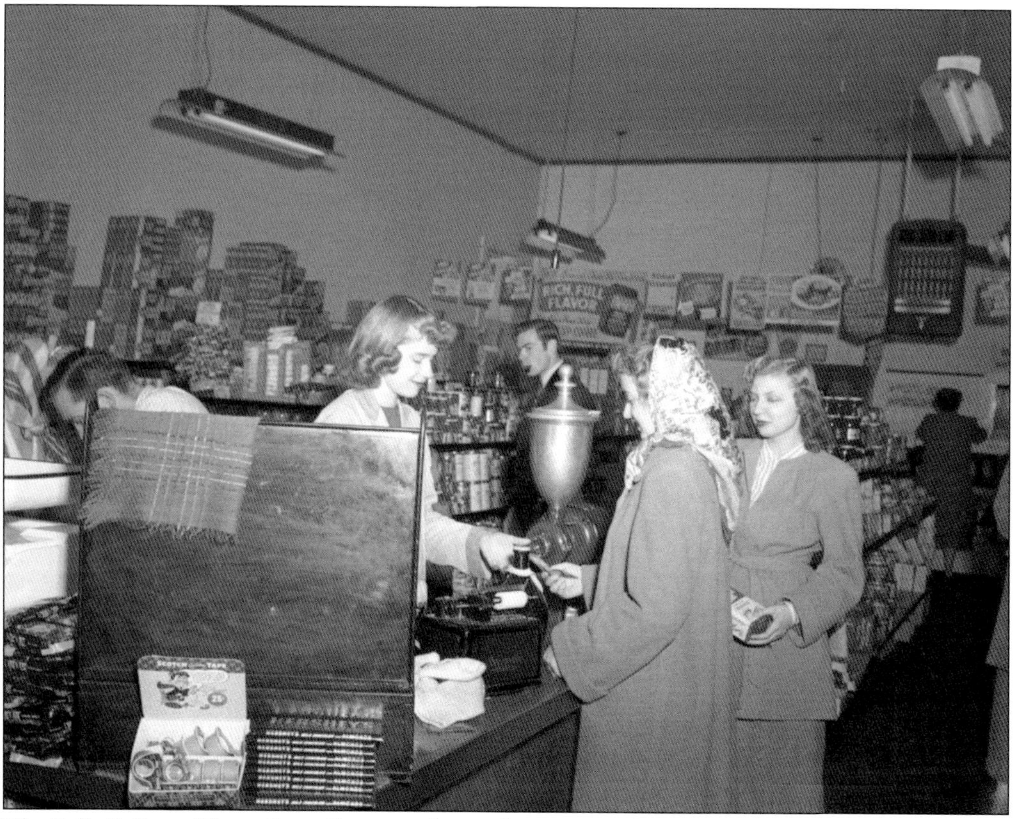

The Falls & Perry Clover Farm Store was located at 336 South Main Street. Newlove Real Estate, Inc. is now located at this site.

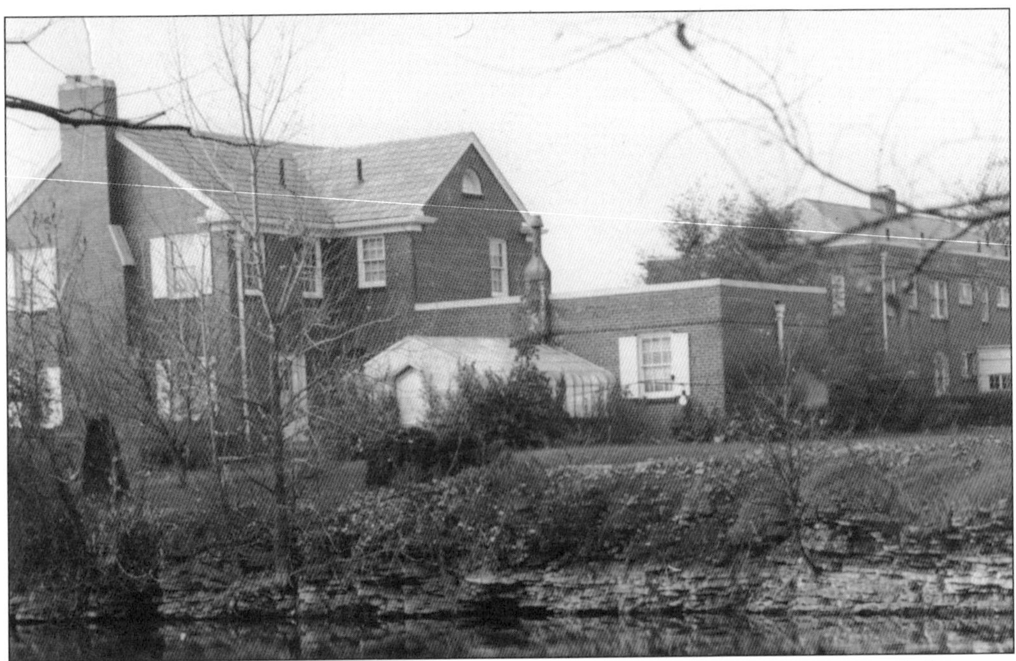

Bertis H. and Lillian Urschel sold their house, faculty apartment complex, stream-fed quarry, and windmill to BGSU in 1949. The house became the guesthouse where visiting dignitaries and celebrities stayed; the apartment complex and the windmill were converted into student apartments, and the quarry became Urschel Pond recreational facility.

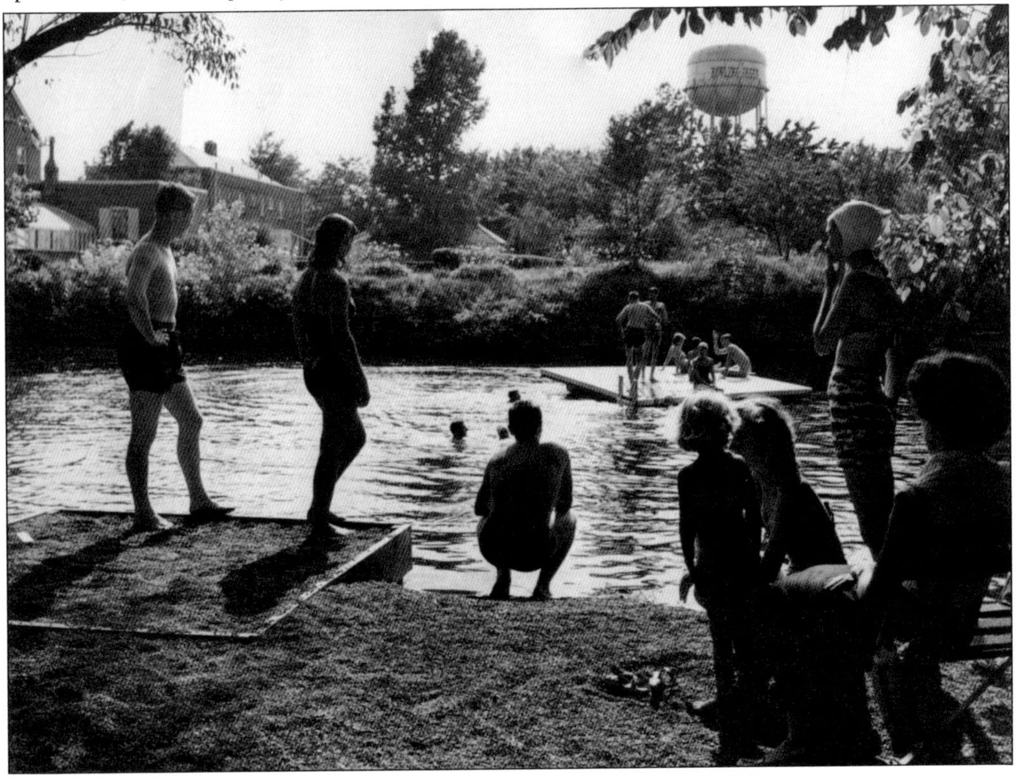

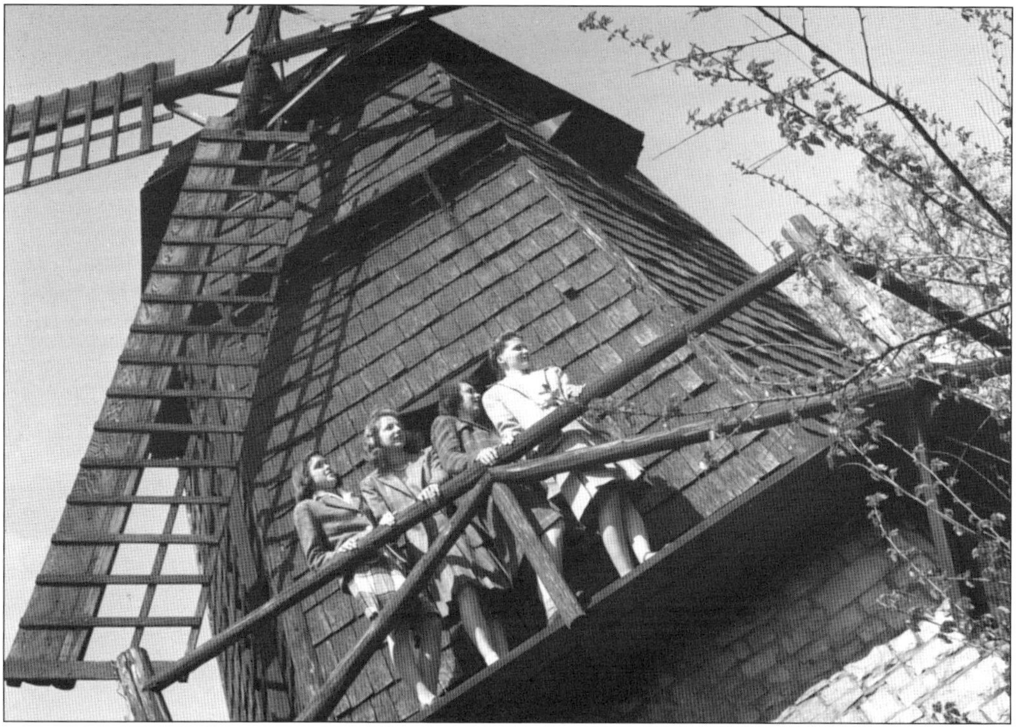

The windmill located at 721 Clough Street was built by B.H Urschel in 1939 to camouflage a pump and a boiler that was used to heat a nearby apartment complex. The interior was later converted into an apartment for students.

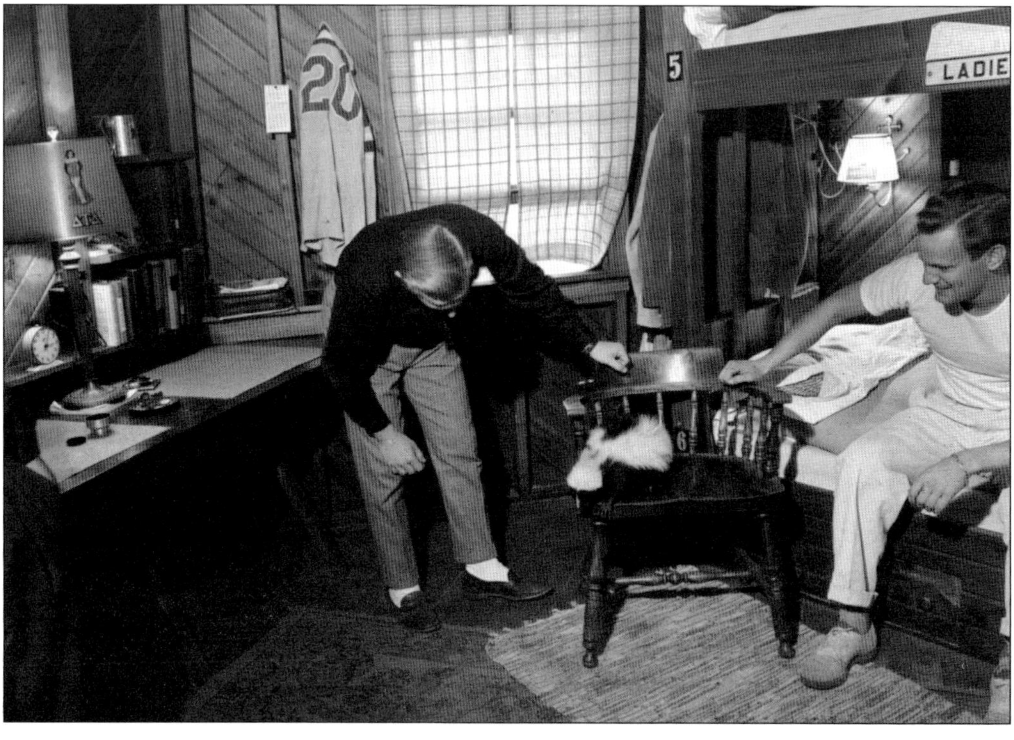

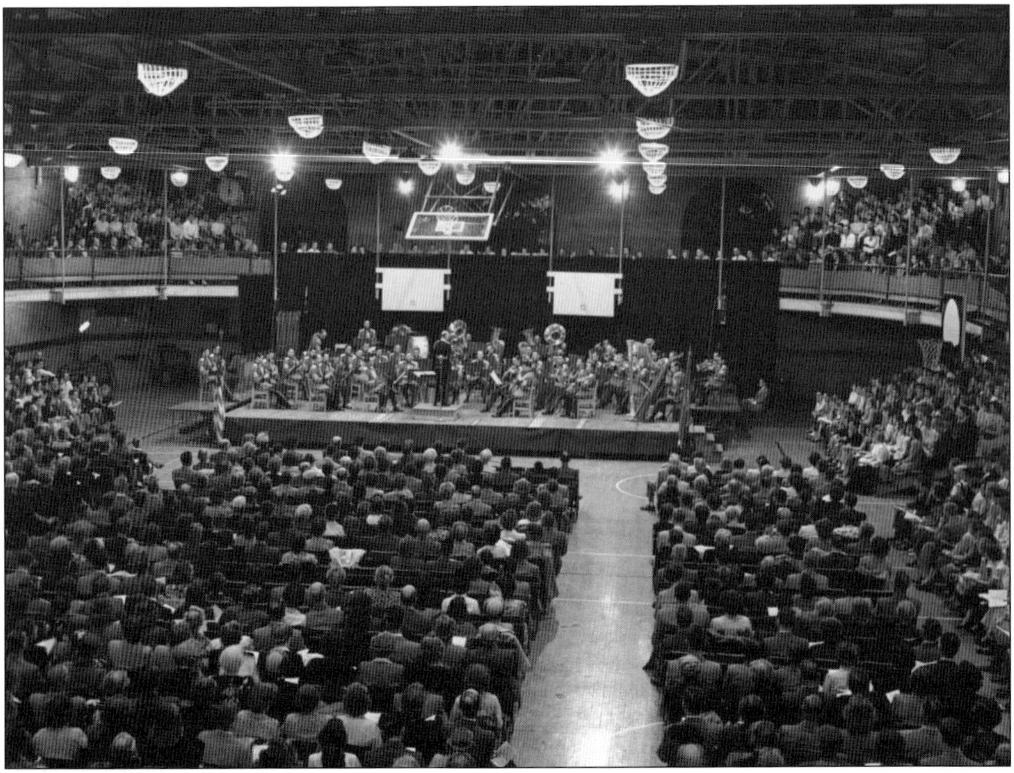

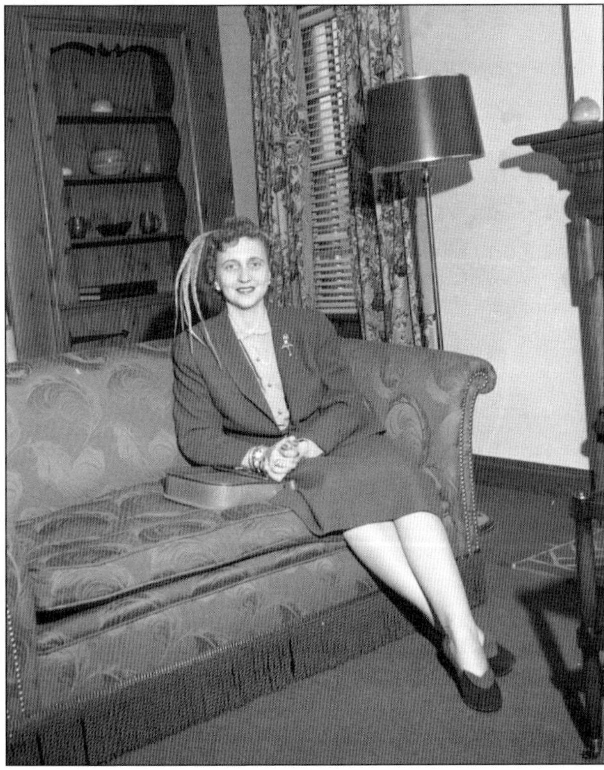

Beginning with the first May Festival in 1915, the university has brought a diverse group of performers to the community. The Artist Series, which had its beginnings in the 1940s, continued that tradition through sponsoring performances by groups such as the US Marine Band and individuals like singer Margaret Truman, who was the daughter of Pres. Harry S. Truman.

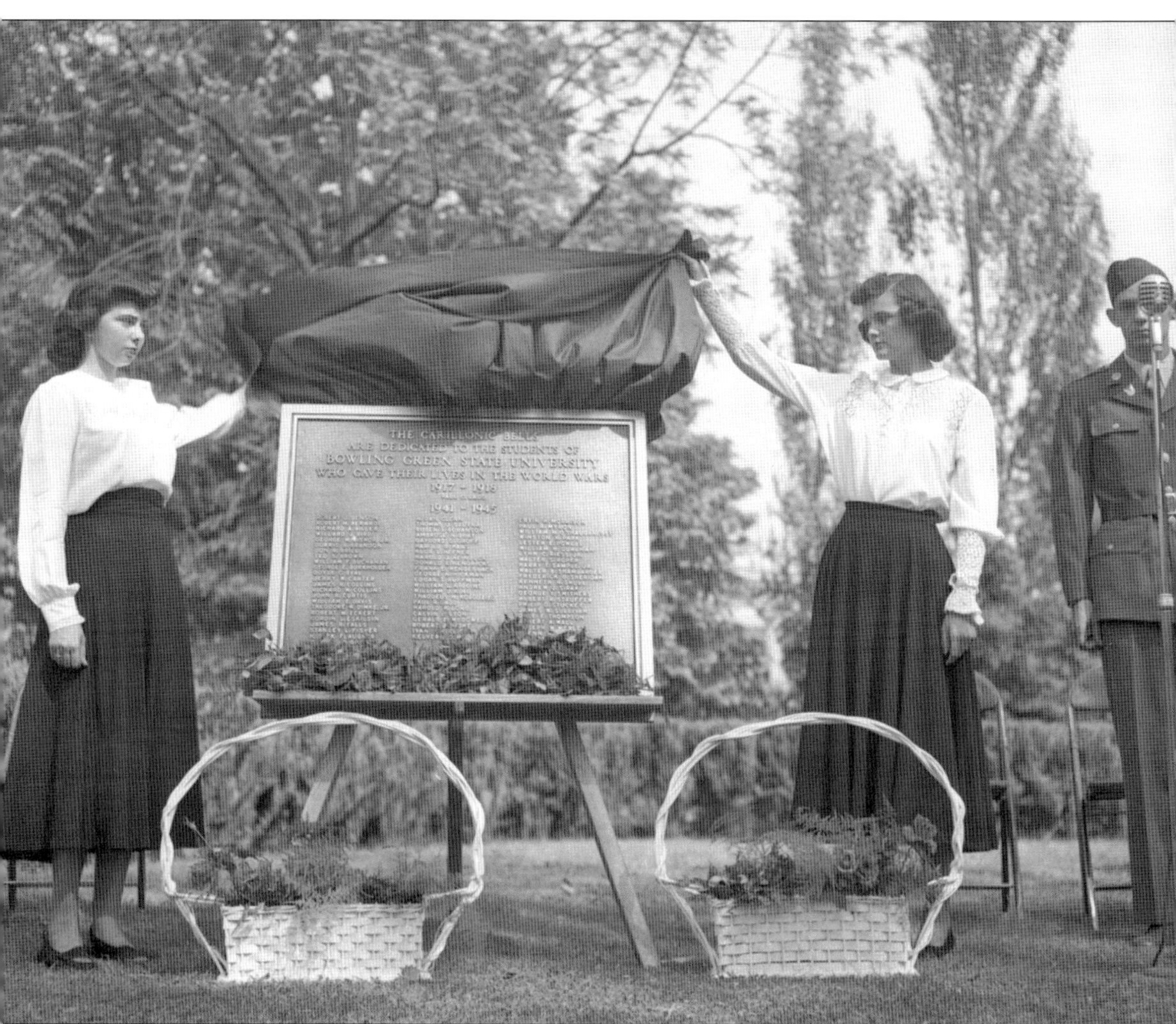

A bronze plaque and two sets of carillon bells were dedicated in 1948 to honor the BGSU alumni and students who sacrificed their lives during World War I and World War II. The names of several local students were among those who are represented on the plaque. The bells were mounted on a bell tower on top of the practical-arts building (Hayes Hall), and the plaque was mounted on in the front entrance.

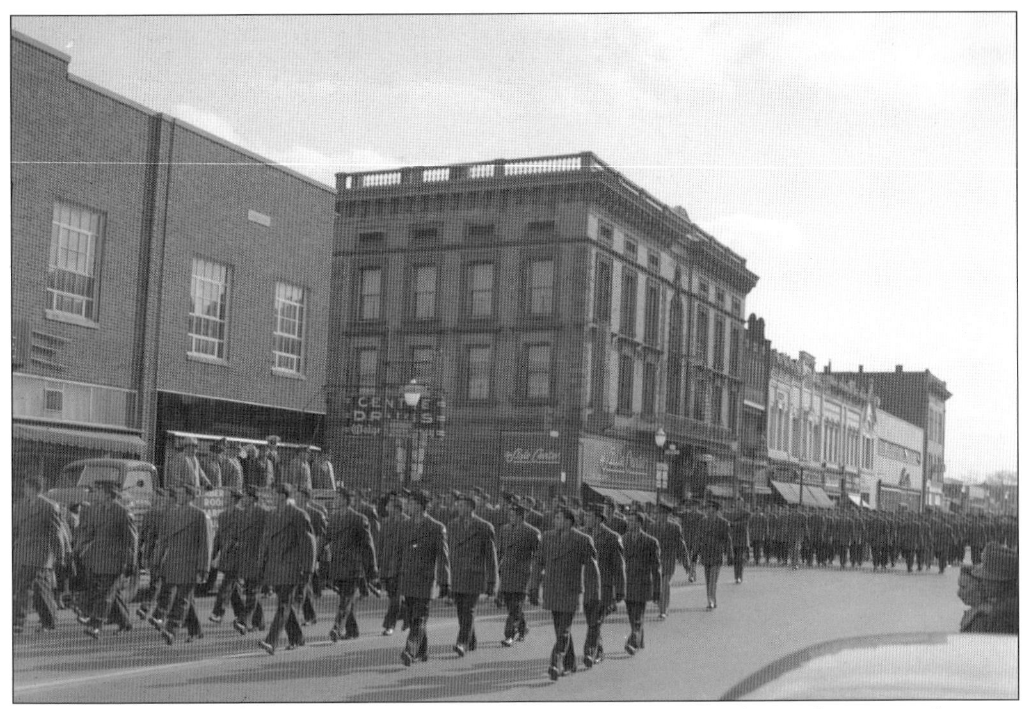

The Bowling Green Armistice Day celebration on November 11, 1950, featured a memorial service at the Wood County Courthouse and a parade of the BGSU ROTC unit.

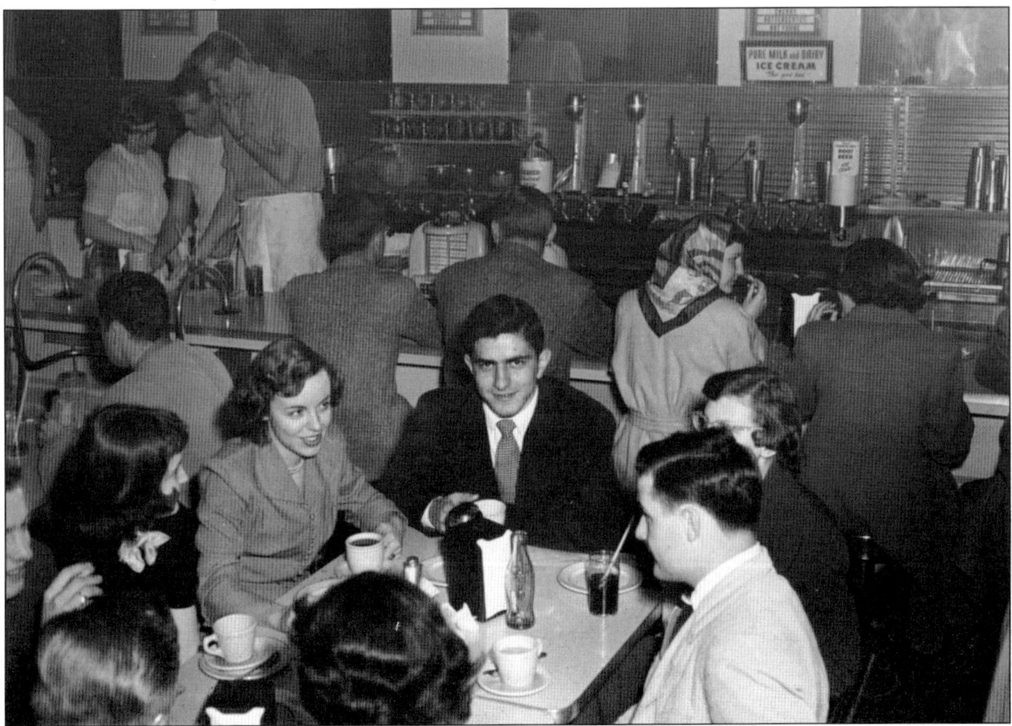

The University Club was located at 530 East Wooster. The club had a backroom dance floor. The Student Book Exchange, which opened in 1958, is currently located at this site.

A neon sign that hung in Howard's Restaurant bearing the mantra "Life Begins at Howard's" is prominently shown in this early 1950s image. The restaurant, located at 213 North Main Street, was always a popular hangout among BGSU students because of its casual, unassuming atmosphere.

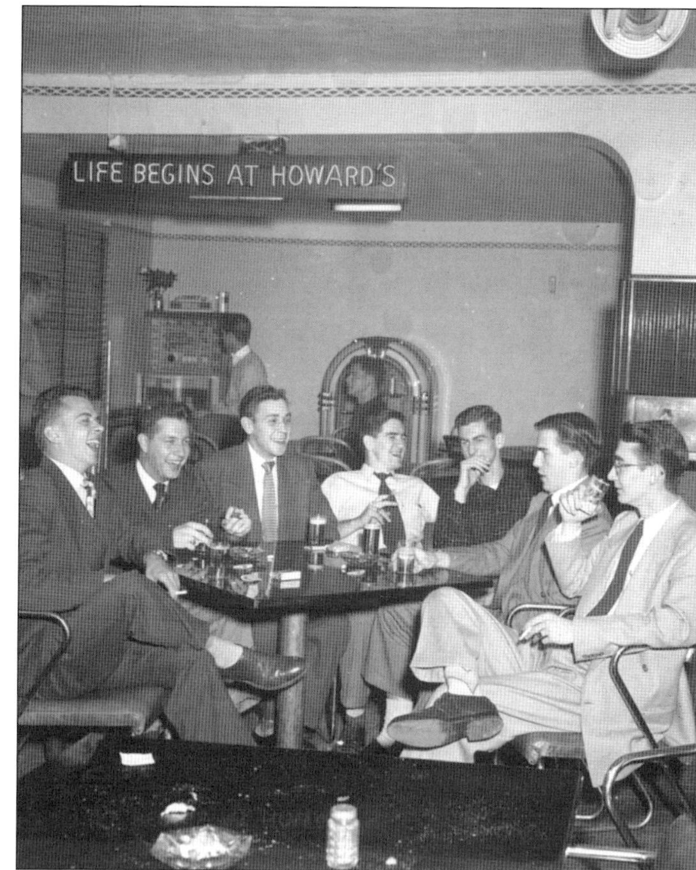

Al-Mar Bowling Alley, formerly Premo Recreational, was originally located at 111 West Washington Street. The Bowling Alley is still in operation at 1010 North Main Street.

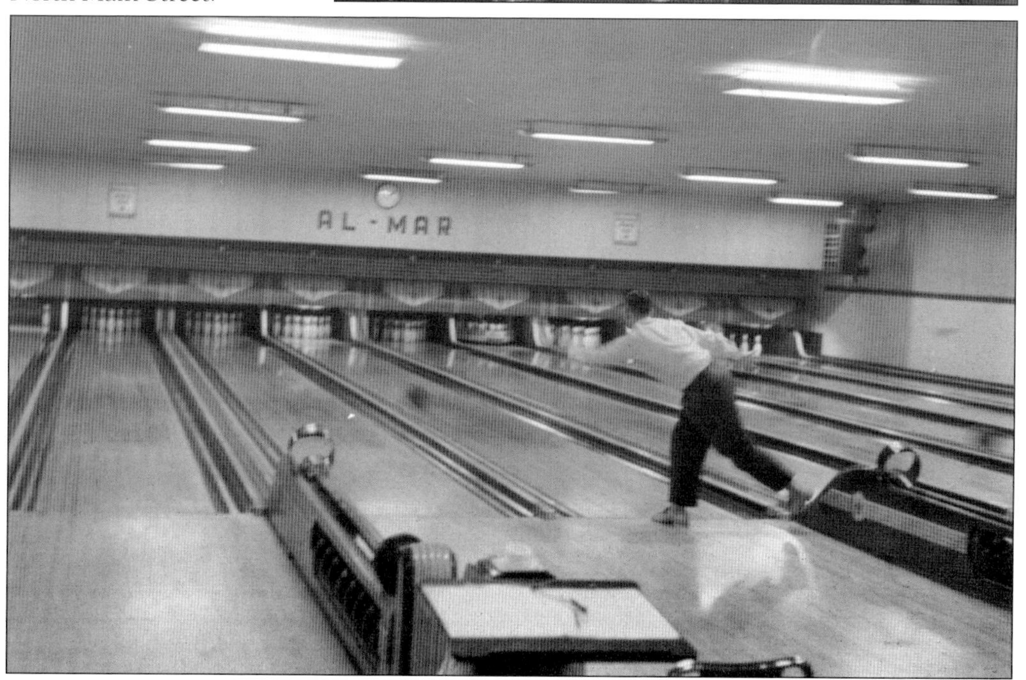

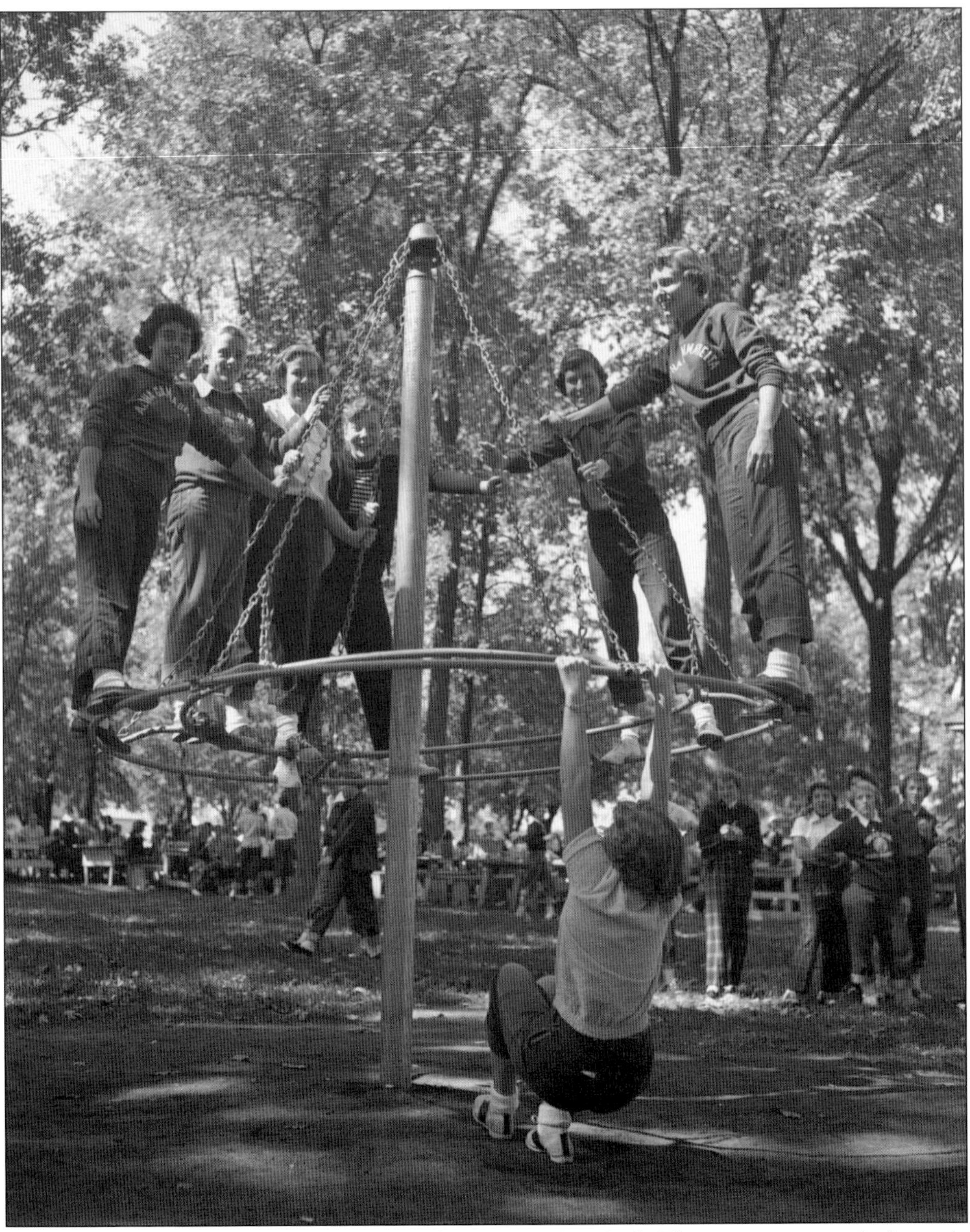

BGSU is located on the site of the first Bowling Green City Park. The current city park, formerly the Wood County fairgrounds, was established in 1929. BGSU students visit the park for individual recreation or organized excursions. Members of the Association of Women Students held their freshman welcome at the park.

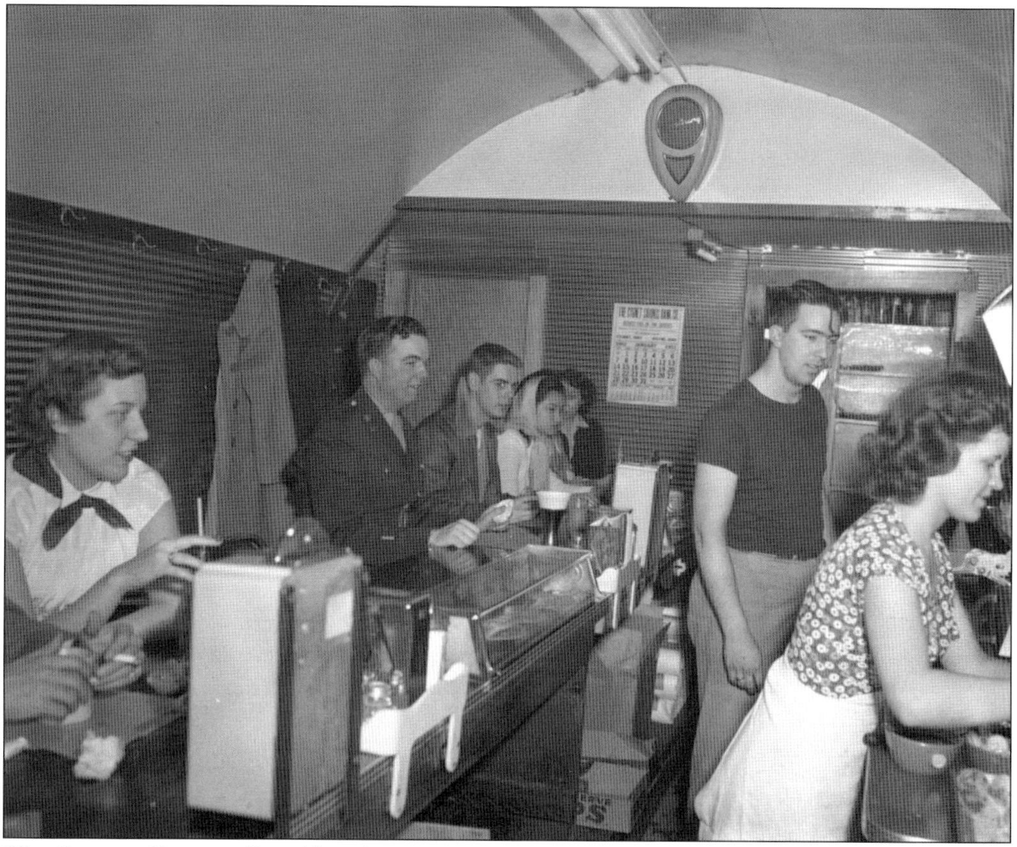

The Coop or Hut, a grill and hamburger stand, was located at 440 East Wooster Street near the New York Central Railroad tracks during the early 1950s. The site is now the parking lot for Myles Dairy Queen at 434 East Wooster Street.

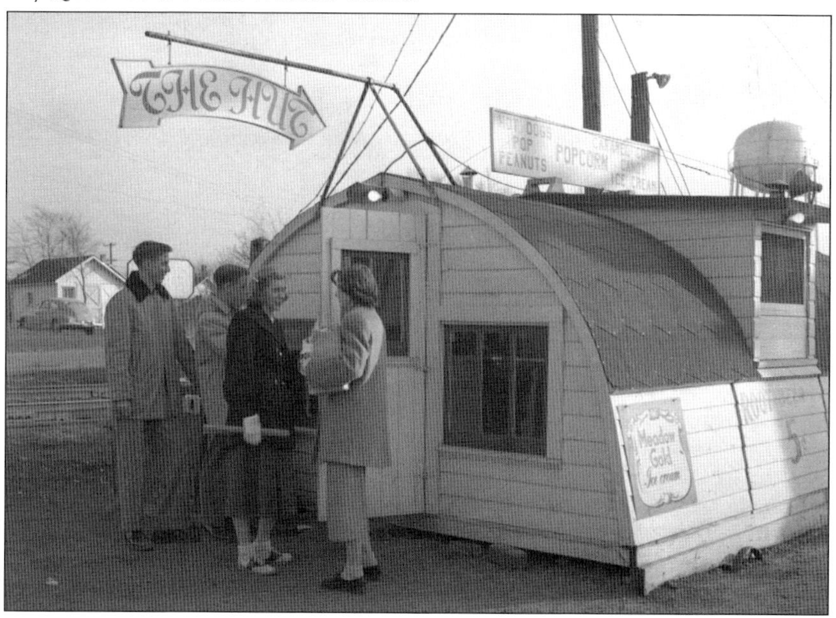

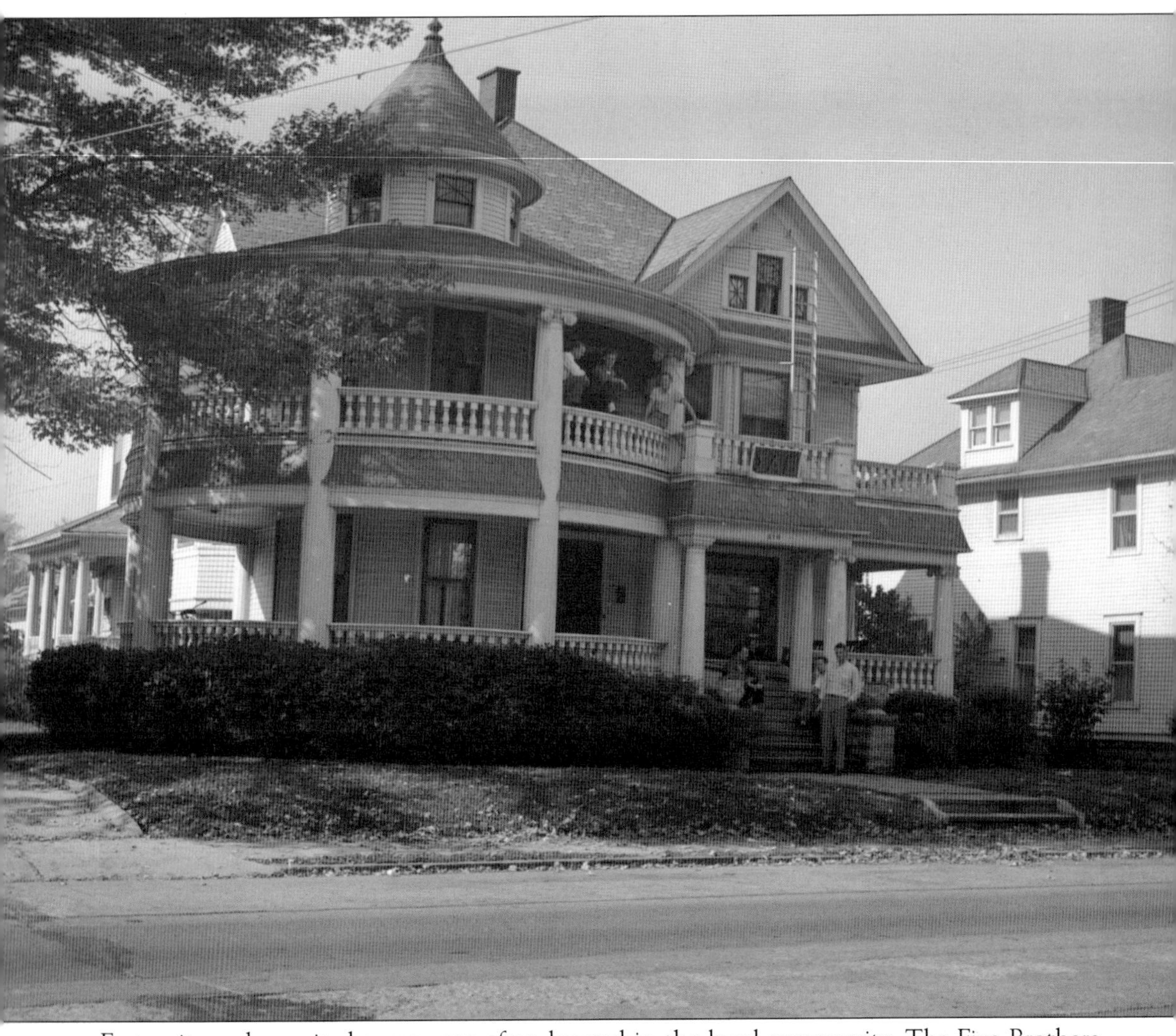

Fraternity and sorority houses were often located in the local community. The Five Brothers Fraternity, now Sigma Alpha Epsilon, or SAE, occupied the house at 410 South Main Street for many years.

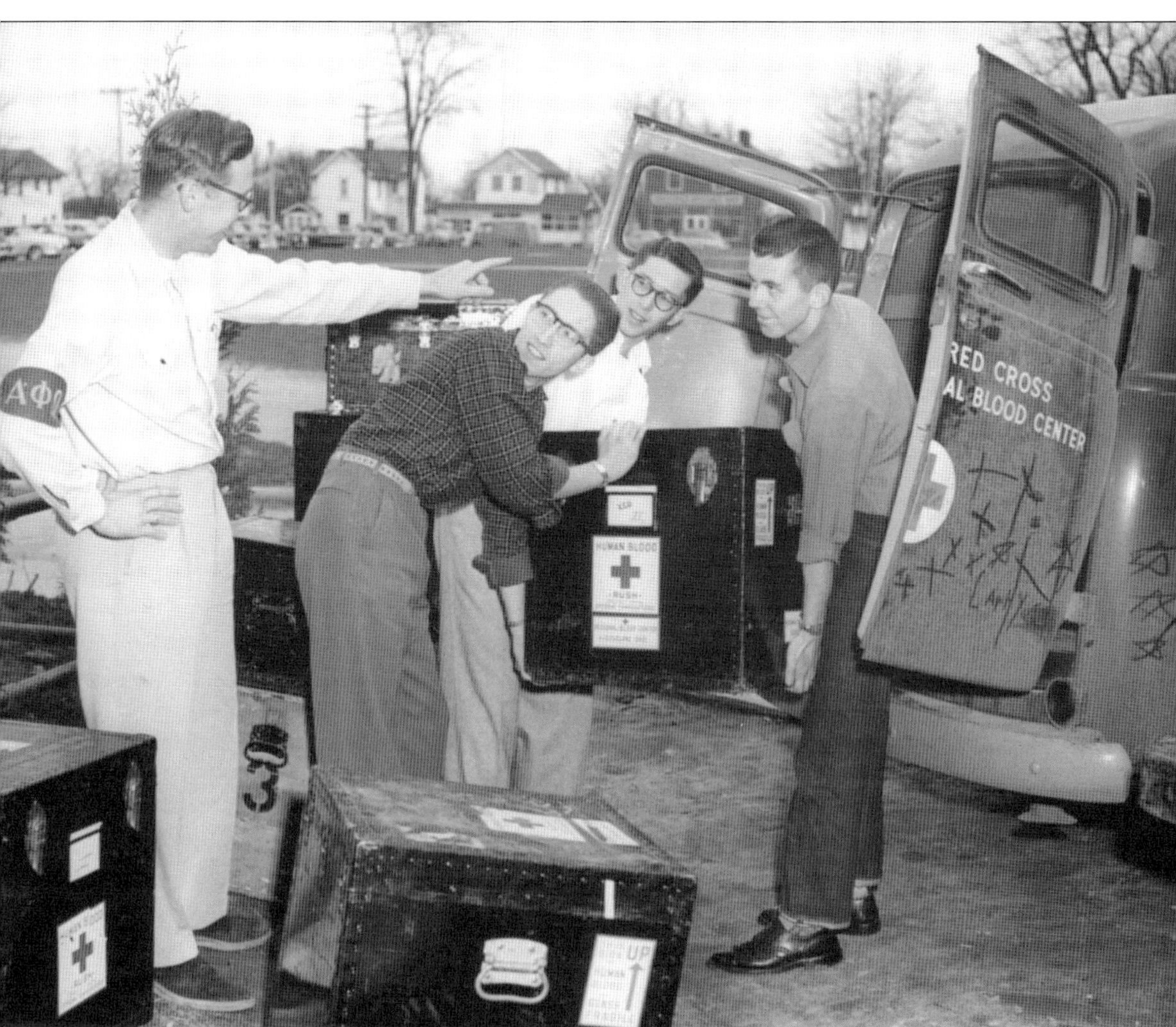

Bowling Green State University students have always provided service to the local community. Members of the Alpha Phi Omega fraternity are shown loading donated blood onto a truck after an American Red Cross blood drive.

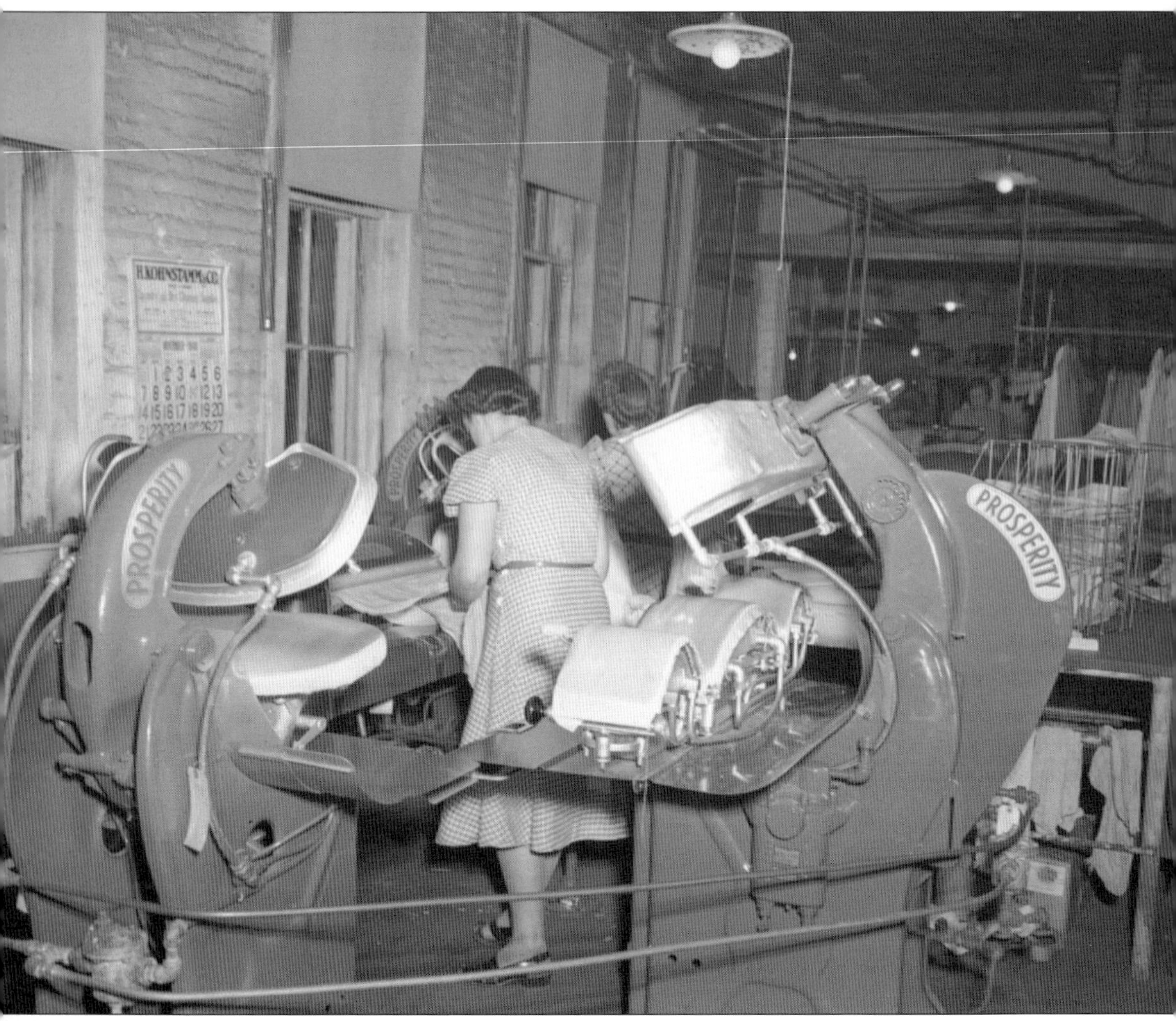

Home Laundry & Dry Cleaners, formerly the Home Steam Laundry, was located at 166 West Wooster Street. The owner's son remembers making deliveries to BGSU students, including Eva Marie Saint. Other dry-cleaning establishments included Hamblin, Longs, Sanitary, and University Dry Cleaners.

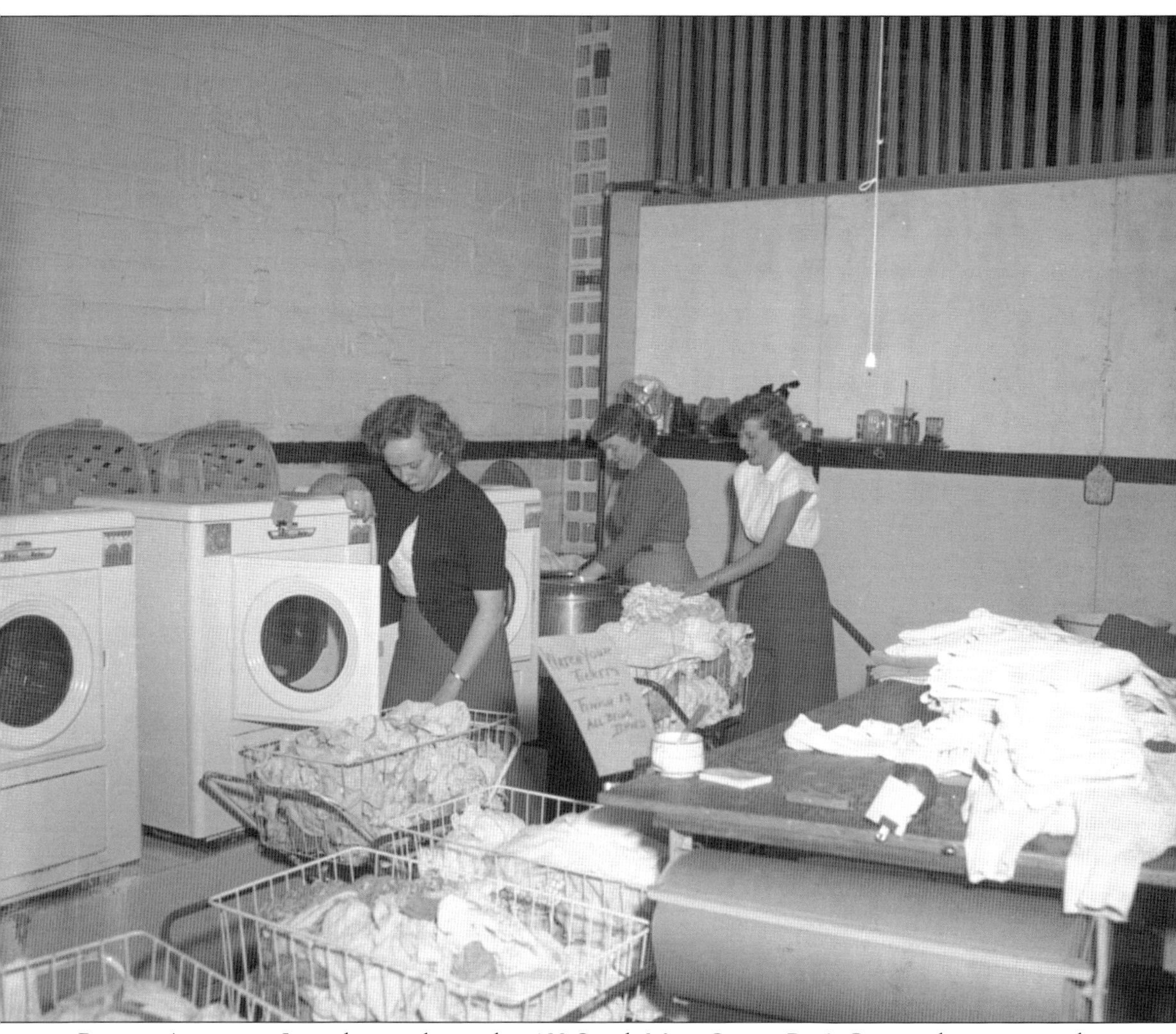

Pioneer Automatic Laundry was located at 182 South Main Street. Pop's Grocery later occupied the site, and Naslada Bistro is the currently located at this address.

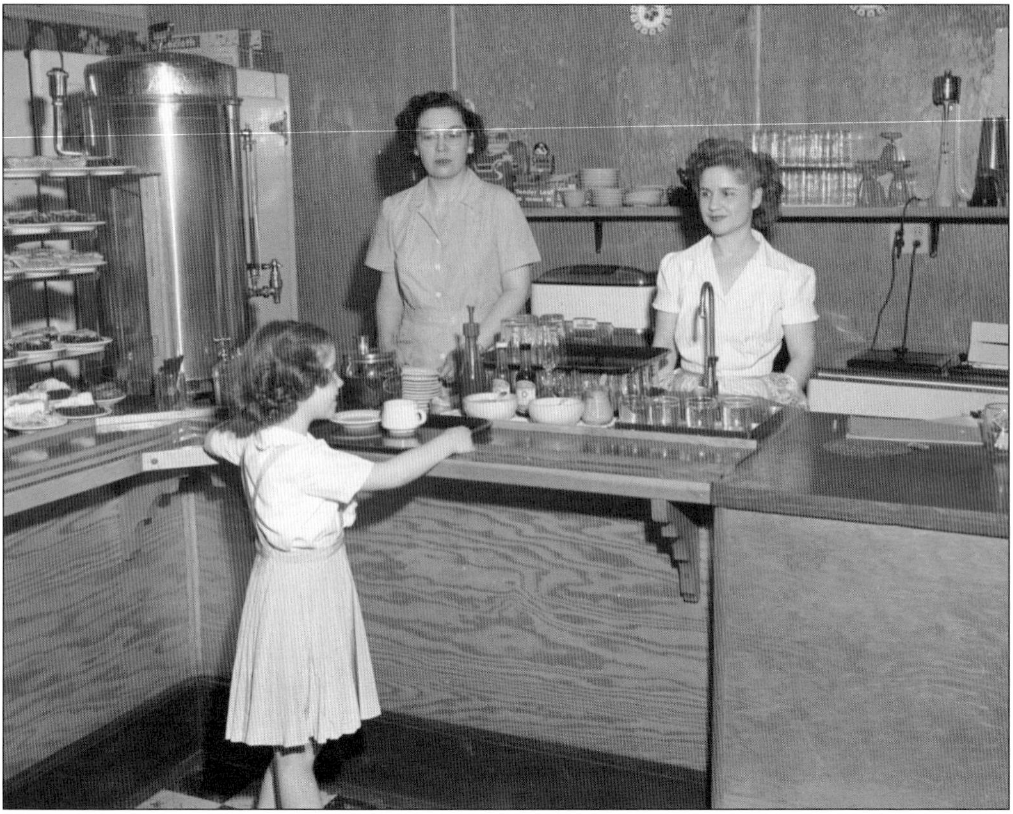

Don & Helen's Cafeteria was located at 117 North Main Street and was one of the few businesses that was open on Sunday. Petit's Pizzeria Restaurant and Petit's Alpine Restaurant later occupied the site.

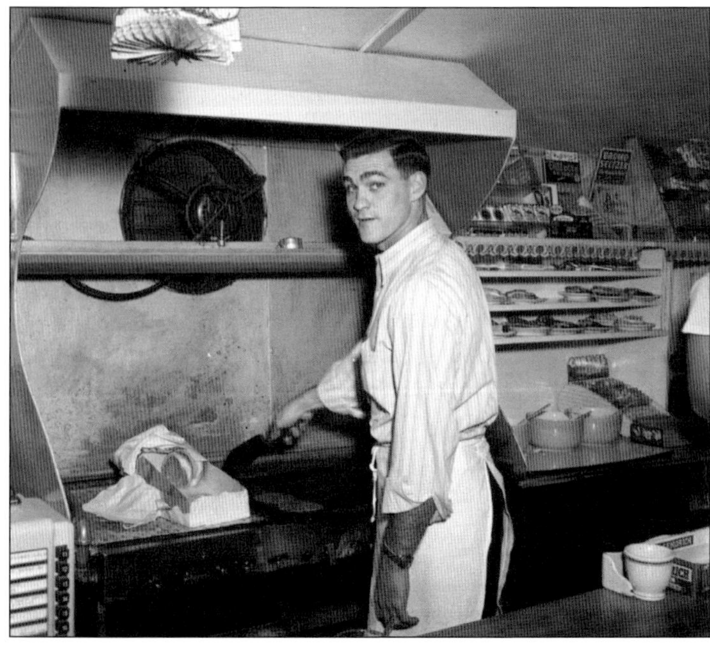

The Giant Hamburg, located at 215 South Main Street, was a typical inexpensive, informal diner.

Klever's Jewelry Store, a family-owned business, was located at 121 North Main Street for many years. Founded by Alexander Klever in 1918, the store later moved to 125 North Main Street and then to 1039 Haskins Road.

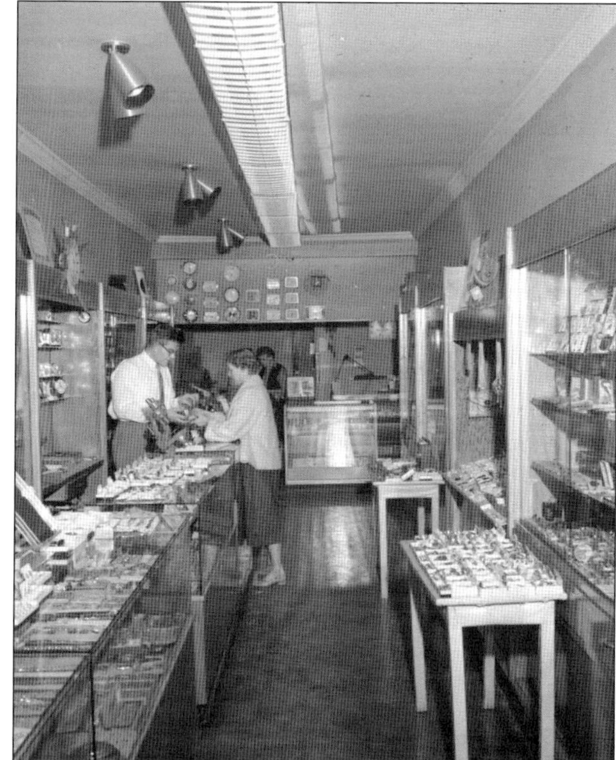

Crosby Jewelers was located at 148 South Main Street. Nestled between Ben Franklin Crafts & Frames and For Keeps, the Busy Thimble is now located at this site.

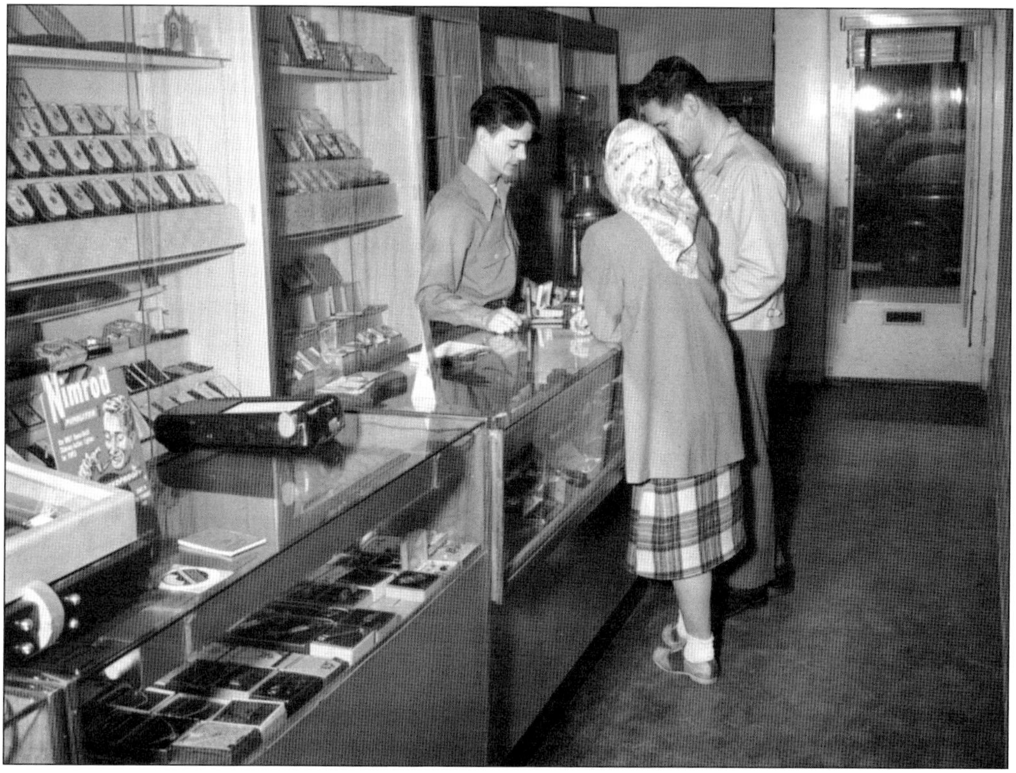

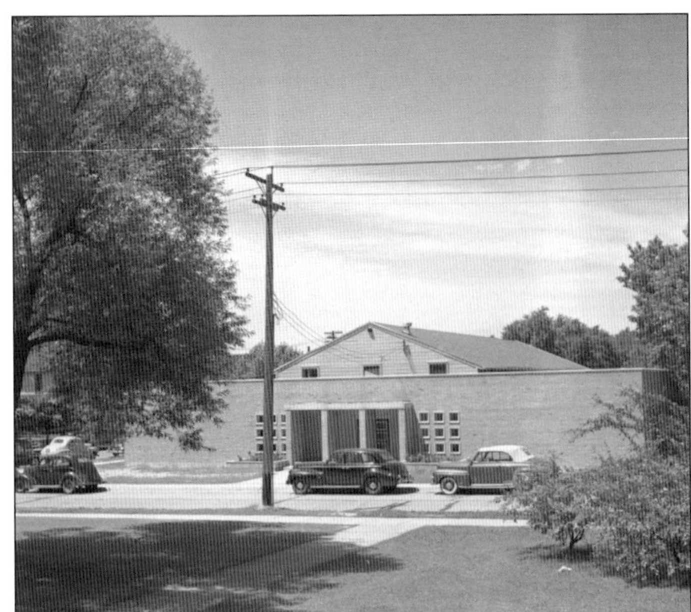

The Campus Gate Theatre, named for the famous Dublin Gate Theatre, was located at the corner of Court and Thurstin Streets. The building was one of four structures purchased, dismantled, and moved to campus from Camp Perry in 1947. It was used for drama classes and simple public studio productions. The speech department, including hearing and speech laboratories, was housed in a brick addition. The building was demolished, due to foundation and structural deterioration.

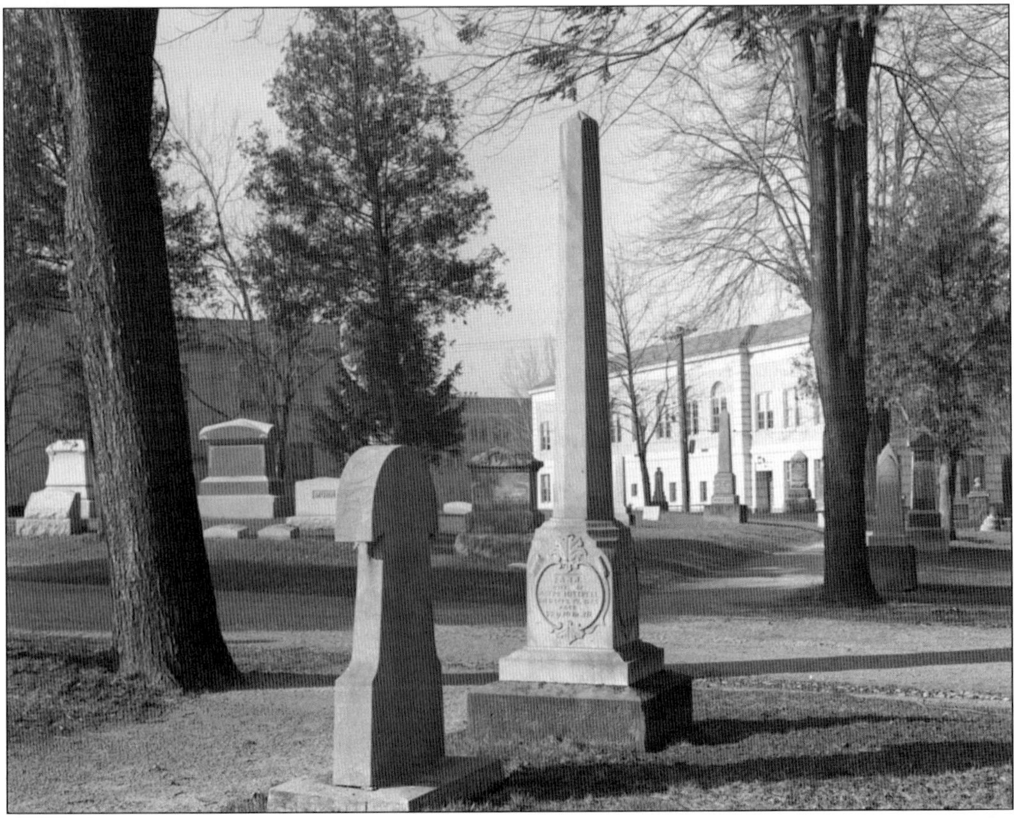

Oak Grove Cemetery was founded in 1873, and the BGSU campus has grown to encompass the cemetery. Pres. Homer B. Williams, as well as many others who have been affiliated with BGSU, are buried in the cemetery. Funeral processions that traversed the campus on Wayne Street were a common sight until the street was closed to outside traffic.

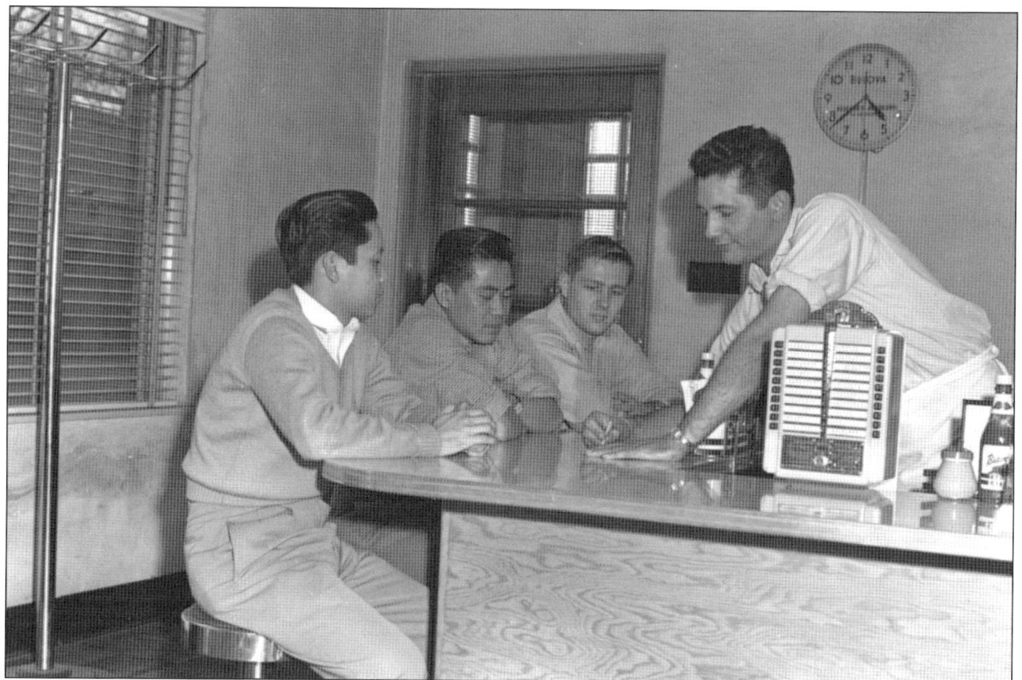

The Wagon Wheel Waffle Shop, noted for its home-style meals and homemade desserts, was located at 307 South Main Street. Kermit's Family Restaurant now occupies the site and maintains the same commitment to leisurely breakfasts and down-home eating.

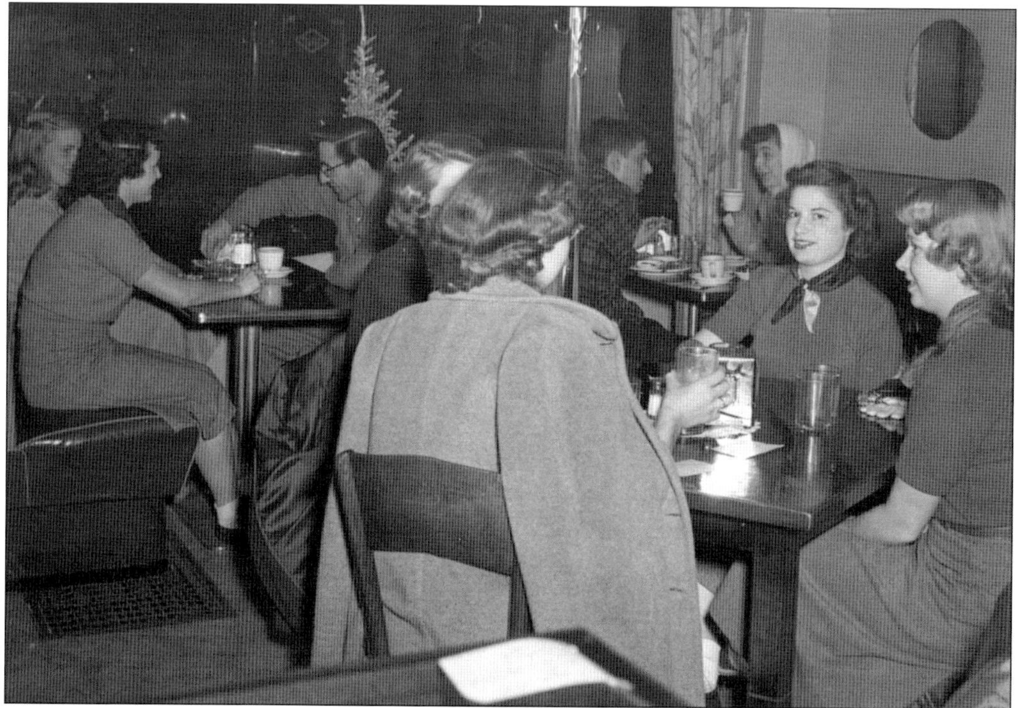

Main Restaurant was located at 163 North Main Street. The site was later occupied by the Bowling Green Chamber of Commerce and the Private Industry Council.

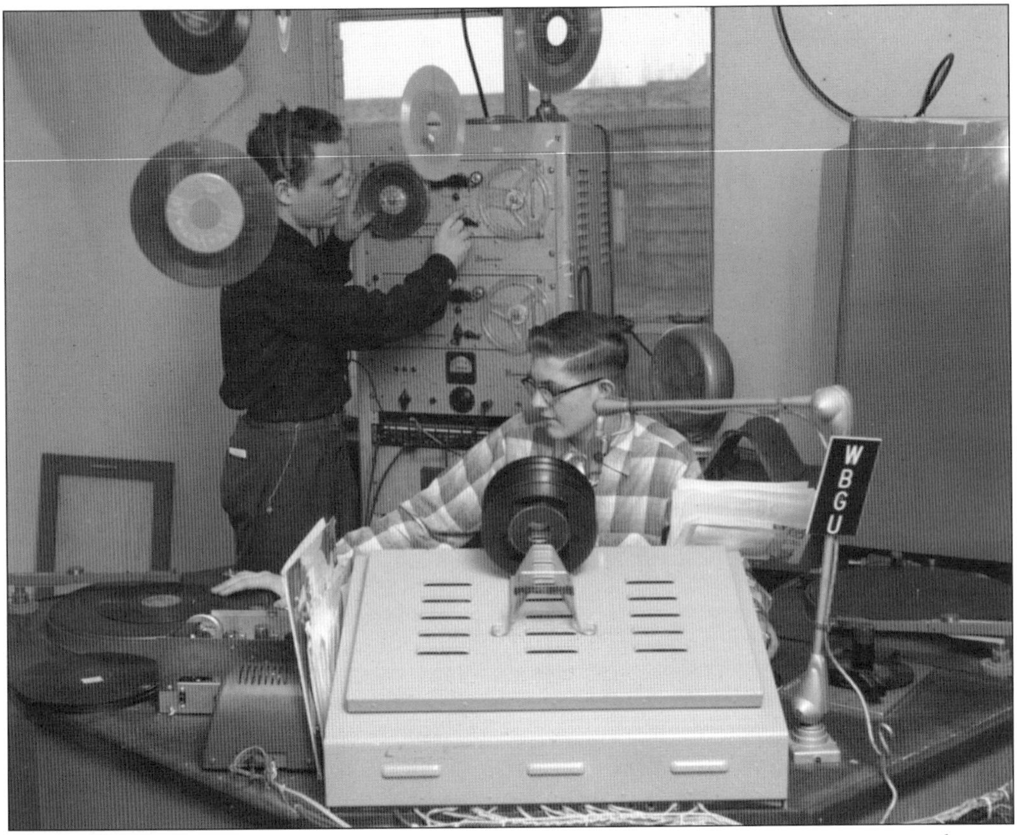

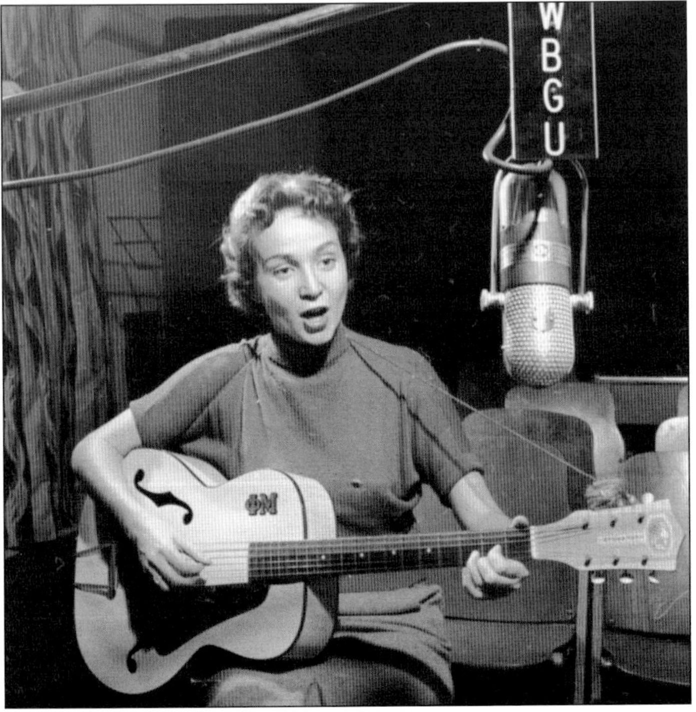

A BGSU campus radio station first appeared in the 1940s. Broadcasts included news, music, drama, commentary, comedy, announcements, and advertisements. WBGU-FM was established in 1951 and operated by BGSU students. In addition to playing popular recorded music, the station featured live performances by community and student talent. The station has had several homes over the years but it is now located in West Hall.

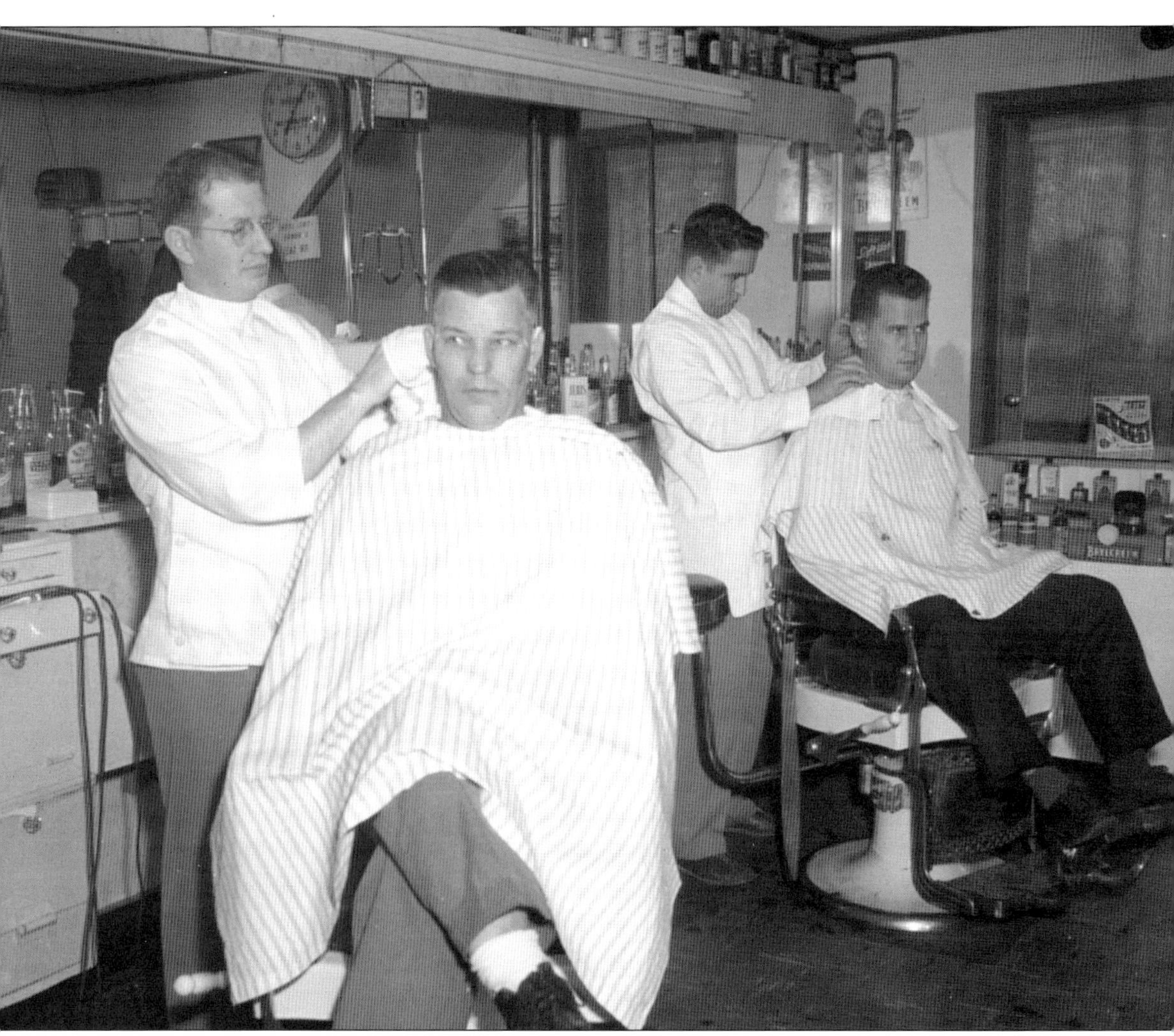

The Service Barber Shop was established in early 1950s by Dallas D. Sockrider and is still located at 426 East Wooster Street.

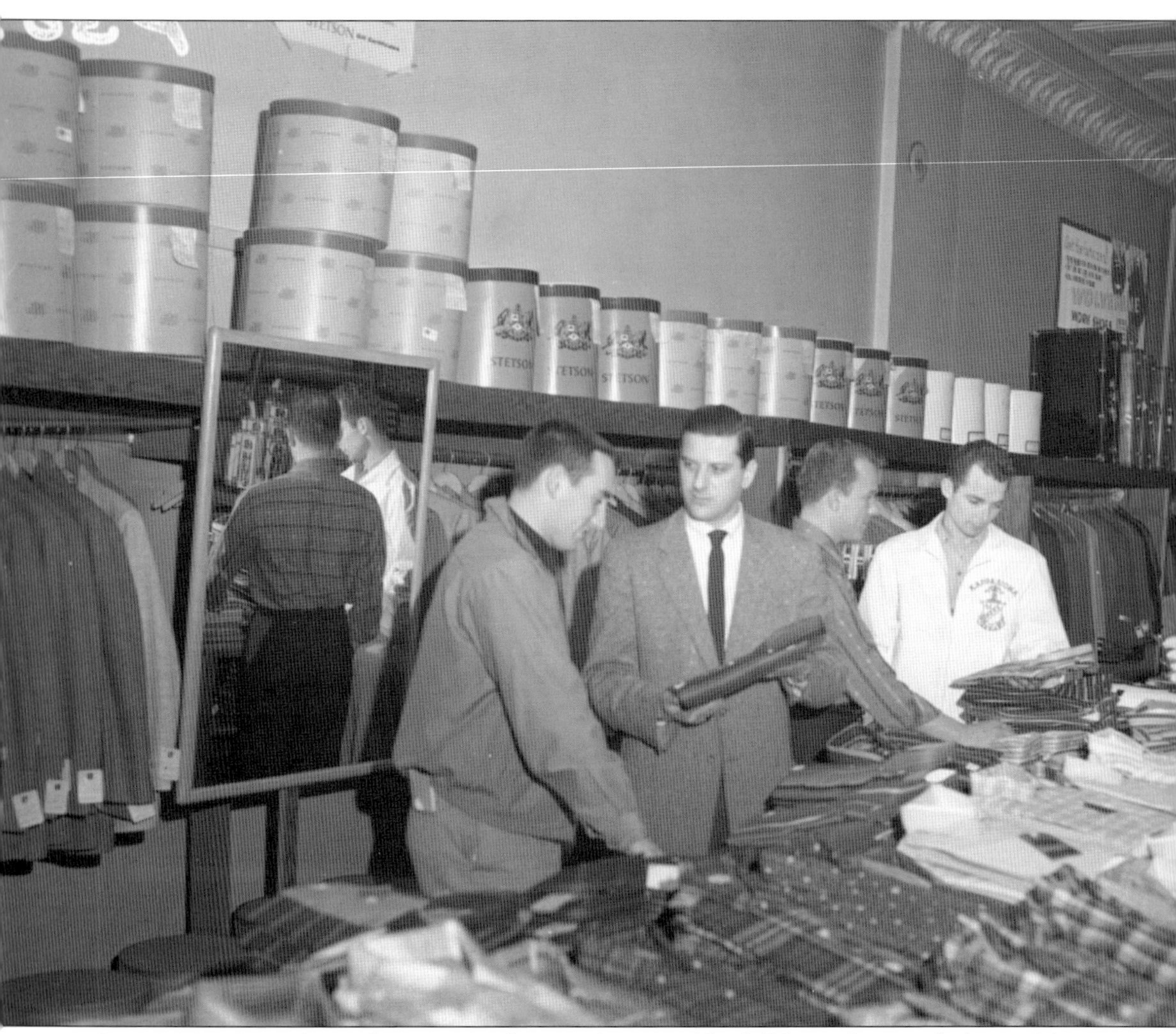

Larry's Men Store, located at 138 North Main Street, sold a full line of men's clothing. Gibson Home Restaurant and Weiss Cut Rate Store were previously located at this site.

A view of South Main
looking north from Clough
Street shows several
businesses, including
Newlove Restaurant
(now Huntington Bank),
Earl's Office Supplies
and Equipment (now
H&R Block), Coen Stove
Shop, Mills Jewelry, and
Randall's Bakery.

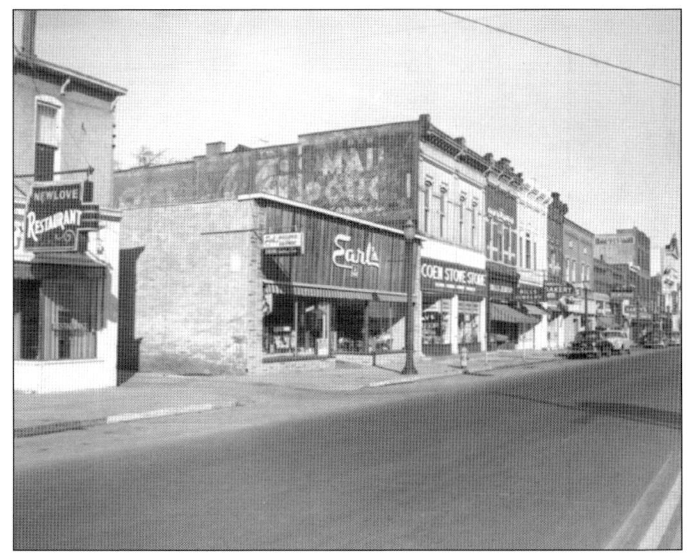

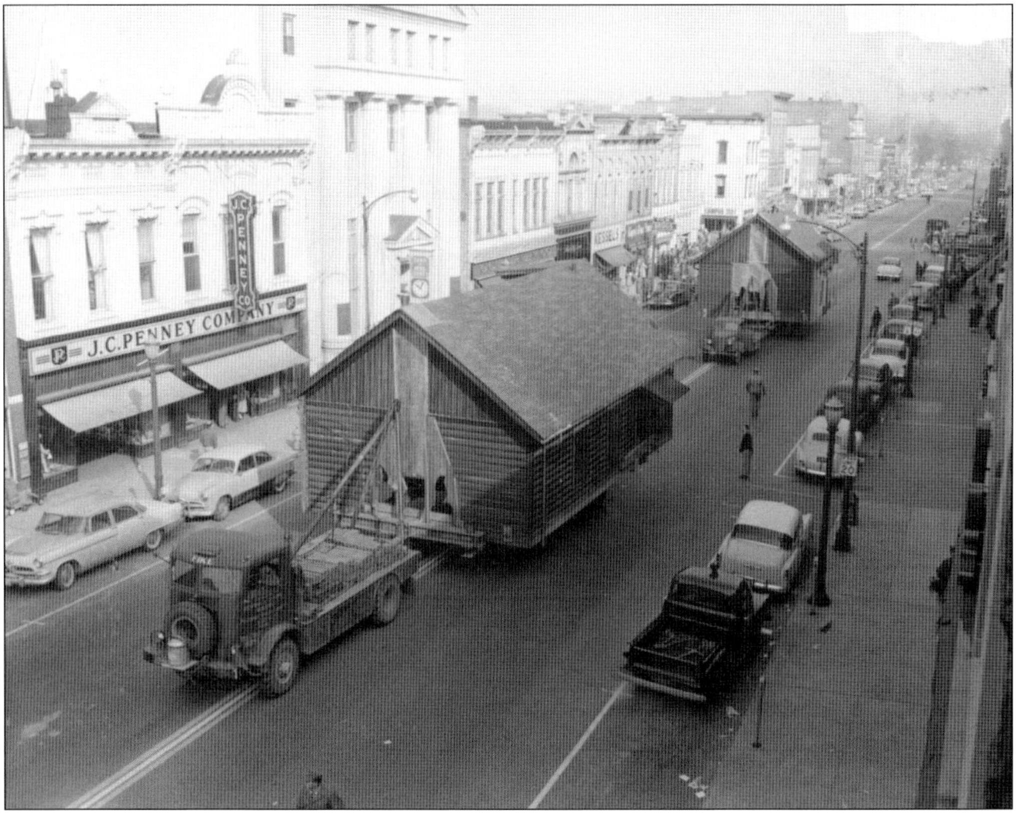

The Falcon's Nest, the first student union, was constructed by BGSU students in 1941. It was sold
and moved from campus in 1955 to make room for construction of the new BGSU student union.
The Nest traveled down East Wooster Street to South Main Street and then to its new home
in Portage, Ohio. Some of the businesses shown on the west side of South Main Street include
JC Penney (now Ace Hardware), Bank of Wood County, G.C. Murphy, City Loan, Kessel's, and
Kiger's Drug. A crowd gathered at the four corners to watch the spectacle.

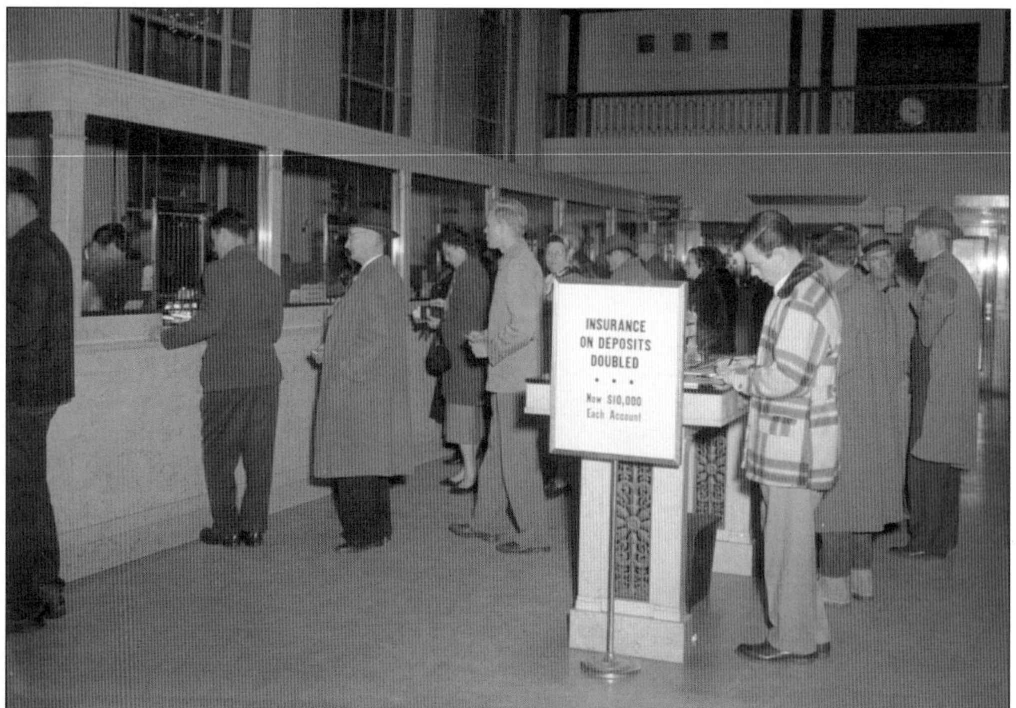

The Bank of Wood County, at 130 South Main Street, was opened on November 16, 1931, in the midst of the Great Depression. The bank was one of several financial institutions that served the needs of BGSU students and the local community. The Bank of Wood County became Huntington National Bank in 1980.

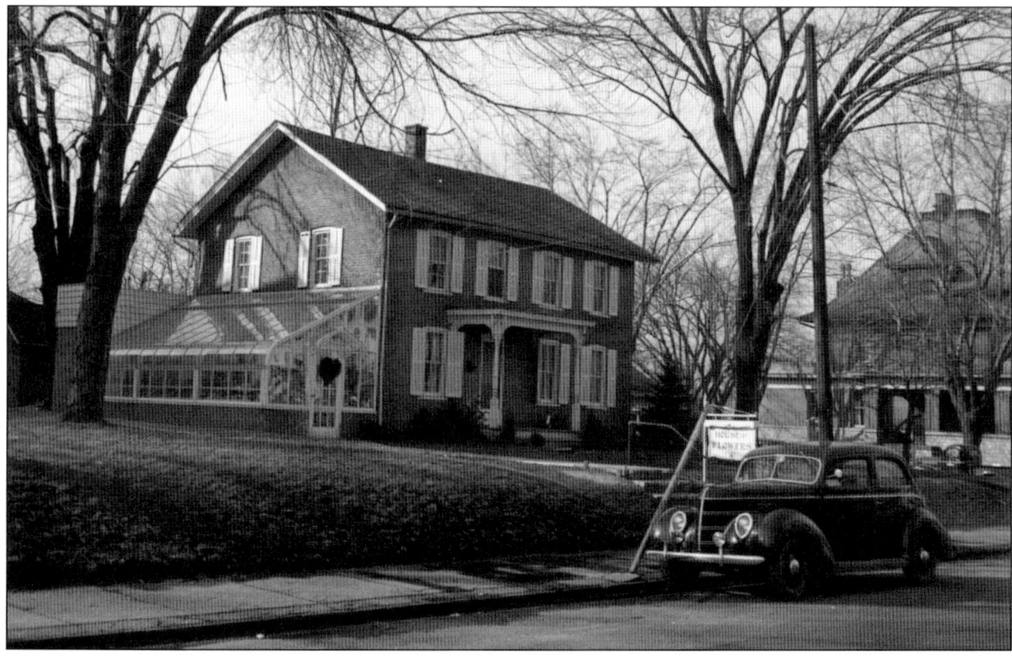

The House of Flowers was located at 331 North Main Street. Established in the 1940s by John E. Cheetwood in his home, a storefront was later added for customer convenience.

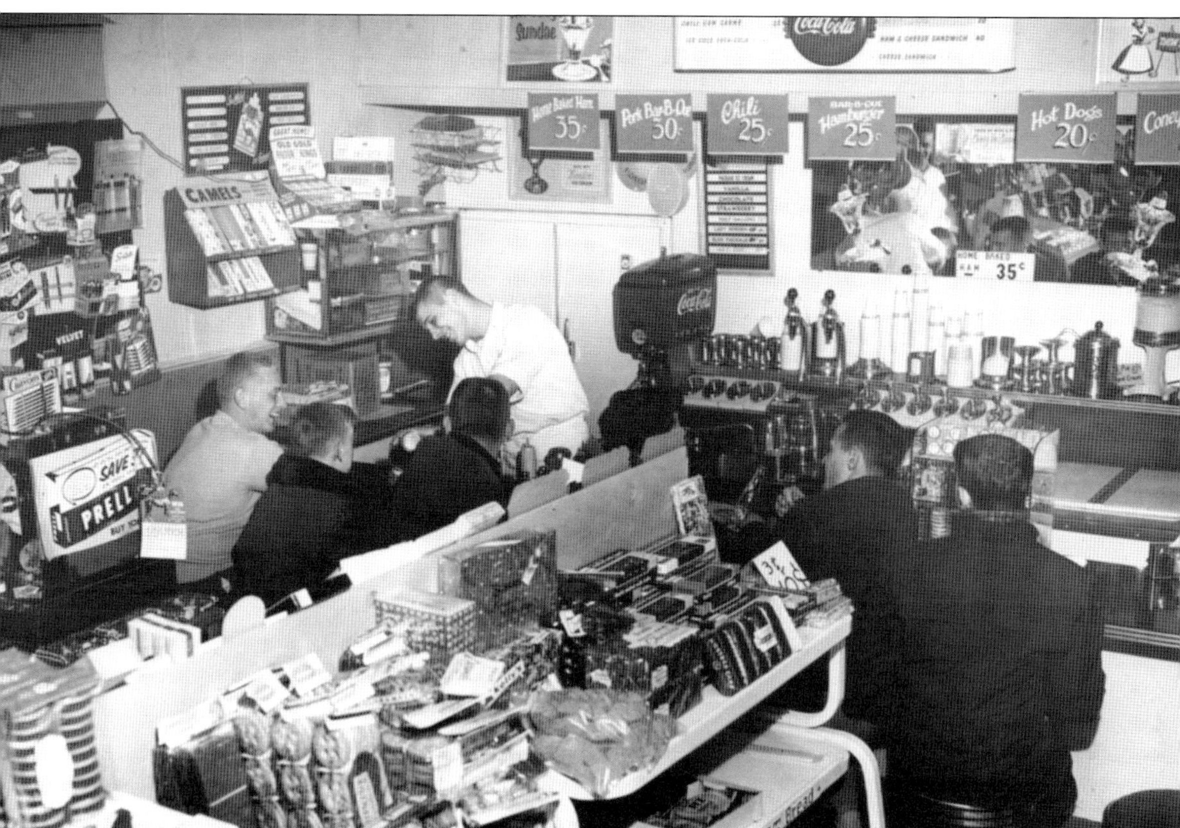

Conveniently located directly across the street from campus at 900 East Wooster Street, TOs provided a diverse variety of products for students to purchase, including snacks, toiletries, and tobacco products. A lunch counter and soda fountain were featured. The business was expanded to include the former Household Appliance Store and became known as the Campus Corner.

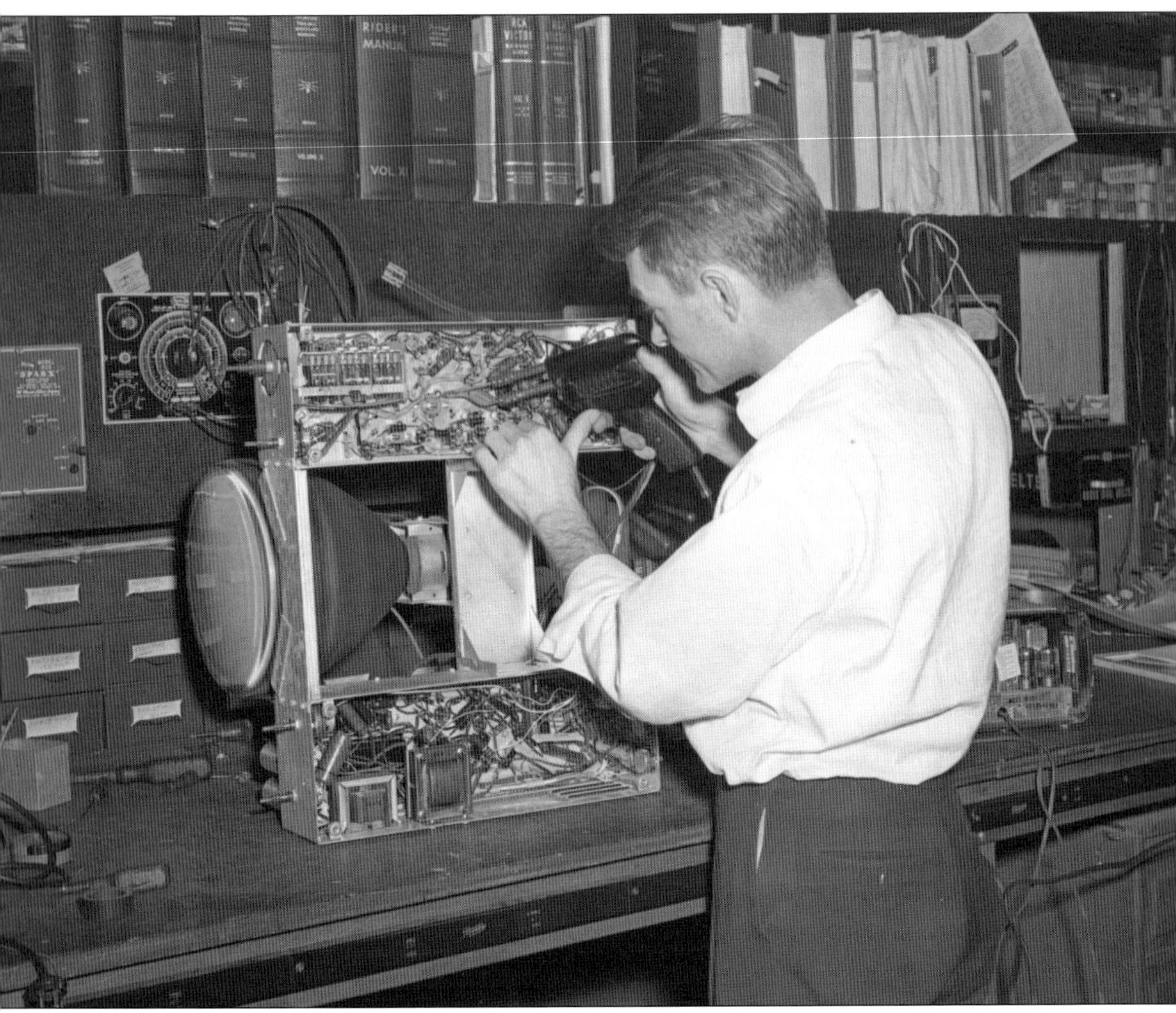

Household Appliance Shop, at 902 East Wooster Street, sold and repaired radios, televisions, and other electronics. Beat the Bookstore is now located at the site.

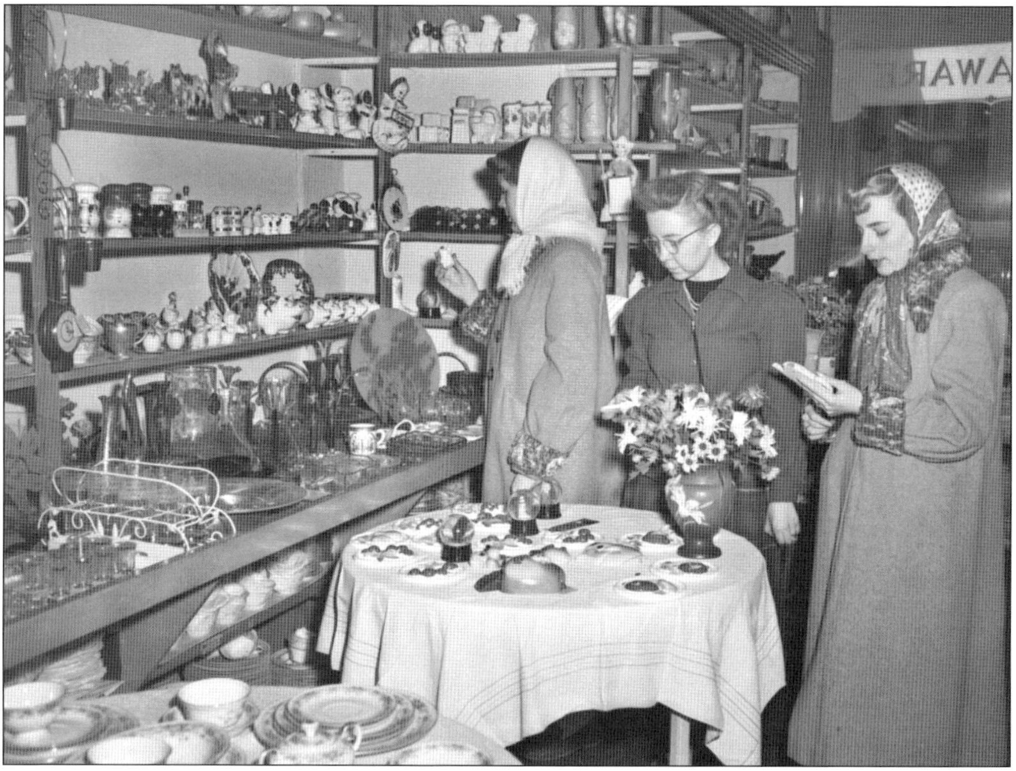

Rappaport's Department Store was located at 127 South Main Street. The store carried a diverse selection of merchandise, including china, glassware, art and school supplies, and candy.

The Campus Men's Shop, located at 101 North Main Street at the corner of West Wooster Street, provided a large selection of clothing and accessories. The Clothes Rack and Pfisterer's-Gladieux Clothiers later occupied the site. Mosaic Consignment Studio is the current occupant.

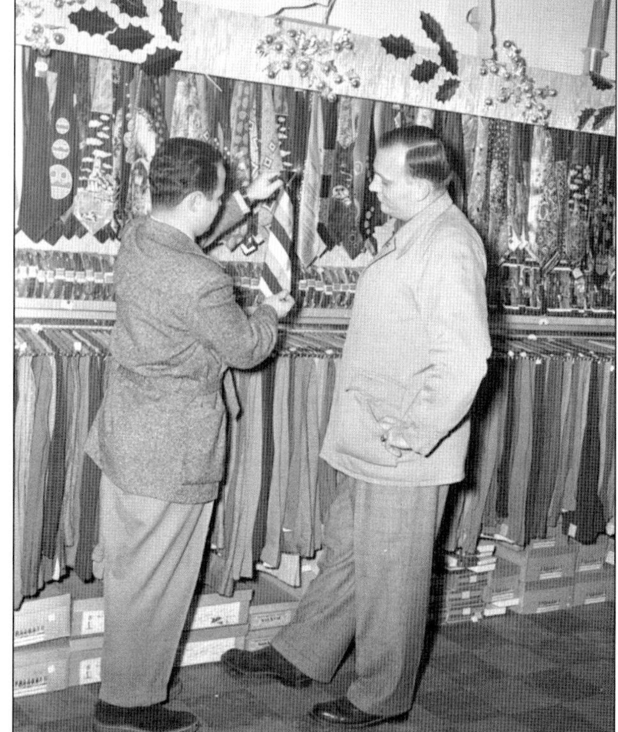

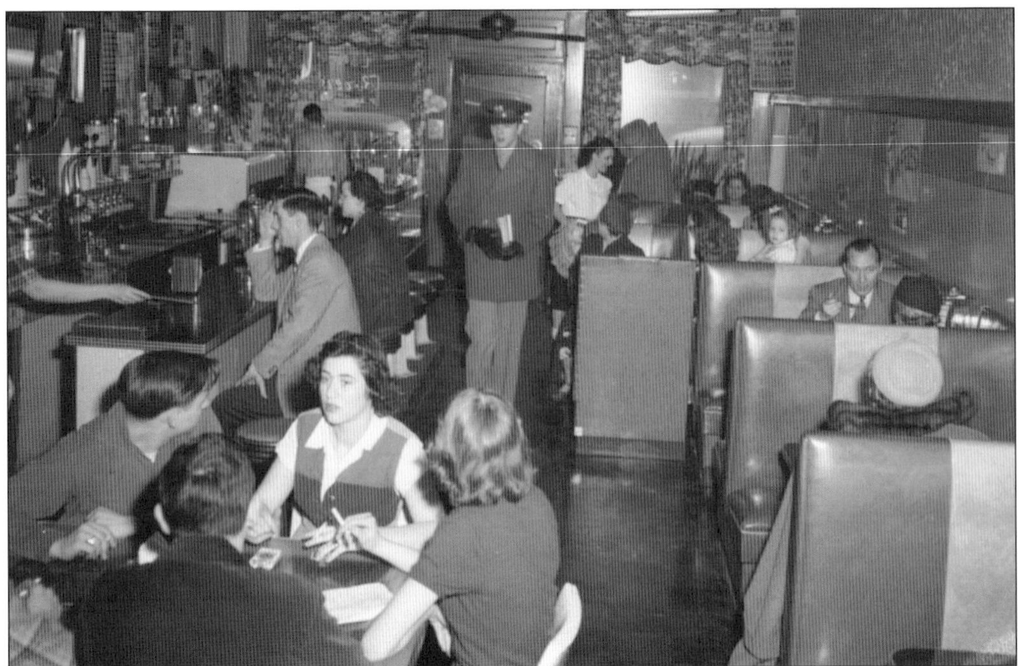

Holland Snack Bar, located at 125 North Main Street, featured the meaty Dream Burger. The Jack & Jill Shop and Klever's Jewelry Store later occupied the site. Broad Wing Tattoo and Body Piercings is the current occupant.

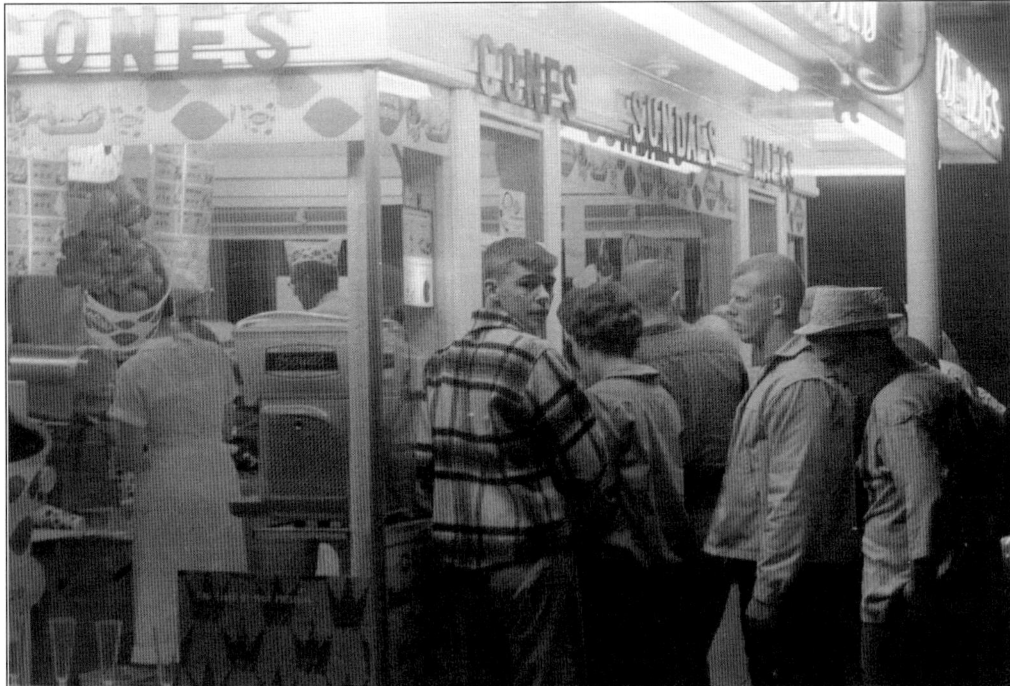

The Dairy Queen Store at 434 East Wooster Street opened in the mid-1950s. Myle's Dairy Queen is located at the same location. The Dairy Queen has been a favorite among BGSU students and local residents.

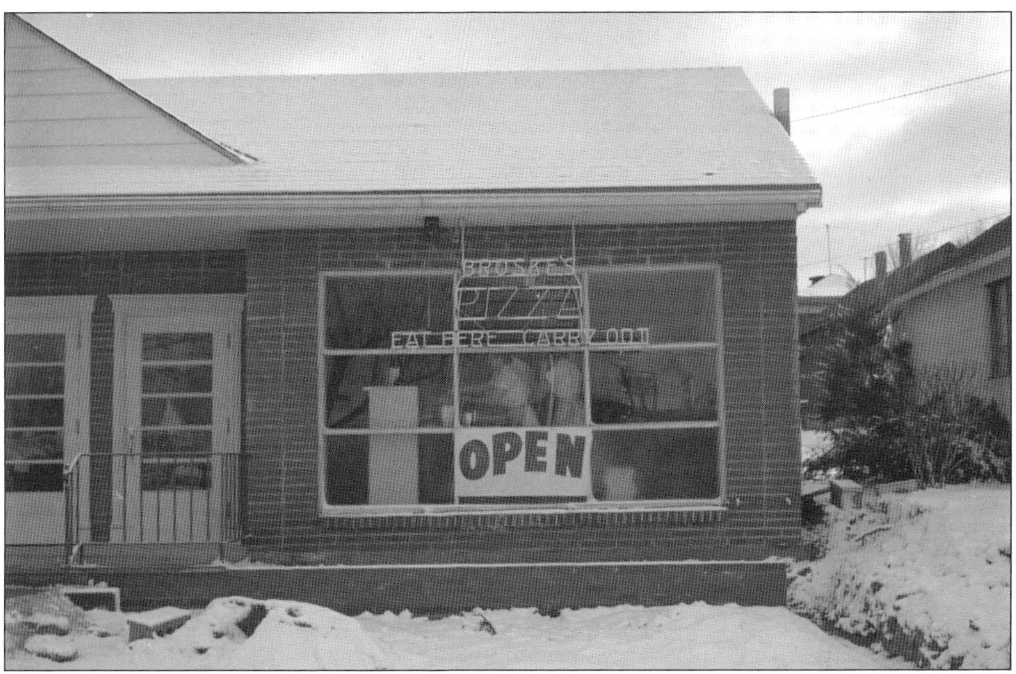

Pizza was first introduced in the United States by Italian immigrants in the late 19th century, but it gained popularity after World War II. The first pizzerias appeared in Bowling Green in the mid-1950s. One of the first, Broske's Pizza, was located at East Wooster Street.

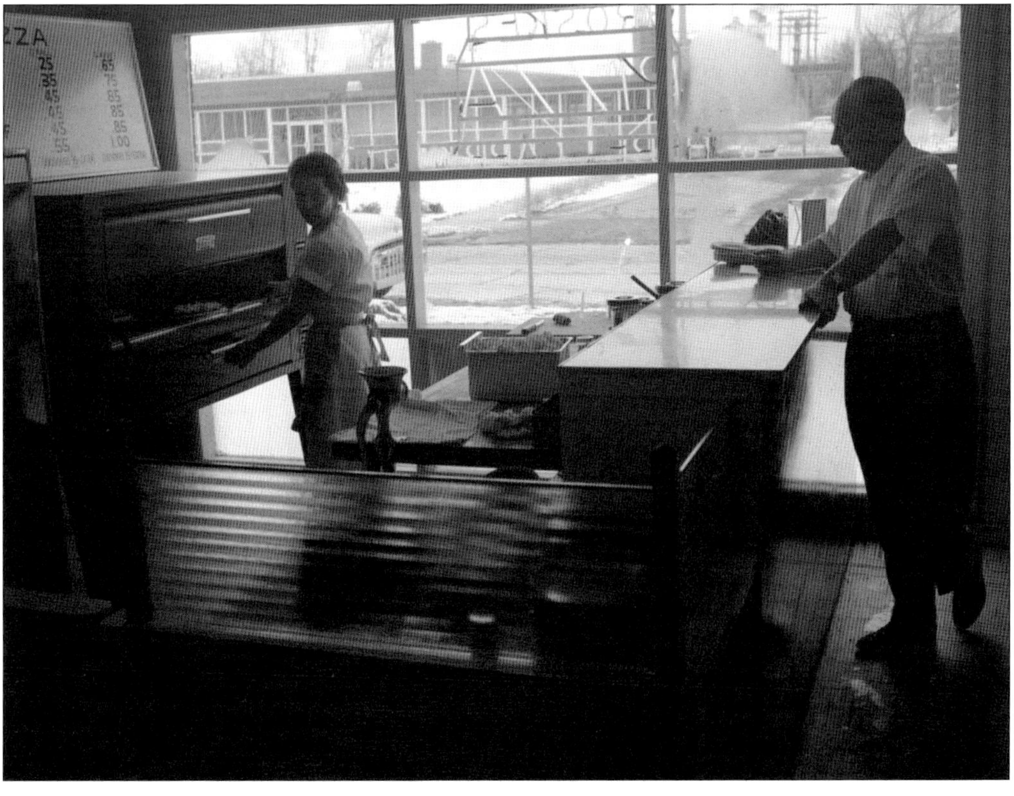

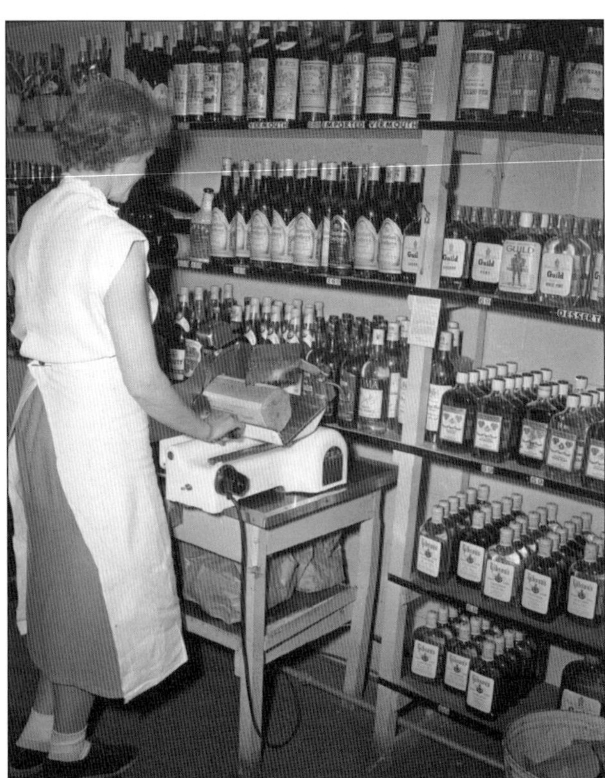

Bee Gee Delicatessen & Carry Out at 115 West Merry Street carried wine, champagne, beer, and kosher foods.

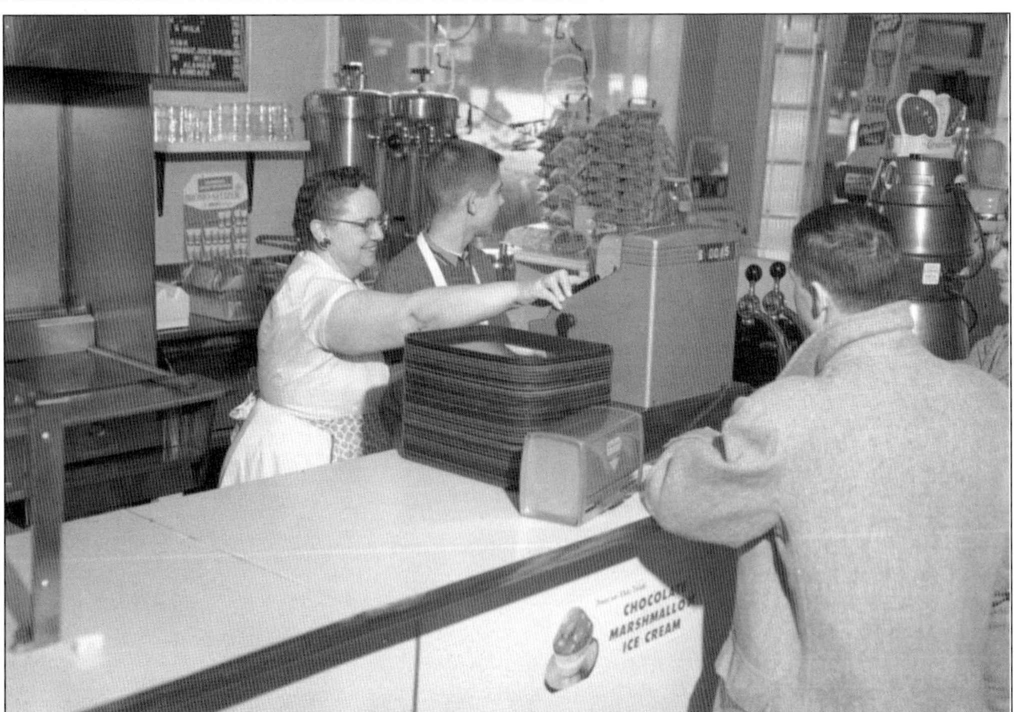

University Dairy Bar was located at 531 Ridge Street at the corner of Thurstin Street and across from Sorority Row. Collegiate Connection later occupied this site.

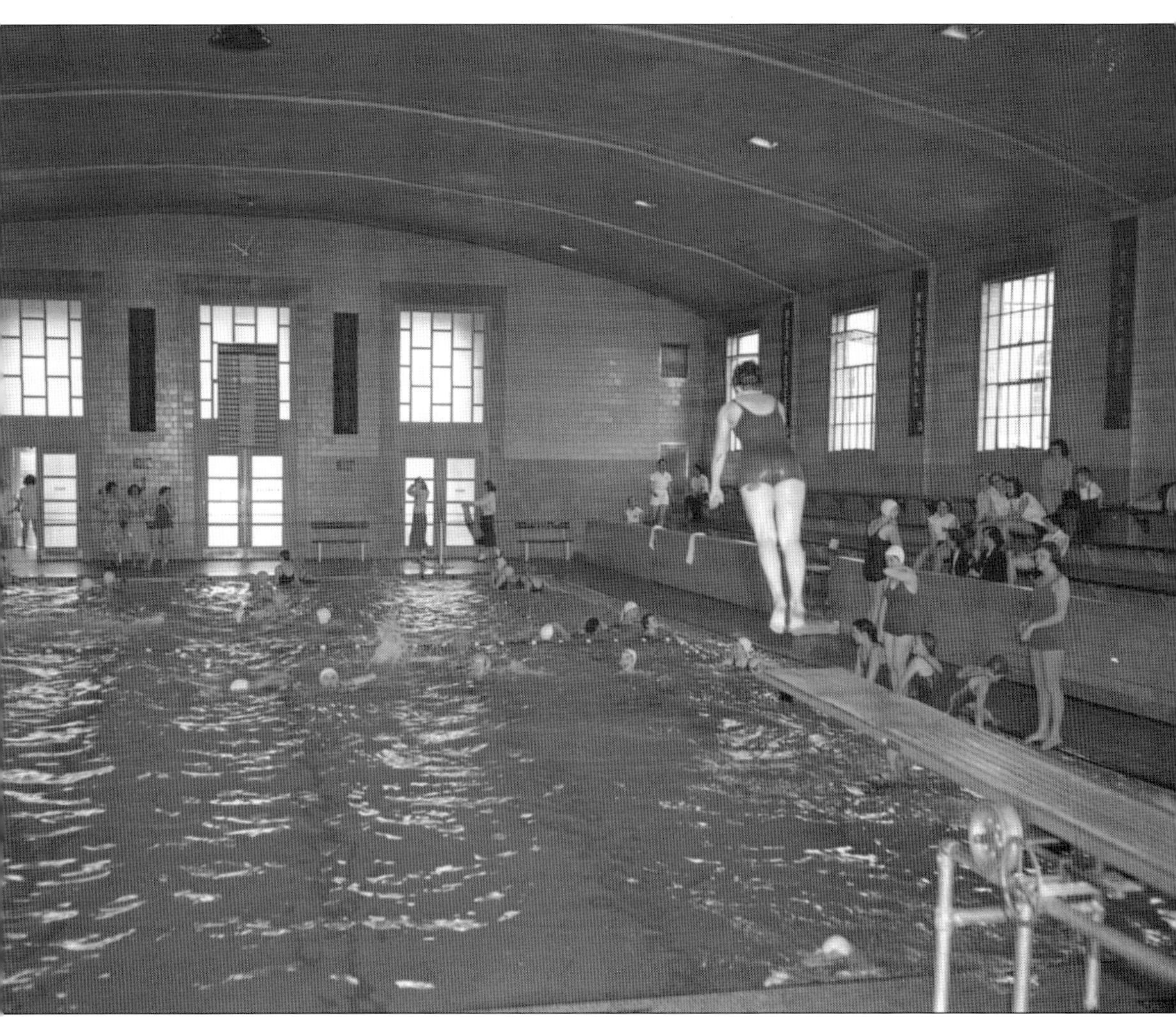

The BGSU women's health and physical education department sponsored an annual Northwest Ohio Sports Day for young women. Recreational activities included bowling, dancing, shuffleboard, swimming, table tennis, trampoline demonstrations, and volleyball.

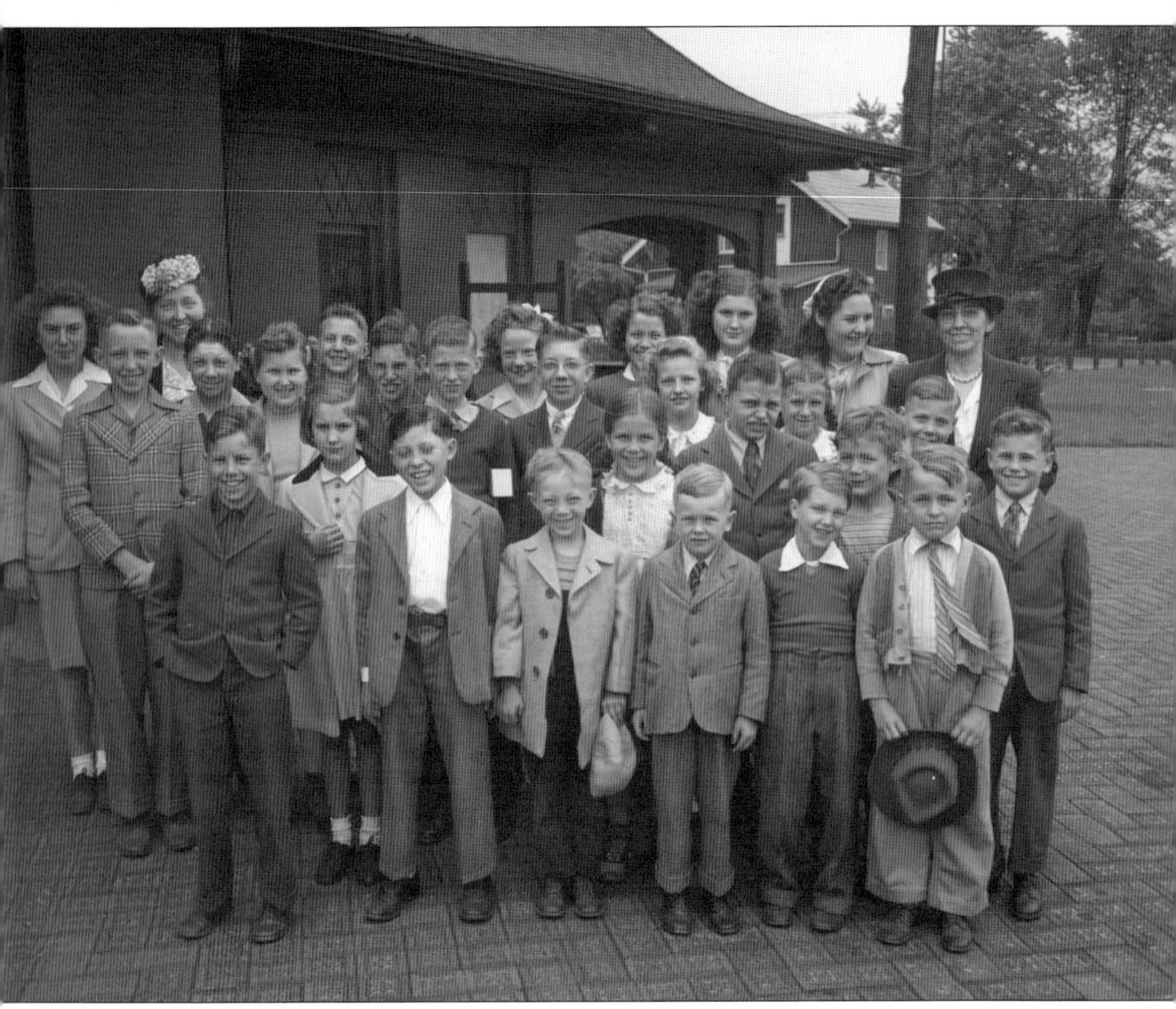

A group of manual-training schoolchildren, dressed in their best clothing, anxiously awaits the arrival of a train that will take them to their field-trip destination. Students visited the Toledo Museum of Art and the Toledo Zoo, among other places of interest.

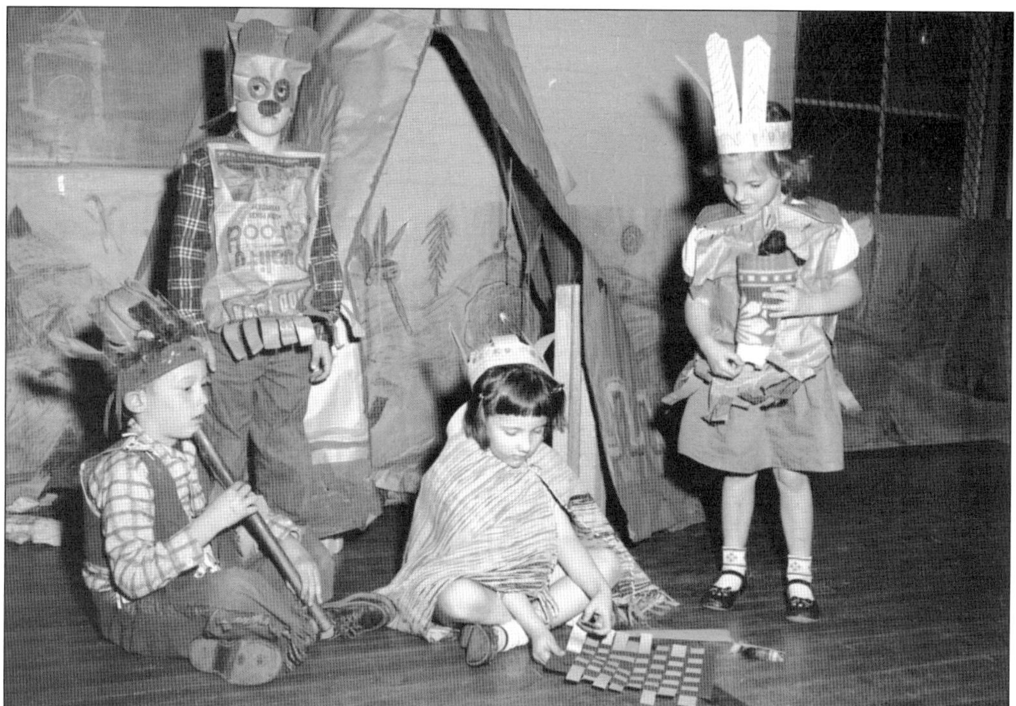

Students of the manual-training school and local schools participated in a number of artistic activities. A group of children show off their talents in a depiction of Native American culture (above), while a group of Kenwood Elementary students create their own necklaces (below).

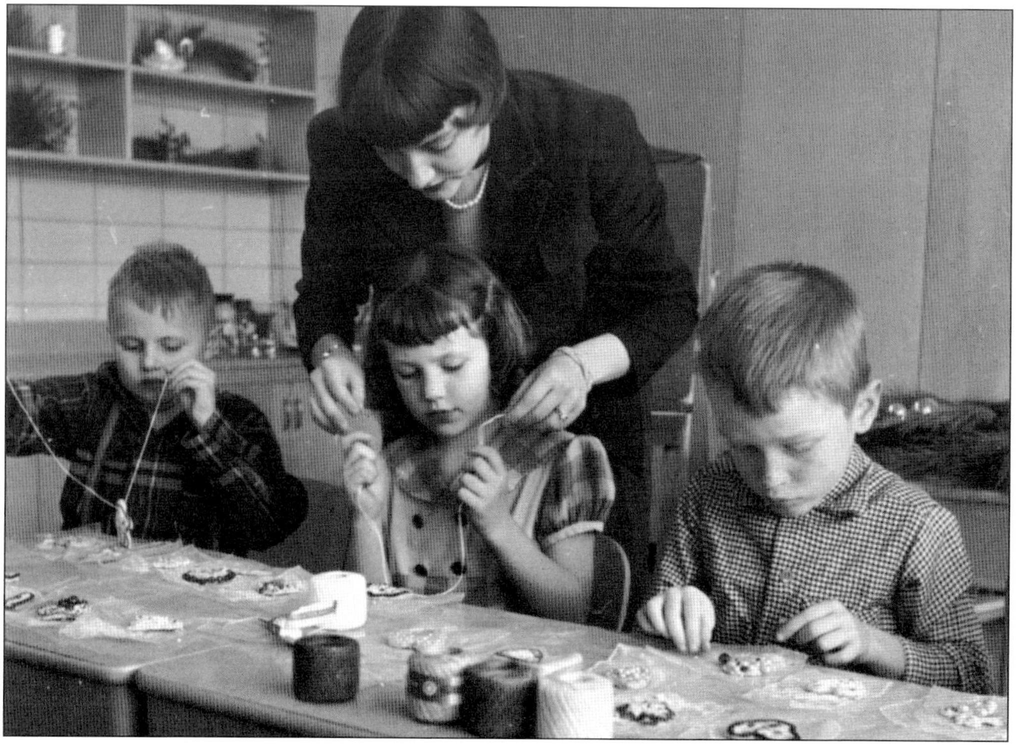

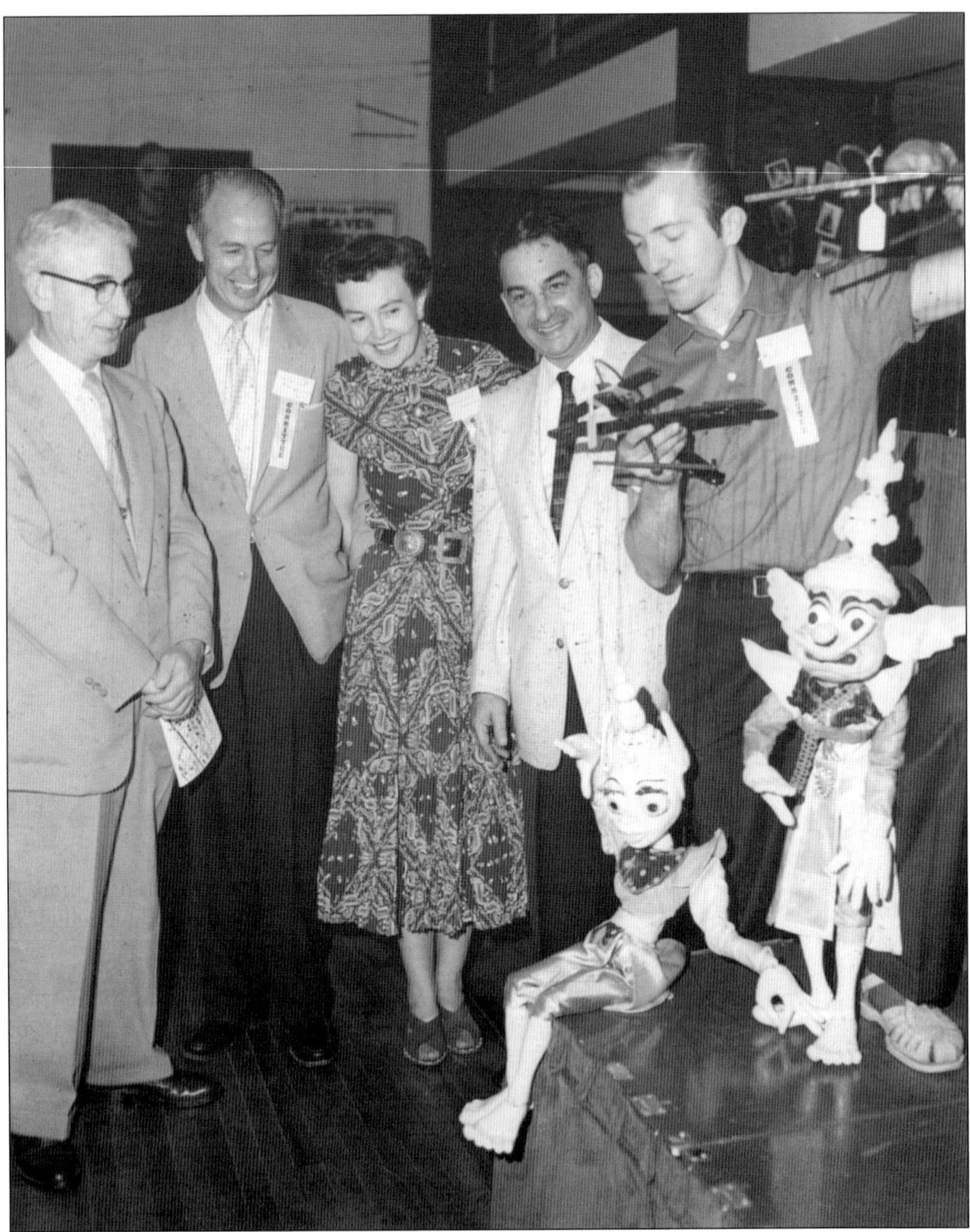

Puppetry is a very early and popular form of theater. It has been used in counseling and therapy, as well as in educational programming. The National Puppeteer Festival, held in 1955, is one of many BGSU-sponsored events that focused specifically on puppetry. The festival featured puppet making and shows. Marionettes Kukla, Fran, and Ollie were featured.

G&M Drug was located at 109 North Main Street. Vatan's Import & Gifts was also located at this site. Call of the Canyon Café is the current occupant.

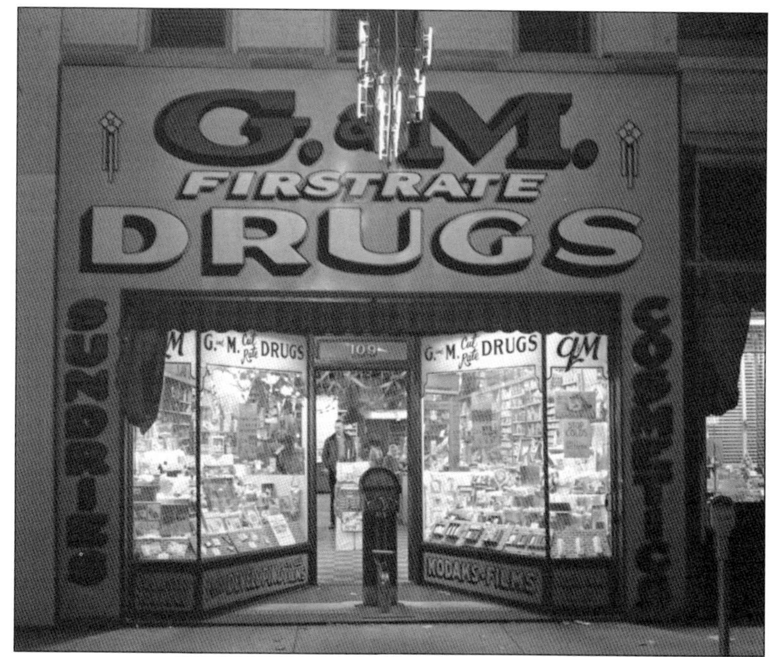

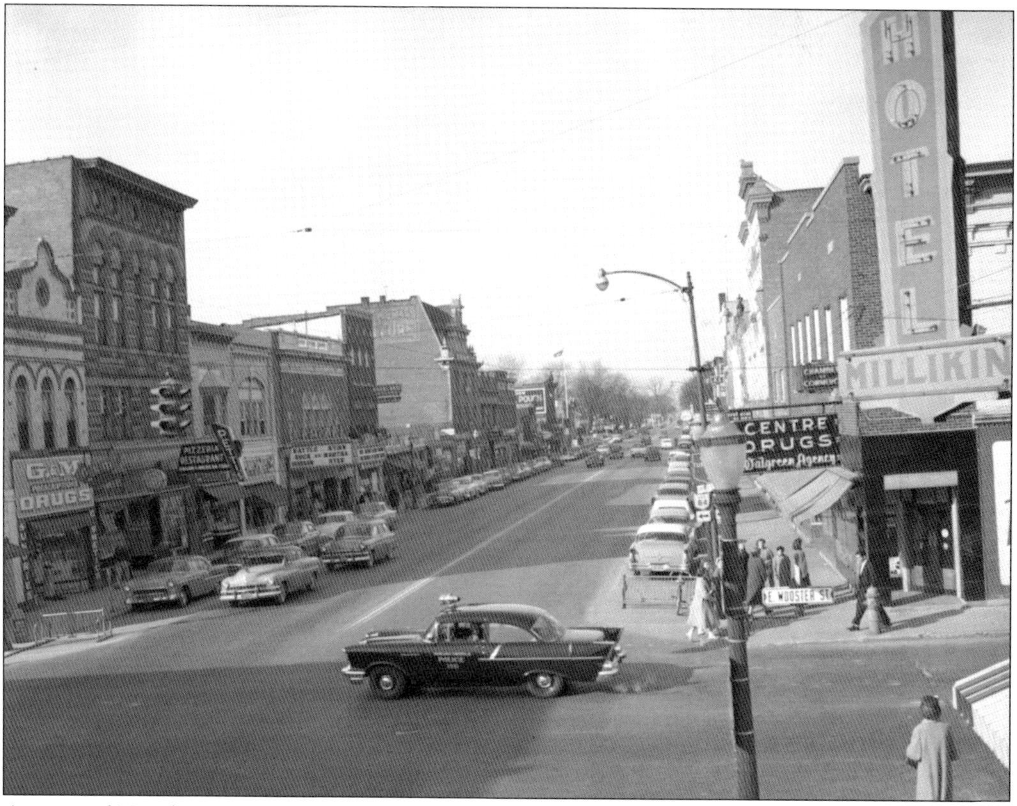

A view of North Main Street from Wooster Street in the mid-to-late 1950s shows the Hotel Millikin in the foreground, Centre Drug, the chamber of commerce, G&M Drugs, Petit's Pizzeria Restaurant, Jack & Jill, The Cla-Zel Theatre, and Rogers Brothers' Drugs.

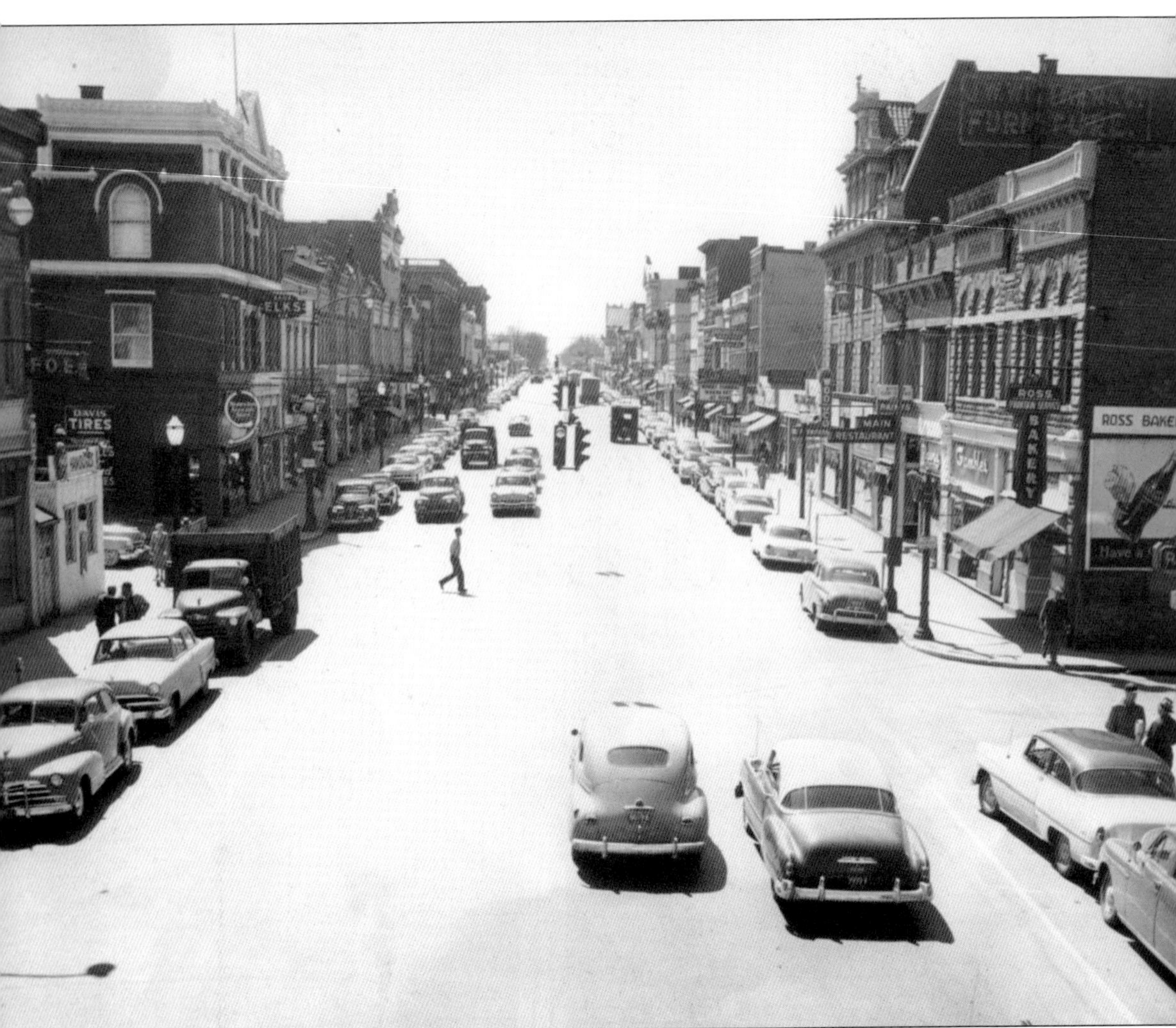

A view of a busy North Main Street, looking south from West Court Street, shows the many businesses, including Ross Bakery (now Pisanello's Pizza), Gamble's, Main Restaurant, Davis Tires (now Corner Grill), Western Auto Associate Store (now Uptown-Downtown), Meade's Restaurant, and Gillespie Plumbing & Heating.

Three

ENROLLMENT BOOM, ACTIVISM, AND UNREST

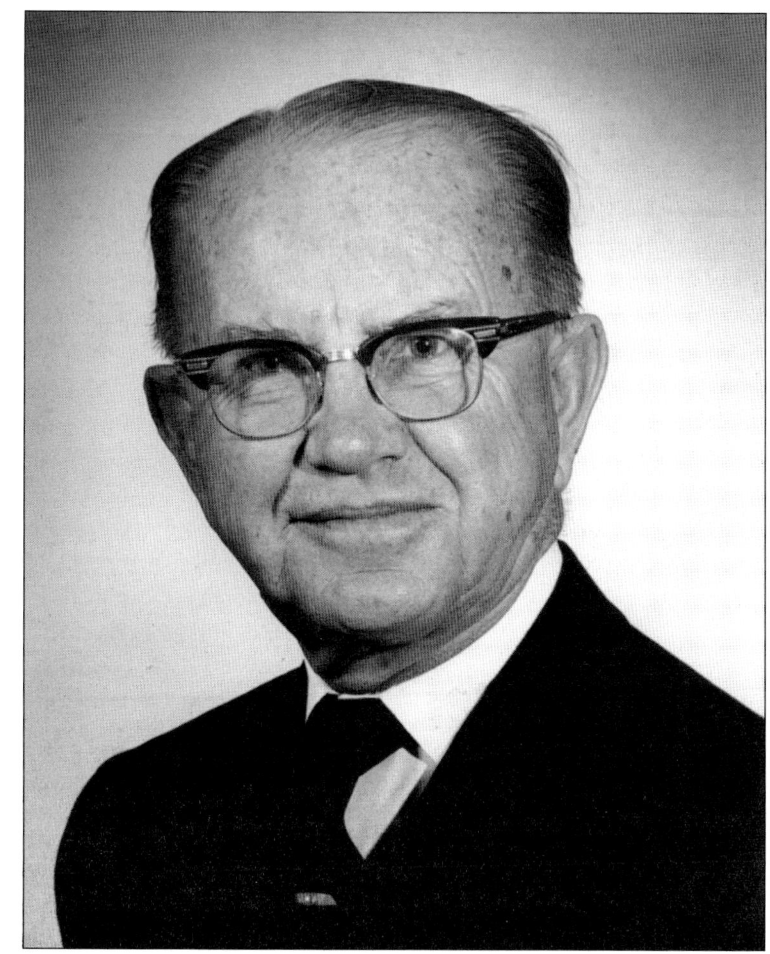

Franklin "Gus" Skibbie, a 1926 graduate of Bowling Green State Normal College, was elected mayor of Bowling Green in 1960 and served until 1972. He was one of the first six inductees into the BGSU Athletic Hall of Fame in 1964 for his work as a football player and basketball and football coach. Over the objection of many local residents, he allowed the peaceful march through downtown following the Kent State shootings. Skibbie was impressed with the way the BGSU community handled its response the event.

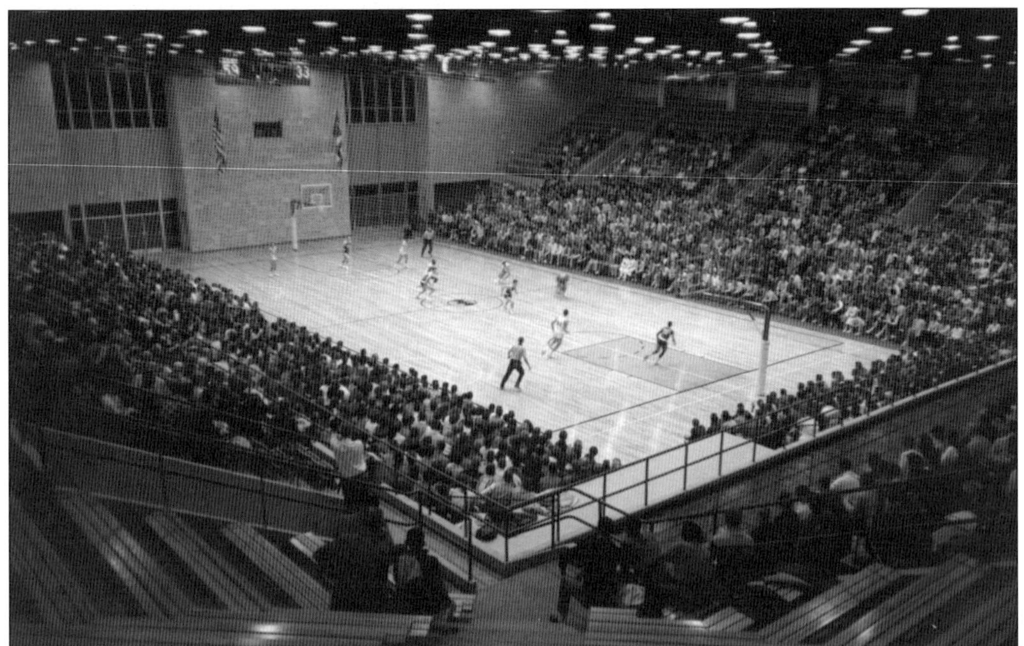

Anderson Arena, inside Memorial Hall, was the venue of many BGSU athletic events, including women's and men's basketball games from 1963 to 2011, as well as other special campus and community events. The championship basketball and volleyball teams practiced in Anderson. The Stroh Center, which opened in 2011, became the new setting for many of these activities.

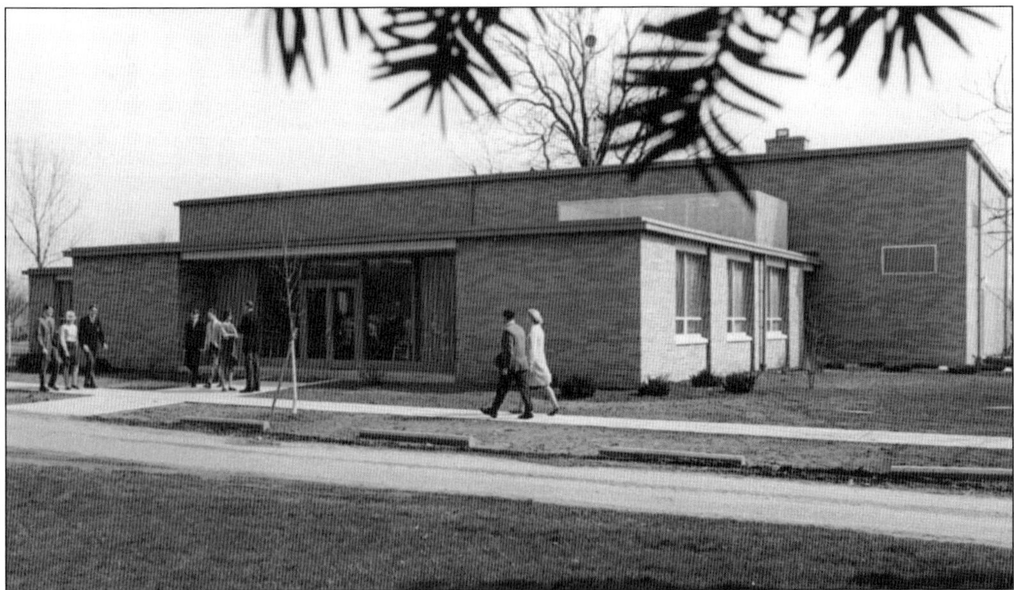

Television broadcasting became a part of the BGSU curriculum after World War II. The construction of a public educational television facility was completed in 1965, and the first broadcast of WBGU-TV took place in January 1966. Since its inception, one of the missions of WBGU-TV has been to provide quality educational programming to Bowling Green and Northwest Ohio residents. The building was named the Tucker Telecommunication Center in 1994 in honor of Duane E. And Margaret J. Tucker.

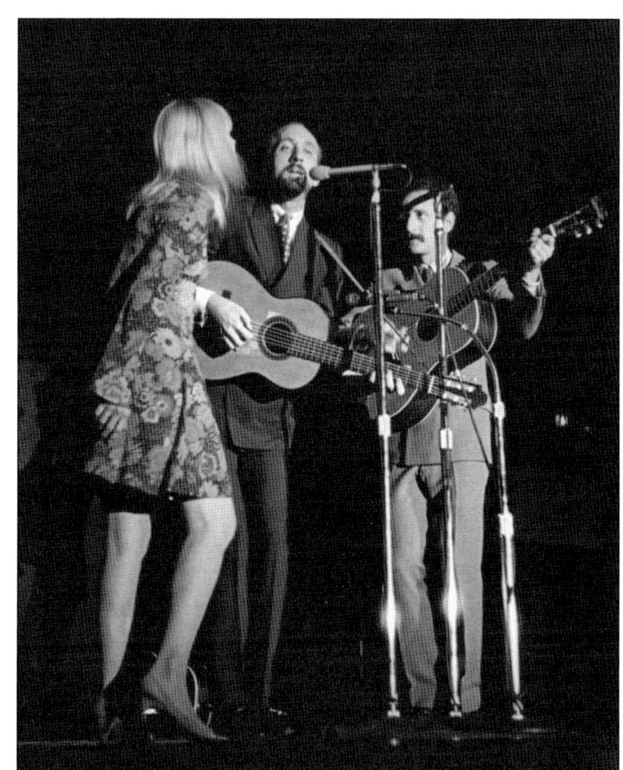

The university has sponsored many concerts that featured popular recording artists in Anderson Arena and other venues. Peter, Paul & Mary came in 1962 and 1993, and John Denver performed in 1972.

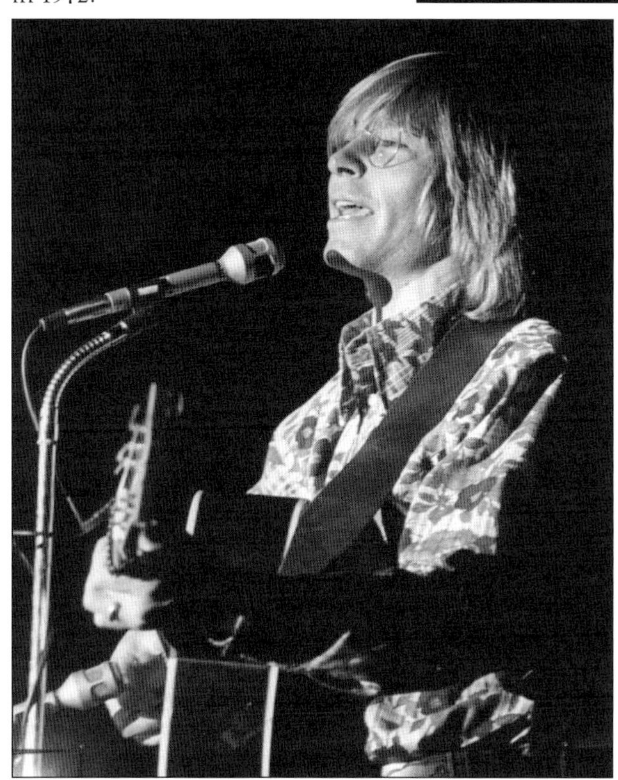

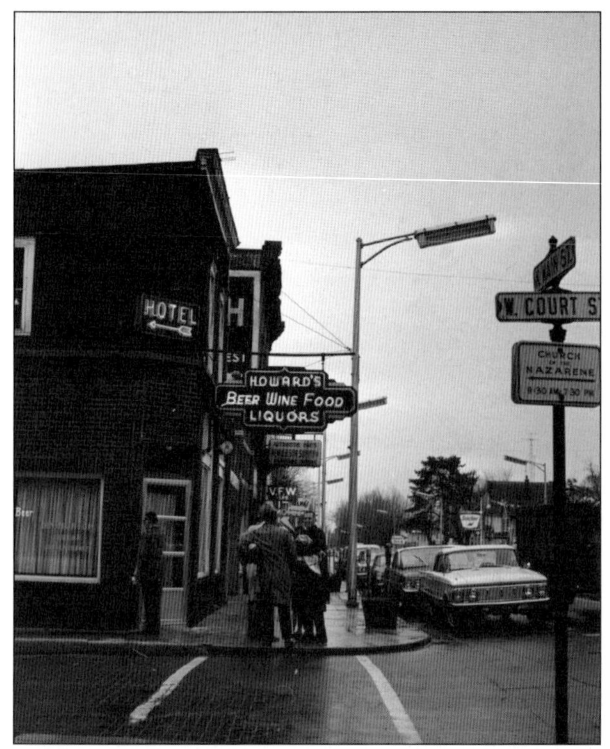

Howard's Restaurant at 213 North Main Street was originally established by Fred H. Howard as Howard's Confectionary Store at 117 North Main Street. It became one of the few businesses that owned a liquor license in a formerly dry community. A hotel was once affiliated with the business. Howard's moved across the street to its current location at 210 North Main Street in 1973 to make way for construction of the new Wood County District Public Library. The name was changed to Howard's Club H. Students have always enjoyed the casual, unassuming atmosphere.

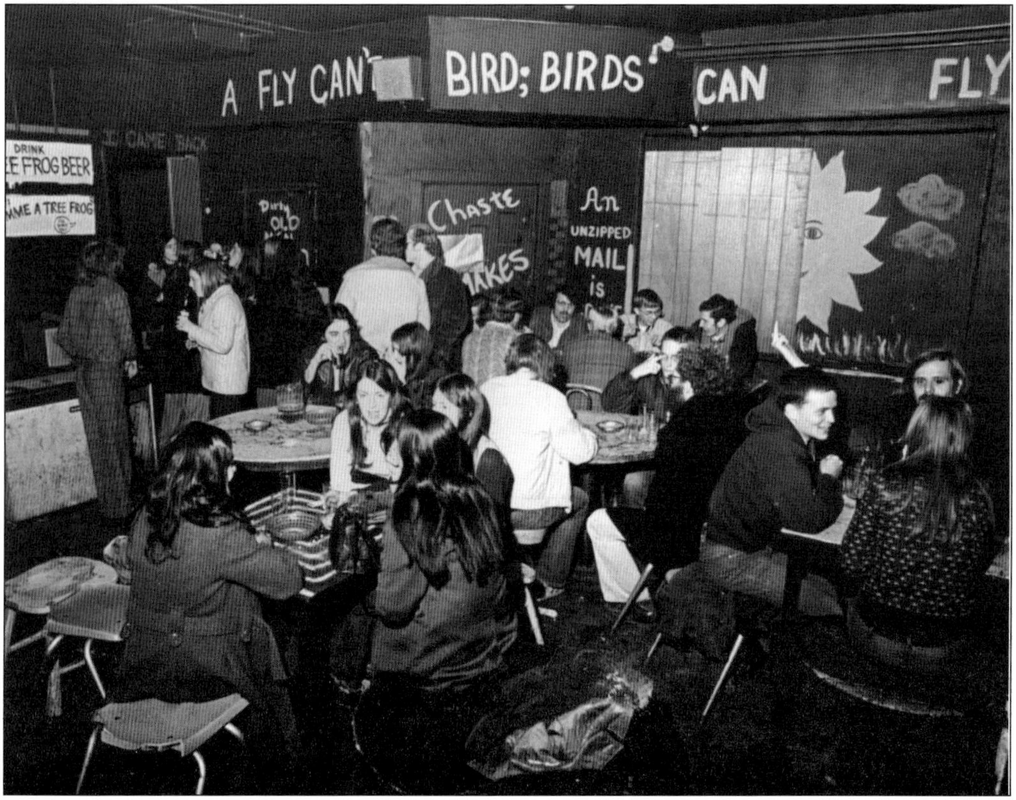

The Falcon,
formerly Broske's
Pizza, was located
at 516 East
Wooster Street.
Myle's Pizza,
which is known
for its rich, hearty
pizzas, is now
located at the site.

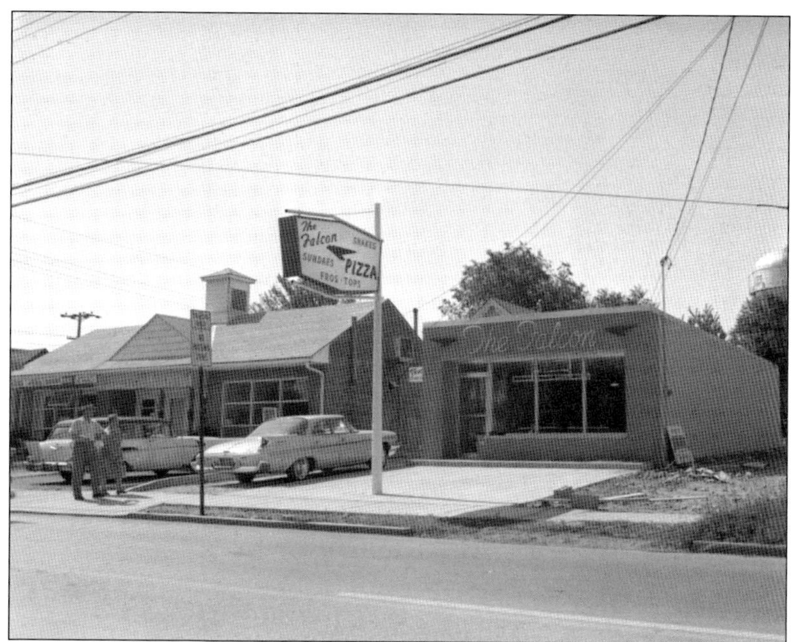

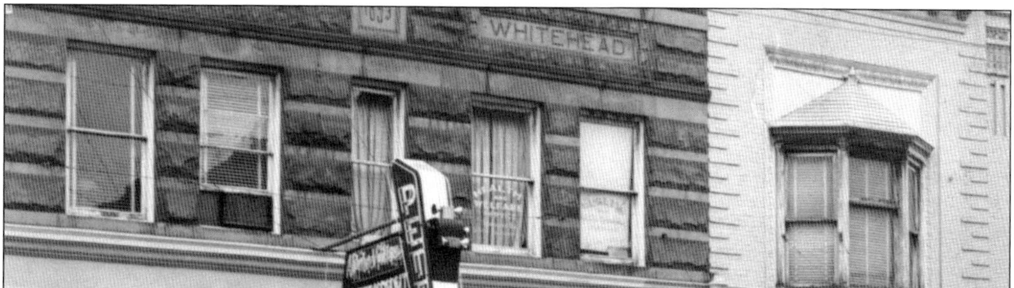

Petit's Alpine Village, formerly Petit's Pizzeria Restaurant, was located at 117 North Main Street.
The restaurant featured Italian cuisine, including pizza. It was especially popular among BGSU
students in the 1960s and 1970s.

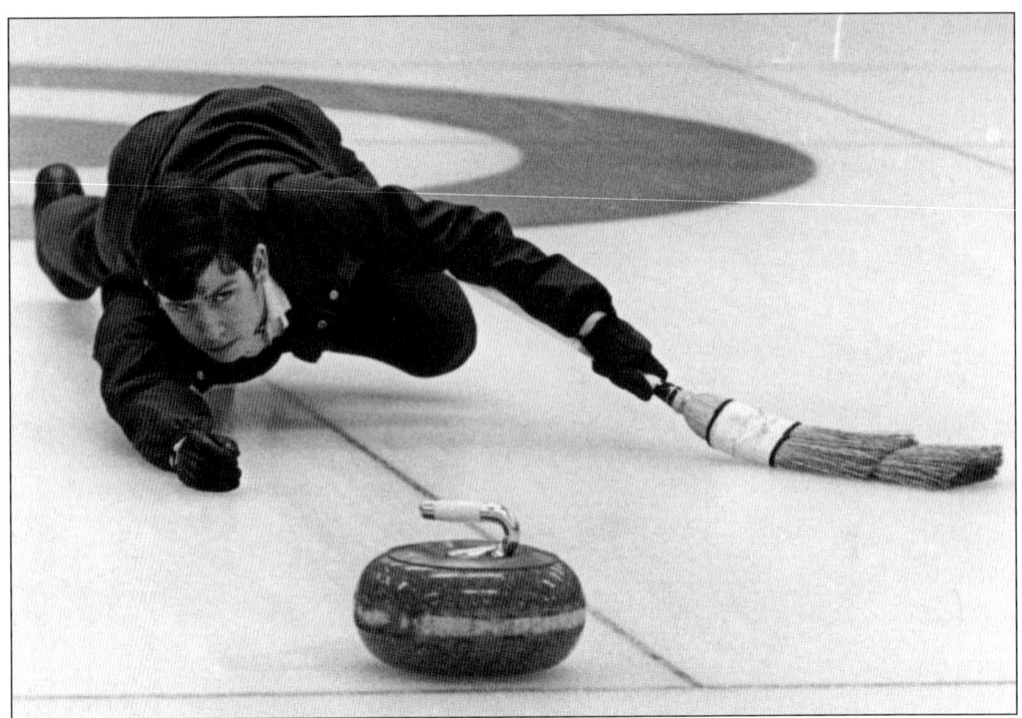

The Ice Arena, which was opened in 1967, serves as the focal point for recreational ice skating, intercollegiate hockey competitions, curling matches, and physical-education activities. Programs offered include basic ice-skating lessons (below), figure skating, public skating, curling (above), broomball, youth hockey clinics and leagues, and recreational adult hockey leagues.

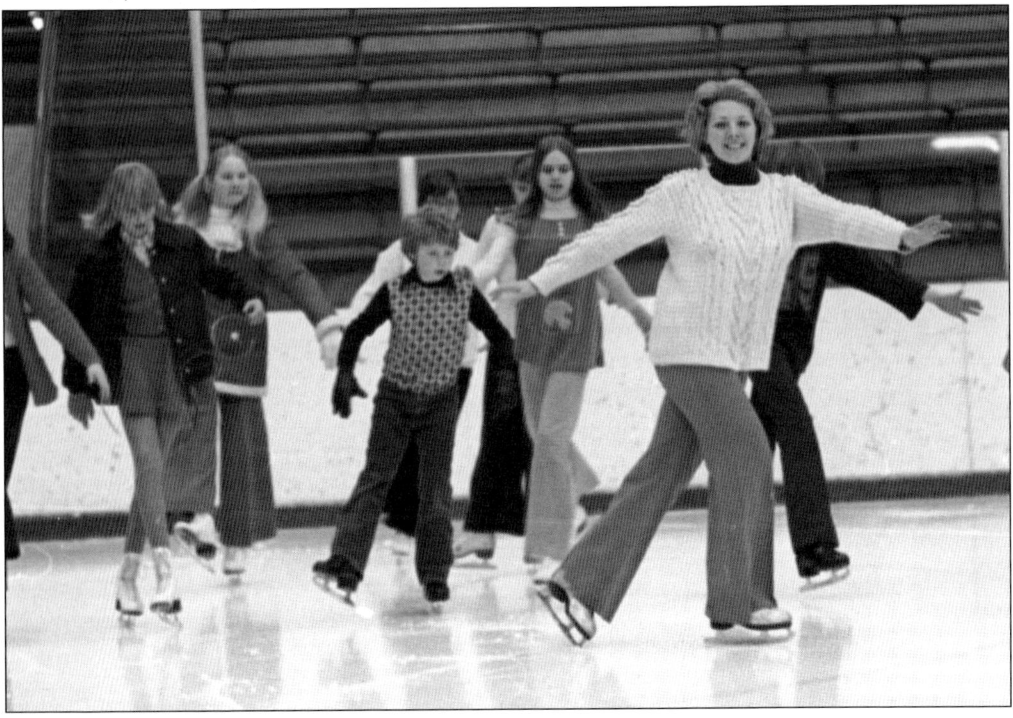

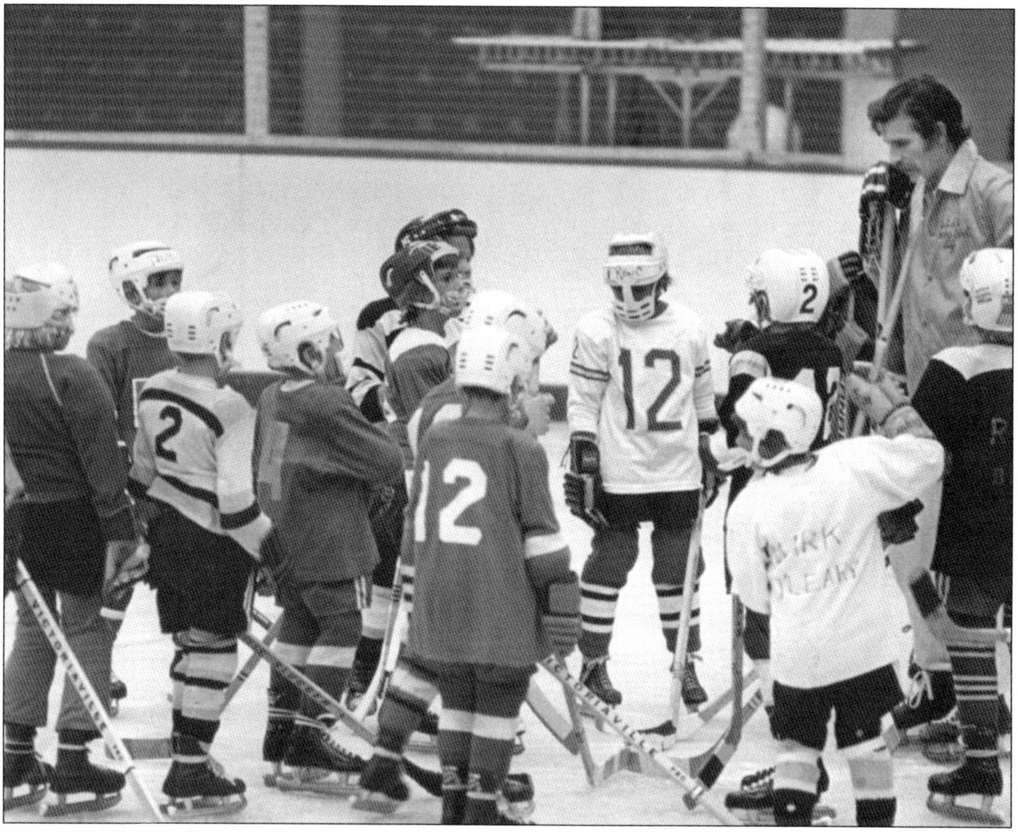

The Ice Arena is home to the champion Bowling Green Senior High School and BGSU Falcon Hockey teams, in addition to the BGSU Club Hockey team. Pictured here are youth hockey groups. The slogan "We Start Them Here" on the 1923 homecoming float that showcased the kindergarten band seems appropriate.

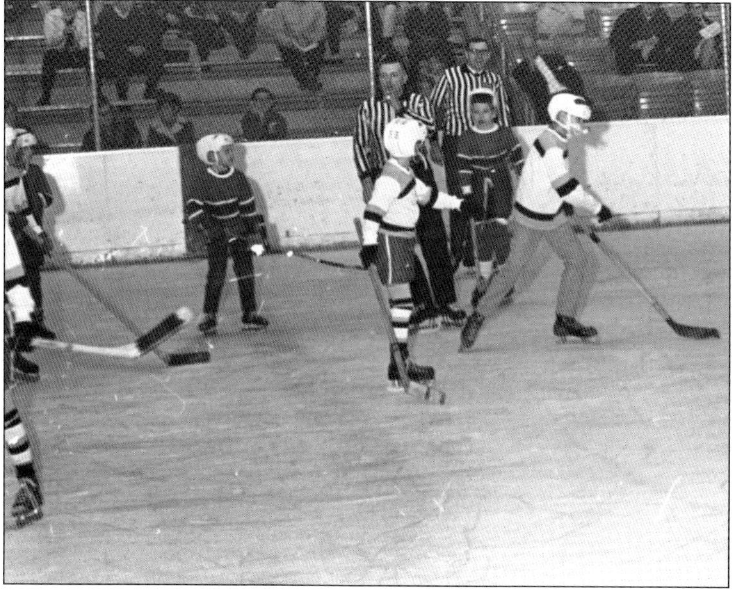

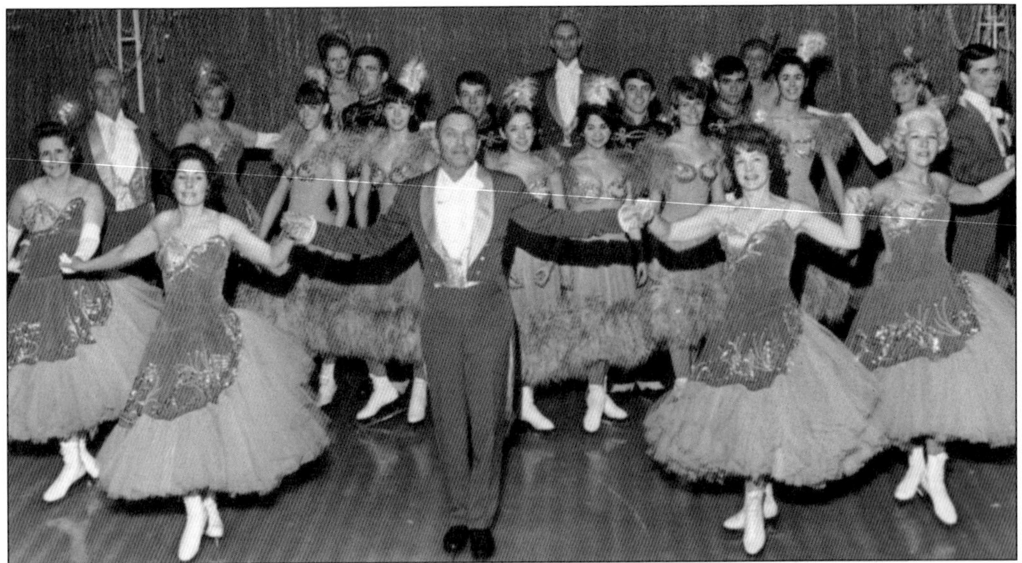

The first amateur ice show in Northwest Ohio, Ice Horizons, was sponsored by the Bowling Green Skating Club on March 29–30, 1968. in the BGSU Ice Arena. The event featured over 200 skaters from the university and local community. Professional skating instructors David and Rita Lowery were program directors. Former resident and Olympic gold medalist Scott Hamilton performed in subsequent shows.

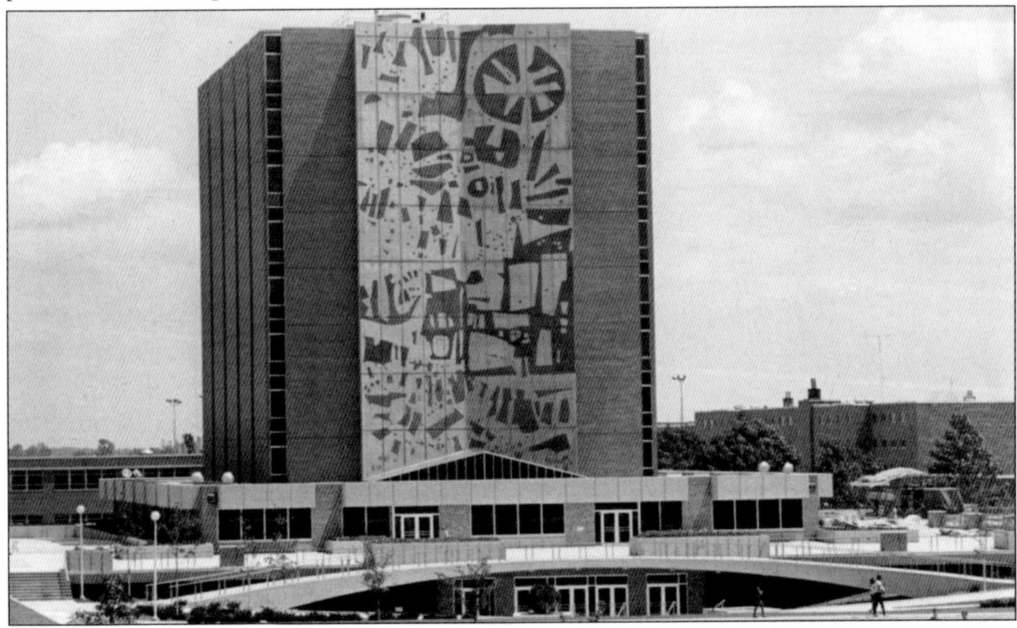

The new BGSU Library was opened in 1967 and in 1982 named the William T. Jerome Library in honor of the former BGSU president. The library has changed to meet the needs of a growing student population. It houses the Learning Commons tutoring service, Student Technology Assistance Center (STAC), the Thinkers Café, as well as individual and group study spaces. The special collections, including the Curriculum Resource Center, music library, and sound-recording archives, Browne Popular Culture Library, and Center for Archival Collections are housed in the library.

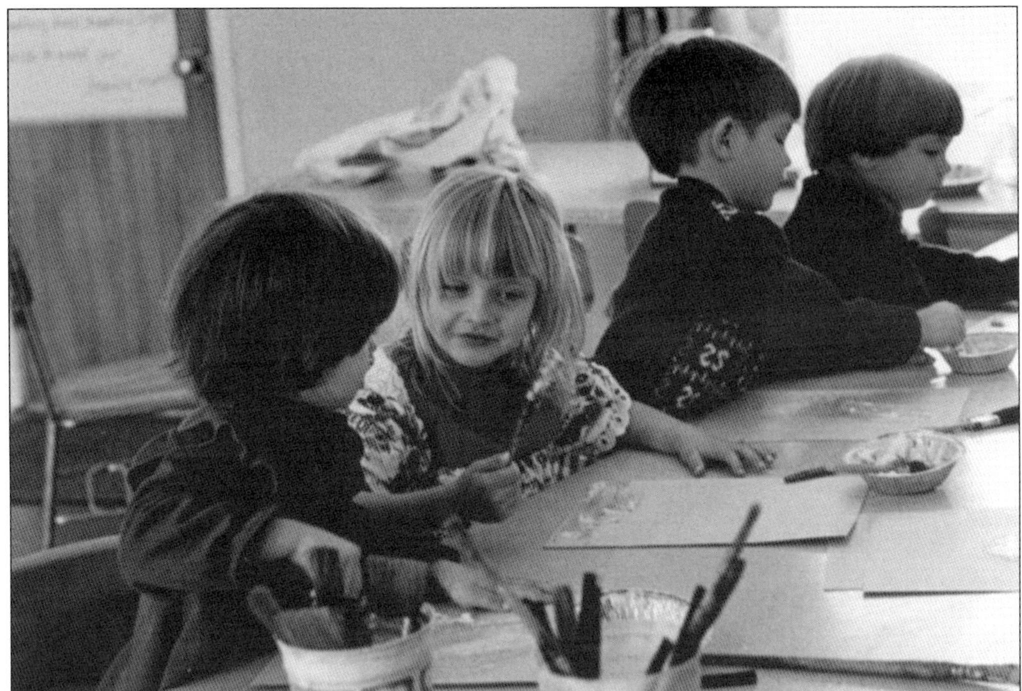

The BGSU Creative Arts Program was established in the 1960s by the school of music to train junior music students and expose children to the fine arts. The program, which operated on a year-long basis after school and during the summer, offered general art and music instruction for children ages three to 17. The program offered group and private lessons in piano, violin, viola, cello, harp, folk dancing, singing, drama, poetry, and storytelling.

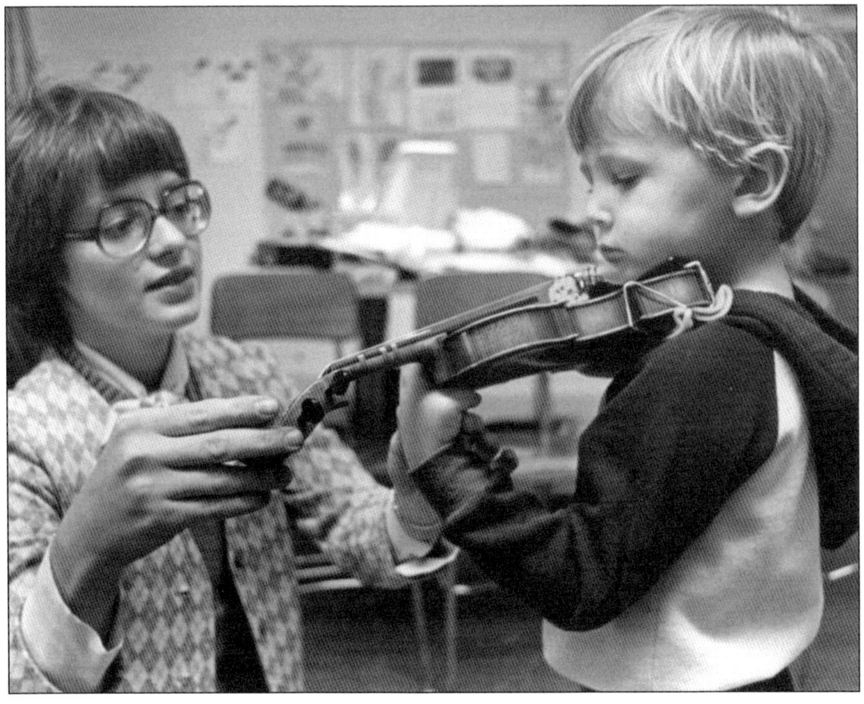

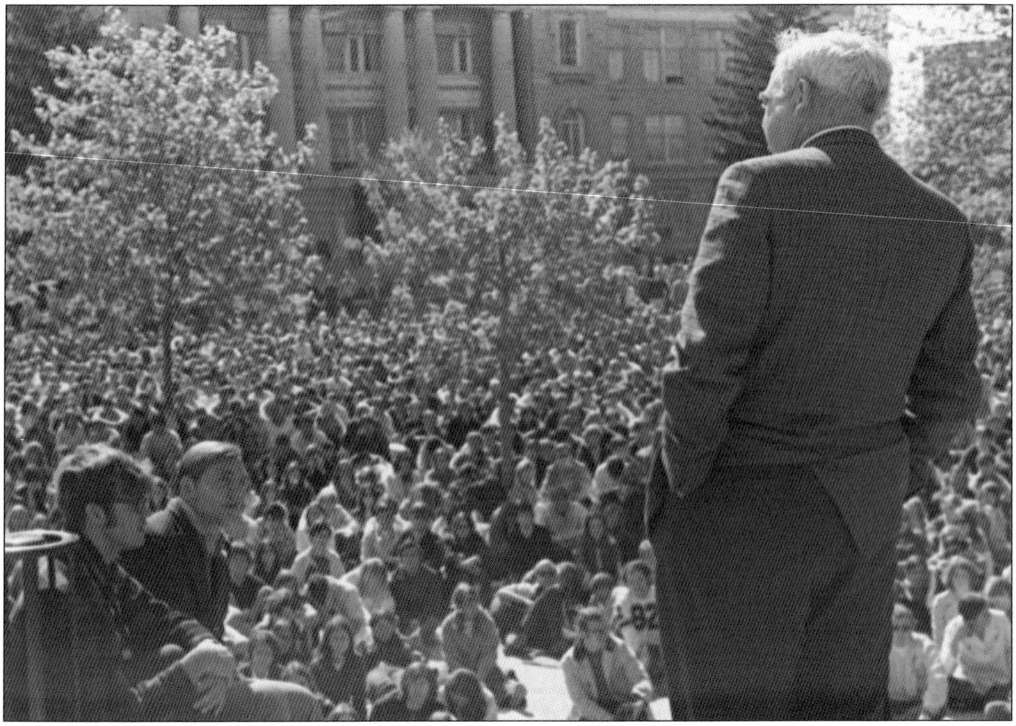

The killing of four Kent State University students by National Guardsmen on May 4, 1970, sparked marches, protests, and violent confrontations with law enforcement on campuses across the nation. Many campuses closed right after the event. Bowling Green State University was the only Ohio campus to remain open. Pres. William T. Jerome worked closely with students, faculty, administrators, and community leaders to formulate strategies for a peaceful reaction. An open forum from the steps of Williams Hall was held, and campus community members could voice their opinions about the situation. A silent candlelight vigil and march through downtown Bowling Green took place on the same evening. Comprised of 7,000 BGSU students, faculty, and staff, the march was led by a flag-draped casket.

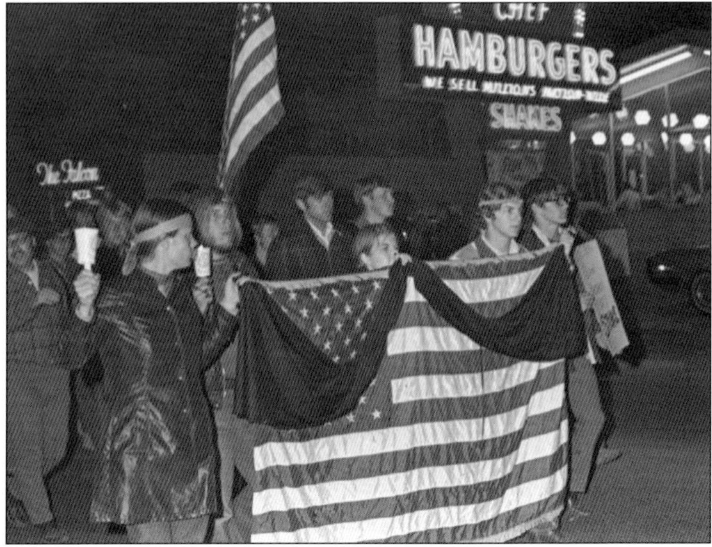

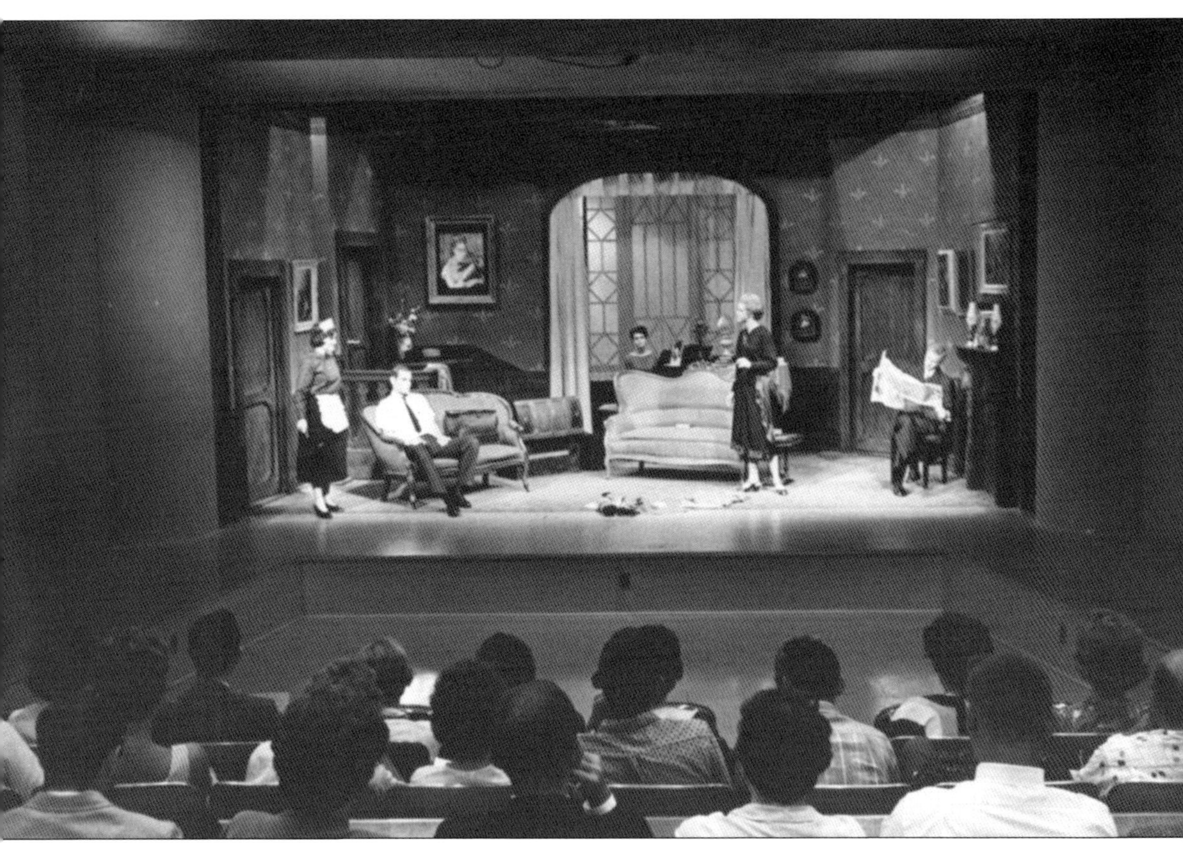

The Joe E. Brown Theatre, located in University Hall, is one of many dramatic-performance venues on the BGSU campus. The space was named in honor of actor-comedian Joe E. Brown in 1961. During his visit for the dedication of the theater, Brown played the role of Elwood P. Dowd in the campus production of *Harvey*. He had been awarded an honorary degree by BGSU in 1949.

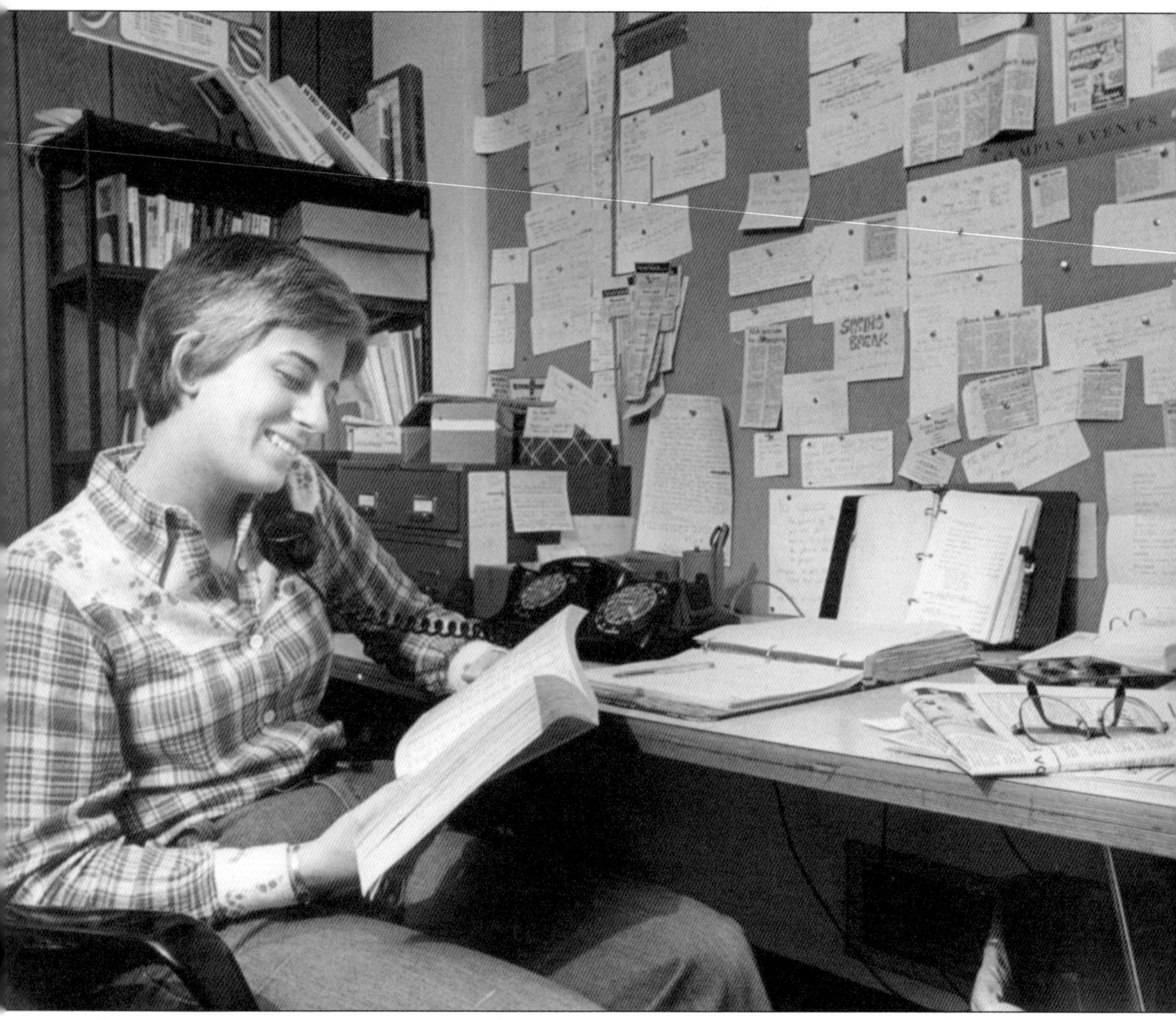

Campus Fact Line, a BGSU campus and community telephone information service, was originally established as the Rumor Center following the Kent State shootings in May 1970. Operators have received questions about a variety of topics, including campus history and traditions.

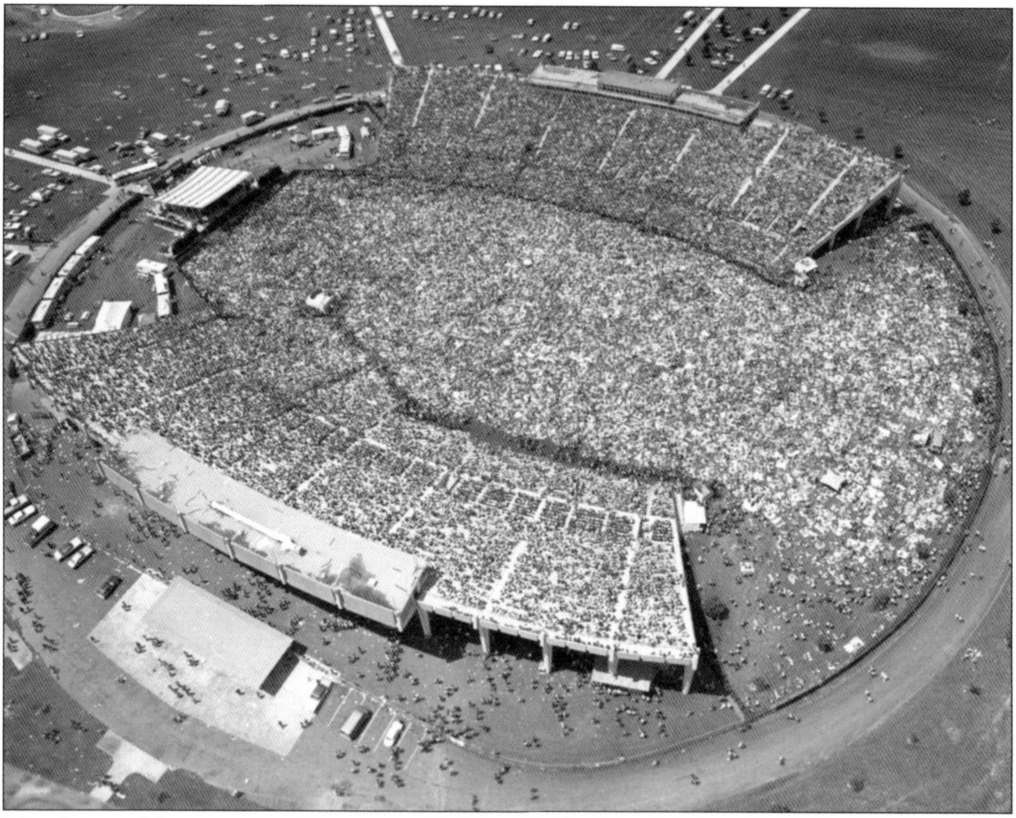

The first and last major rock concert, the Poe Ditch Music Festival, was held in the Doyt L. Perry Stadium on June, 1, 1975 (above). The crowd was estimated at 30,000 to 40,000, including approximately 3,300 BGSU students. The lineup included the Nitty Gritty Dirt Band (below), Montrose, Richie Havens, and others.

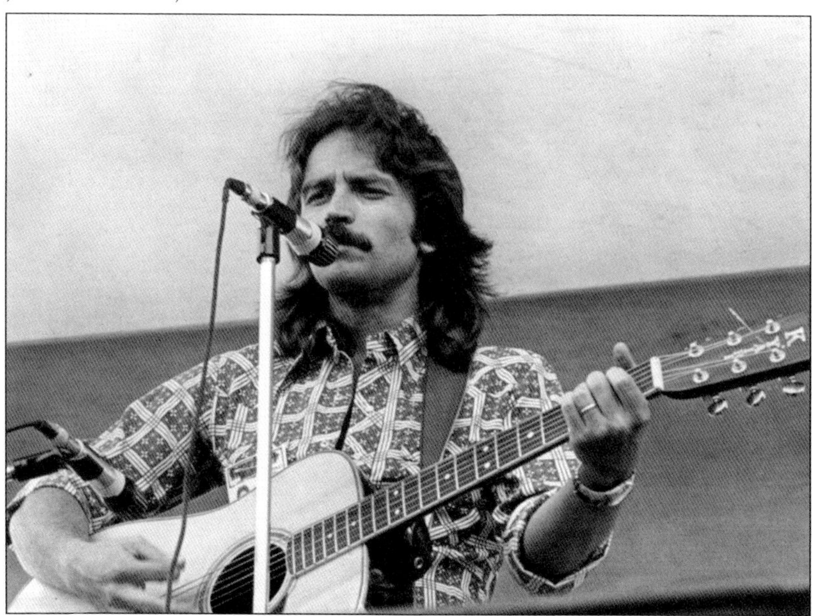

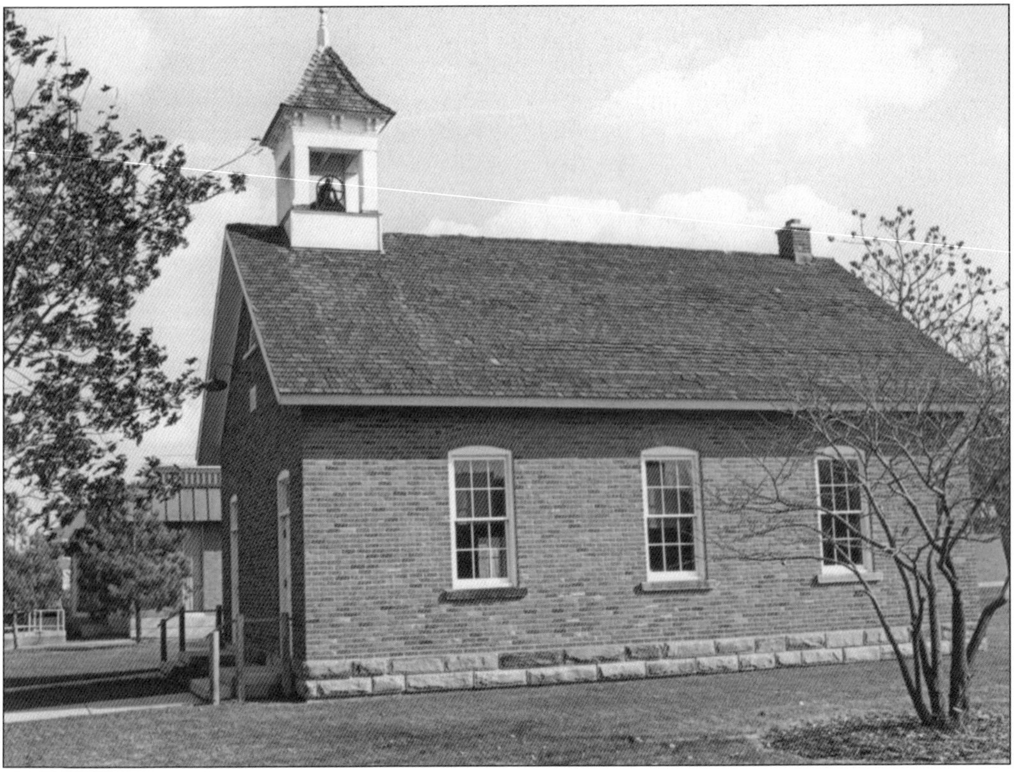

The educational memorabilia center or "Little Red School House" was dismantled and reconstructed on the BGSU campus in 1975 to serve as a living history museum. Originally built in 1875, the building is an example of a typical rural one-room schoolhouse. Decorated with period furnishings, the museum is visited by hundreds of children each year. Jan Wahl, children's author, was a special guest reader for one of the school groups.

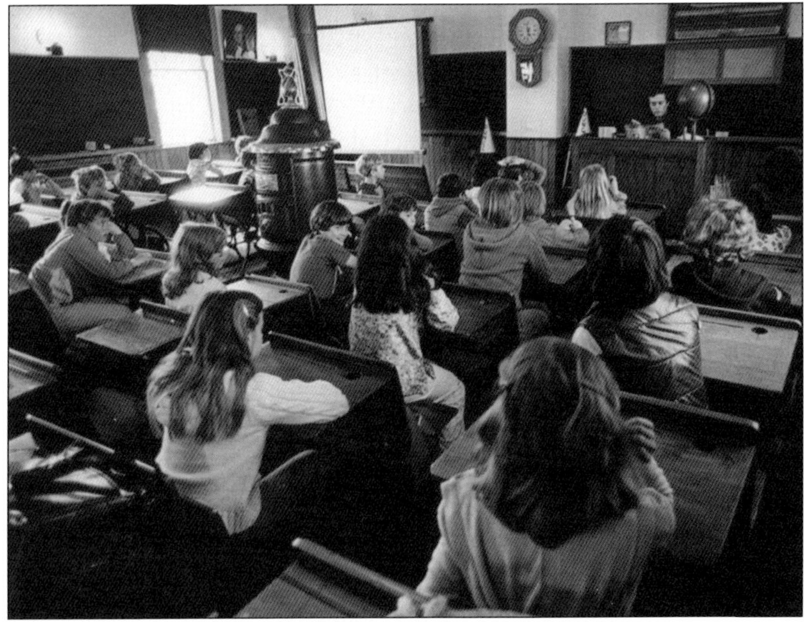

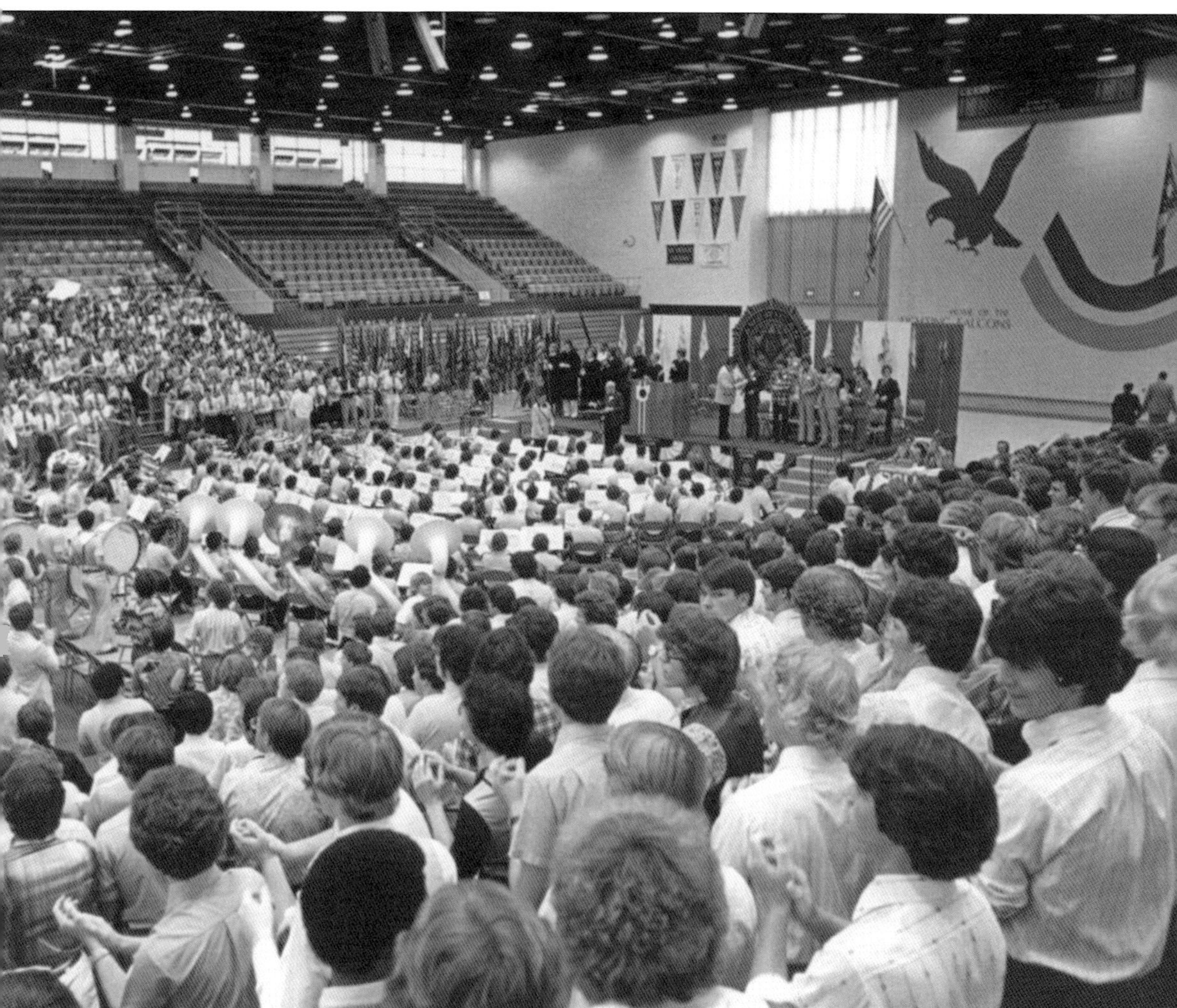

The American Legion Buckeye Boys State first appeared on campus in 1978. The Boys State program is an eight-day, hands-on experience for young men, high school juniors, in the operation of the democratic form of government, the organization of political parties, and the relationship of one to the other in shaping Ohio government.

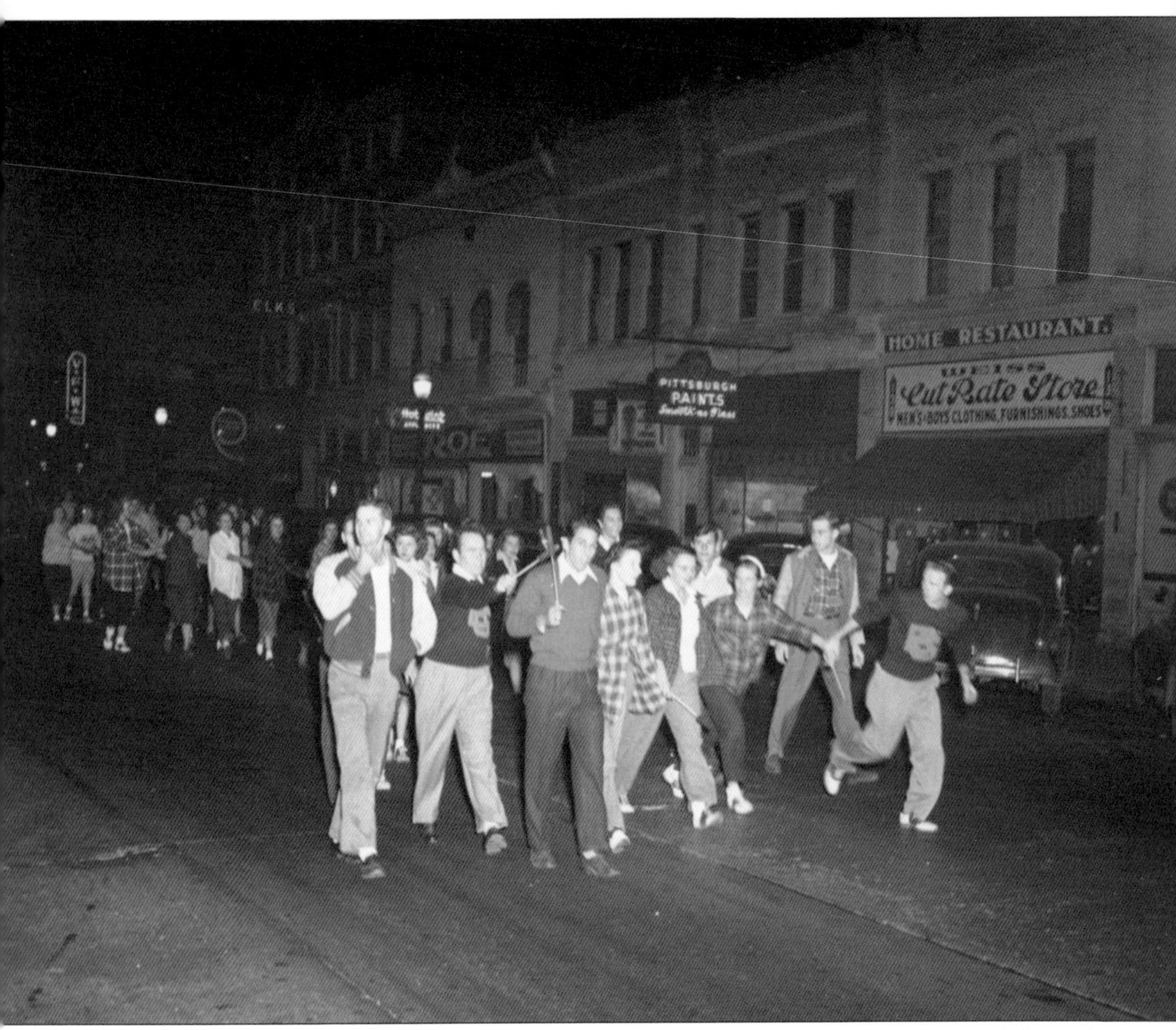

The snake dance was first featured in the 1922 homecoming celebration and wound through campus and city streets. BGSU set a world record for the activity in 1975.

The opening of
Interstate Highway
75 in 1979 provided
improved access
to community and
college. A flurry
of service business
development ensued
along East Wooster
Street near the
Bowling Green State
University campus.
Several of the
businesses are still
situated in the same
locations today.

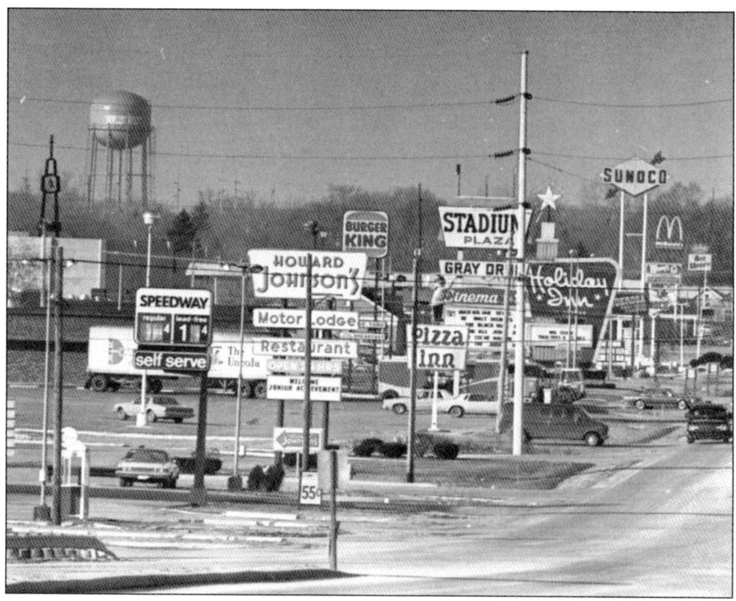

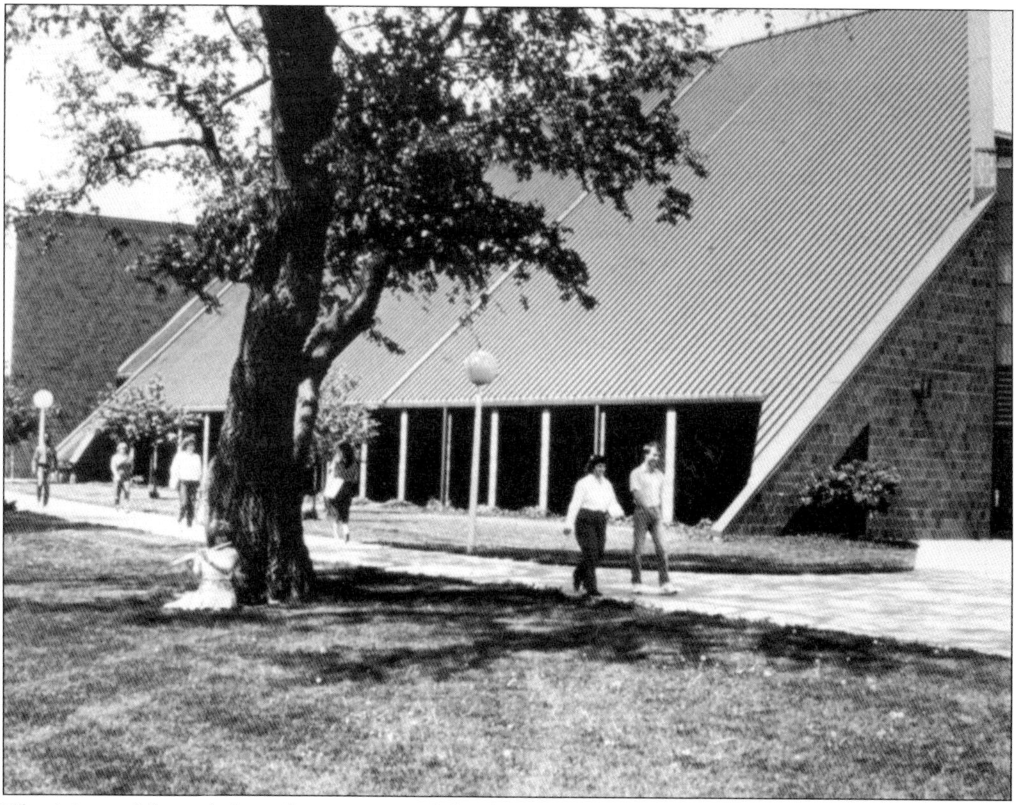

The Moore Musical Arts Center, named for former BGSU president Hollis A. Moore and his wife, Marian, has been the home of the BGSU music program since it opened in 1979. The center houses the College of Musical Arts, the Lenore and Marvin Kobacker Hall, the Dorothy and Ashel Bryan Recital Hall, practice and performance rooms, classrooms, and offices. Activities such as the New Music Festival, educational programs, and performances are offered in the center.

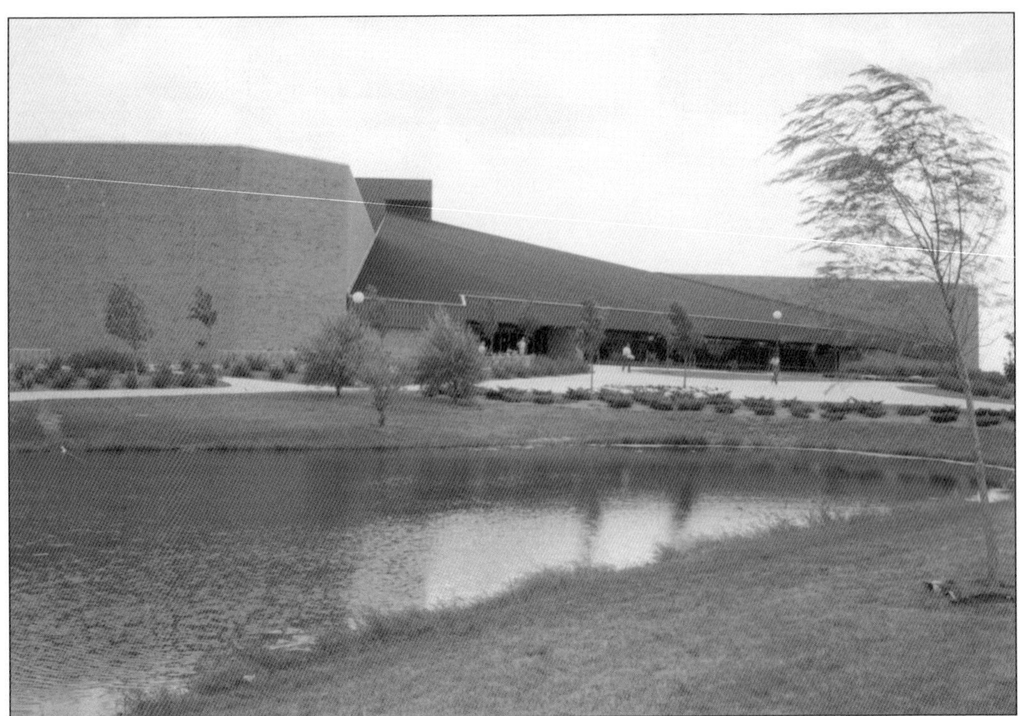

The newly renovated Student Recreation Center, which houses the Department of Recreation and Wellness, was opened in 1979. The facility features the Olympic-sized Cooper swimming pool, the Andrews club pool, a banked running track, multipurpose sports center, golf room, exercise rooms, handball rooms, weight rooms, and locker rooms. The center offers programs that promote a fit and healthy lifestyle for BGSU and local community members.

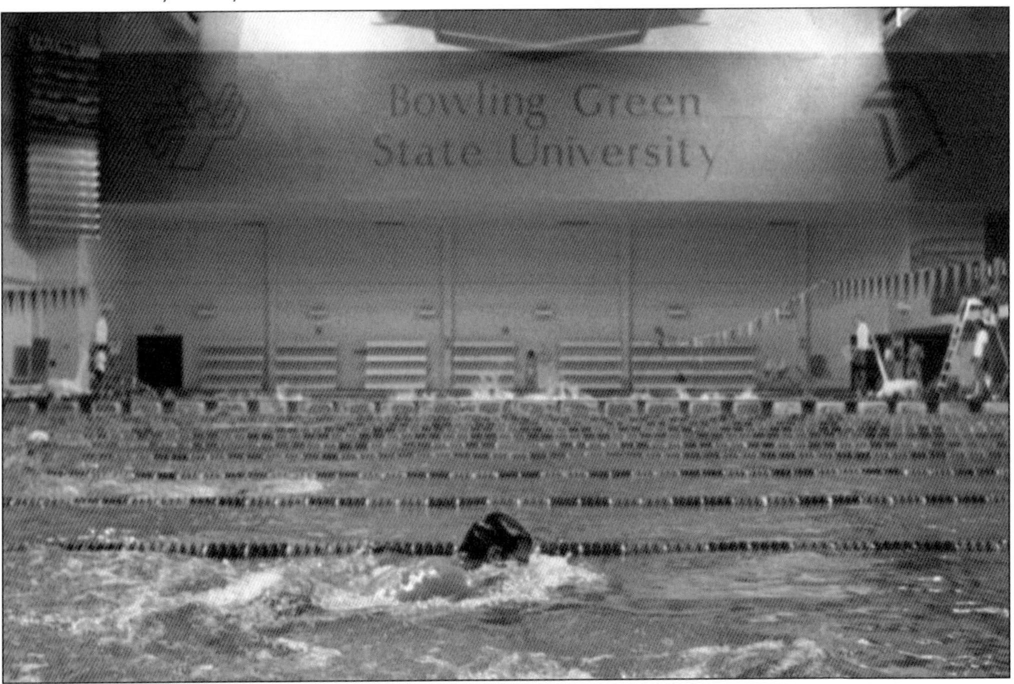

Uptown-Downtown, which is located at 162 North Main Street, is a popular night spot for BGSU students. It is a bar and grill, sports bar, and nightclub. Constructed in the 1890s, the building was originally the New Ross Hotel and later the Brown Hotel.

Construction of the Physical Science Laboratory was completed in 1984. The building houses laboratories, a planetarium, and a rooftop observatory. A series of educational programs have been presented to BGSU and local community members, including school groups, since the planetarium opened.

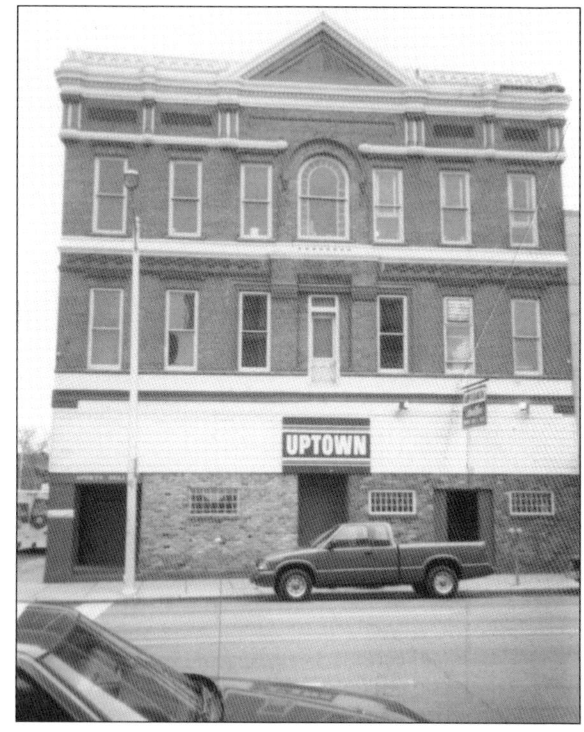

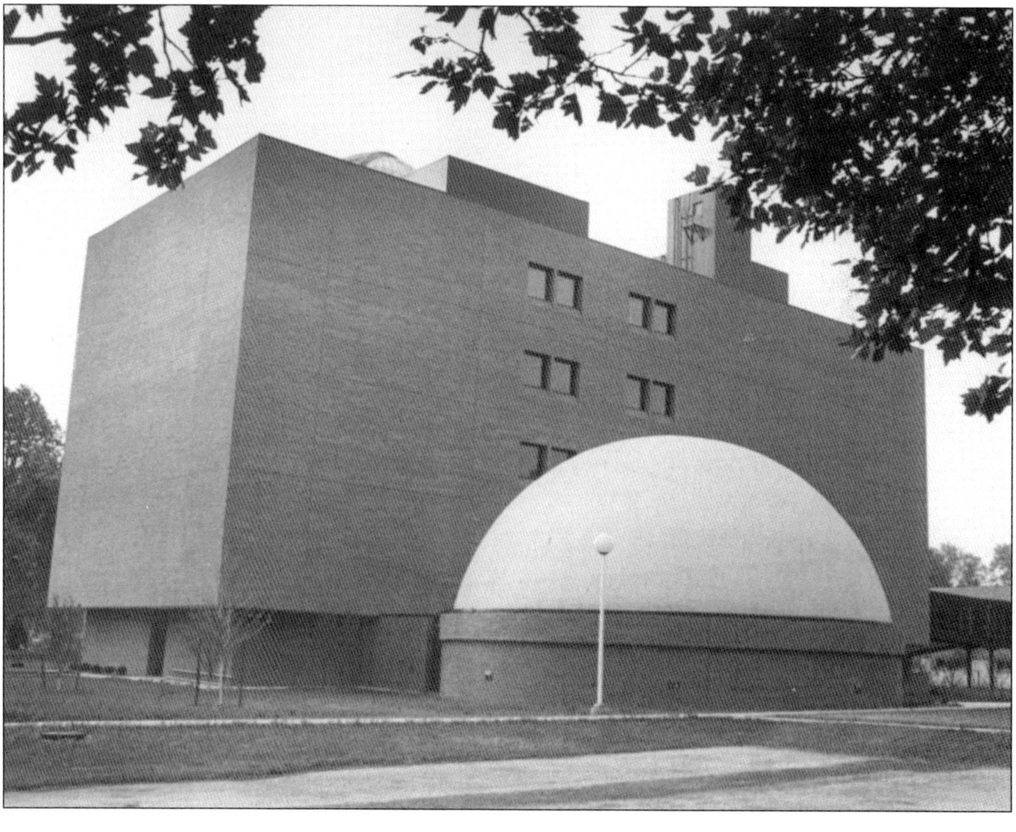

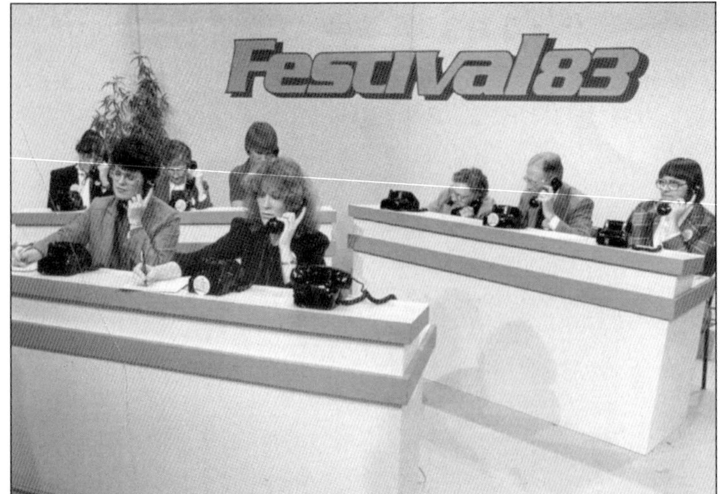

The BGSU public television station, WBGU-TV, enlisted the aid of BGSU employees and local residents in their targeted fundraising telethons. Members of the Bowling Green Sesquicentennial Commission participated in the Festival 83 membership drive.

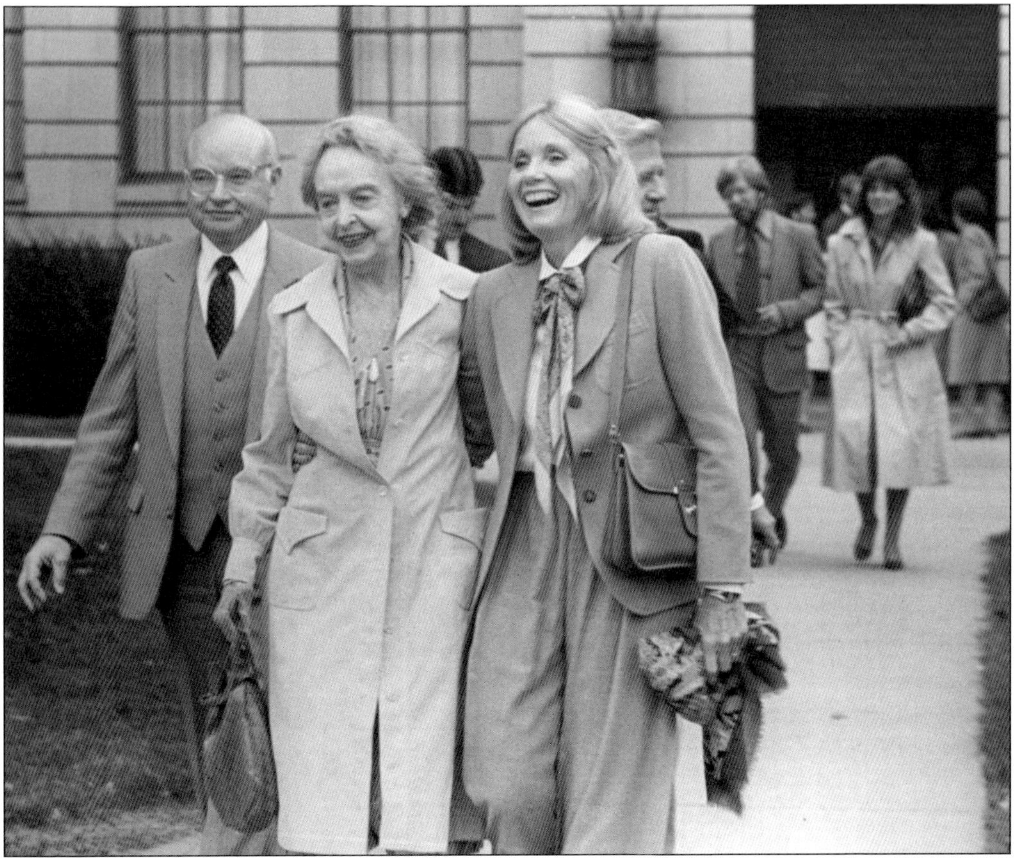

Actresses Lillian Gish (left) and Eva Marie Saint (BGSU class of 1946) appear in front of McFall Center with Dr. Ralph H. Wolfe, founder and curator of the Gish Film Theater in 1982. Both were on campus to attend the Gish Film Theater dedication of a retrospective photographic exhibit of Gish's career previously presented by the Museum of Modern Art in 1980. Saint, who made her Broadway debut with Lillian Gish, was among the guests paying tribute to her. During this same visit, Saint was awarded an honorary doctor of performing arts degree.

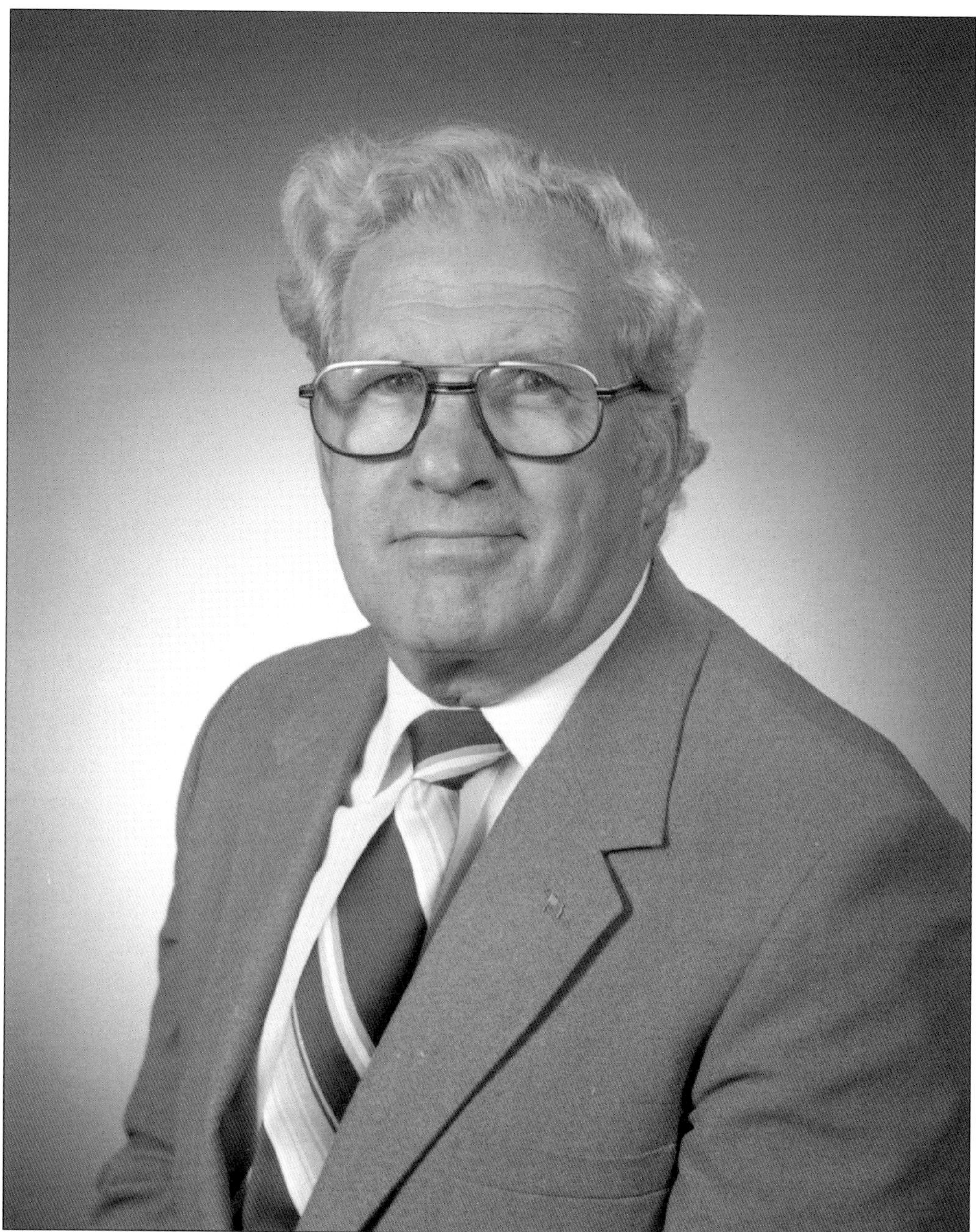

Bruce Bellard came to Bowling Green to attend BGSU but left to serve in the Navy during World War II. He returned to obtain bachelor's and master's degrees. He played on the football team and then served as assistant football coach from 1948 to 1959 and as wrestling coach from 1952 to 1977. He taught for the physical education department from 1948 to 1981. He served on the city council from 1977 to 1982, as mayor from 1983 to 1986, and was inducted into the BGSU Athletic Hall of Fame in 1989.

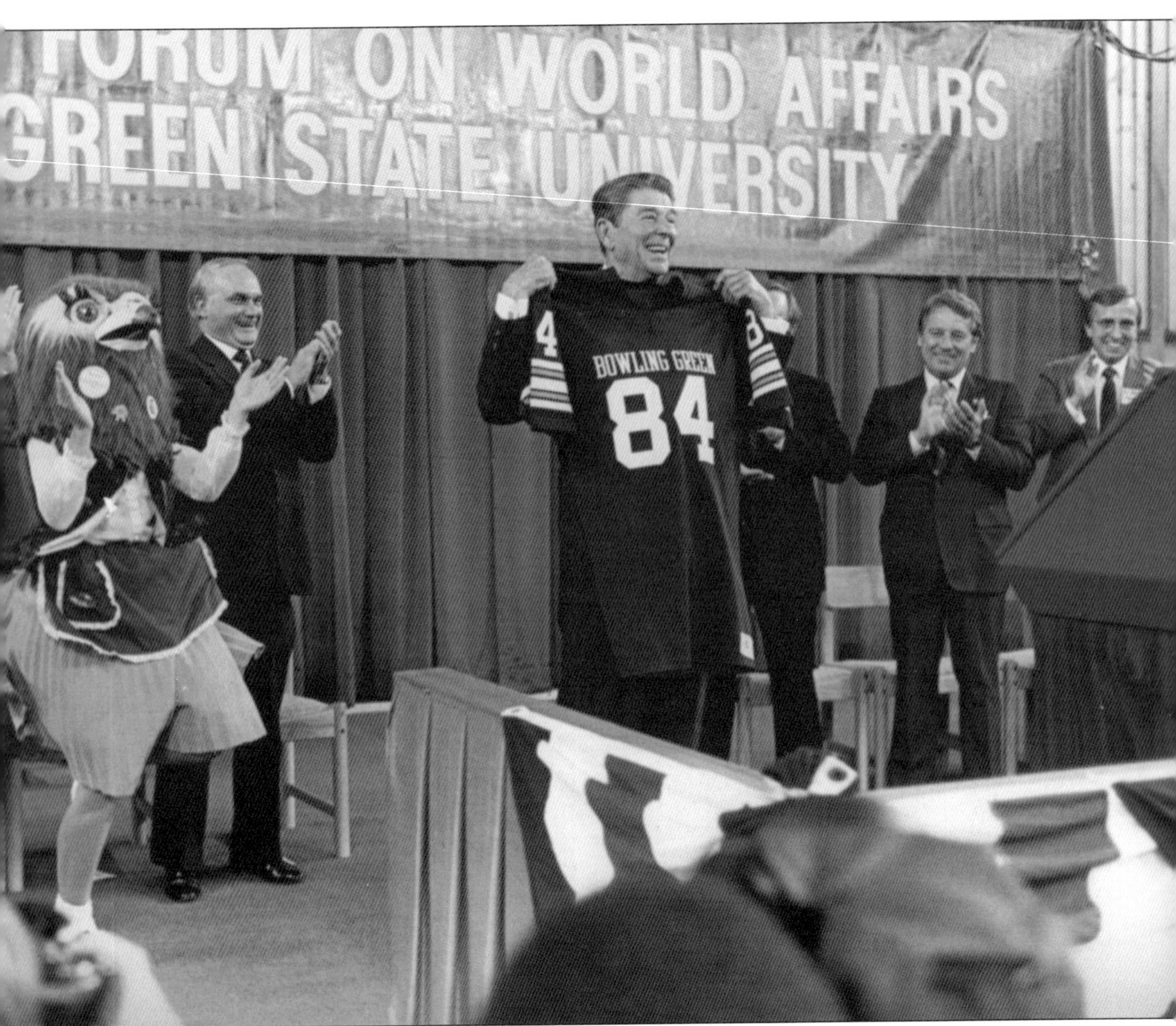

Pres. Ronald Reagan visited the BGSU campus on the campaign trail in 1984. In addition to Reagan, BGSU and Bowling Green have been host to Presidents Theodore Roosevelt, Taft, Harding, Kennedy, Ford, George H.W. Bush, Clinton, and Obama.

Four

BUILDING COMMUNITY

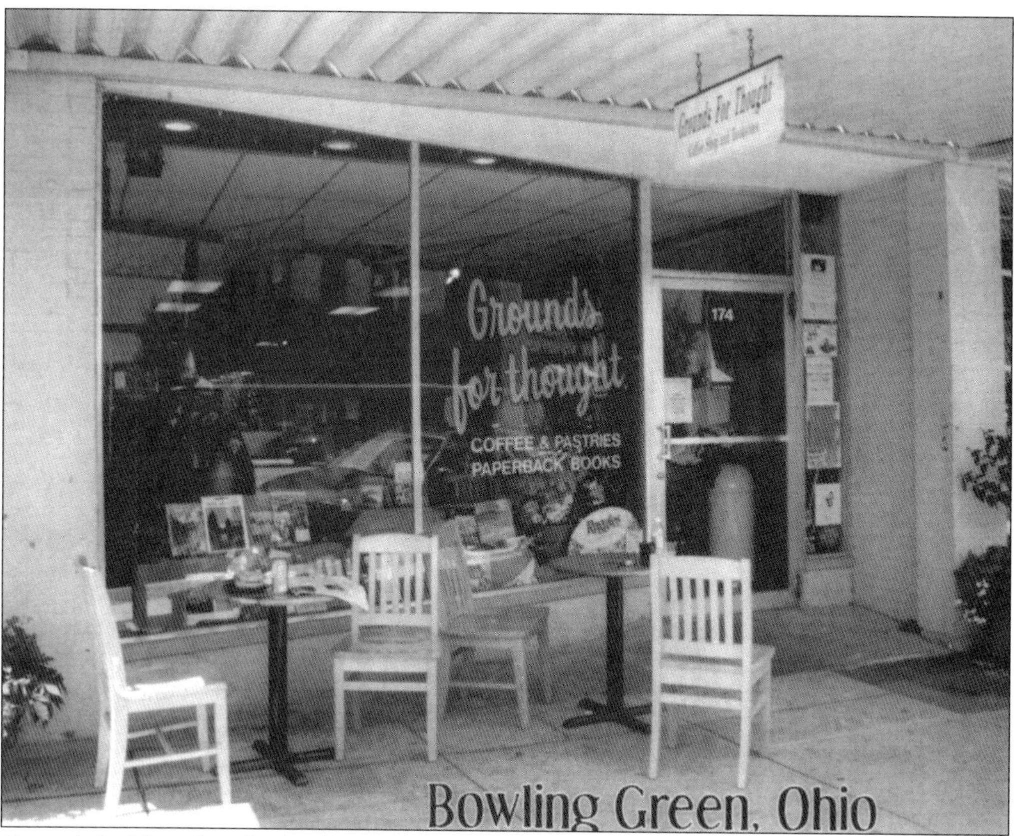

Grounds for Thought, which is located at 174 South Main Street, was established in 1989. Grounds is not a typical coffee house. Members of the BGSU and local communities congregate as individuals or in groups to discuss issues, meet political candidates, study, talk, read, attend a lecture, seminar, or intimate performances by world-renowned musicians, or to just unwind. Paperback books, locally hand-roasted coffee, flavored syrups, cocoa, and teas are offered for sale.

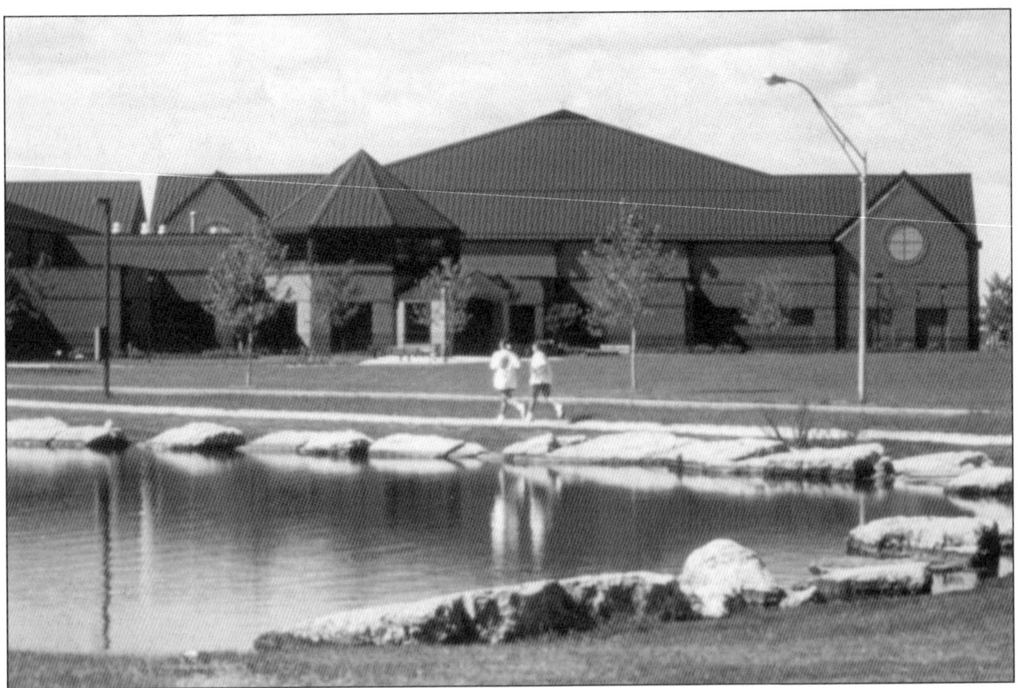

The Charles Perry Field House (above) opened in 1992. The facility contains a 200-meter track, 90-yard field, and four courts that can be used for tennis, basketball, and field events. The field house is the home of off-season training programs for intercollegiate sports teams as well as other team sports practices (below) and competitions. Local community and BGSU Wellness Center activities are also held in the field house.

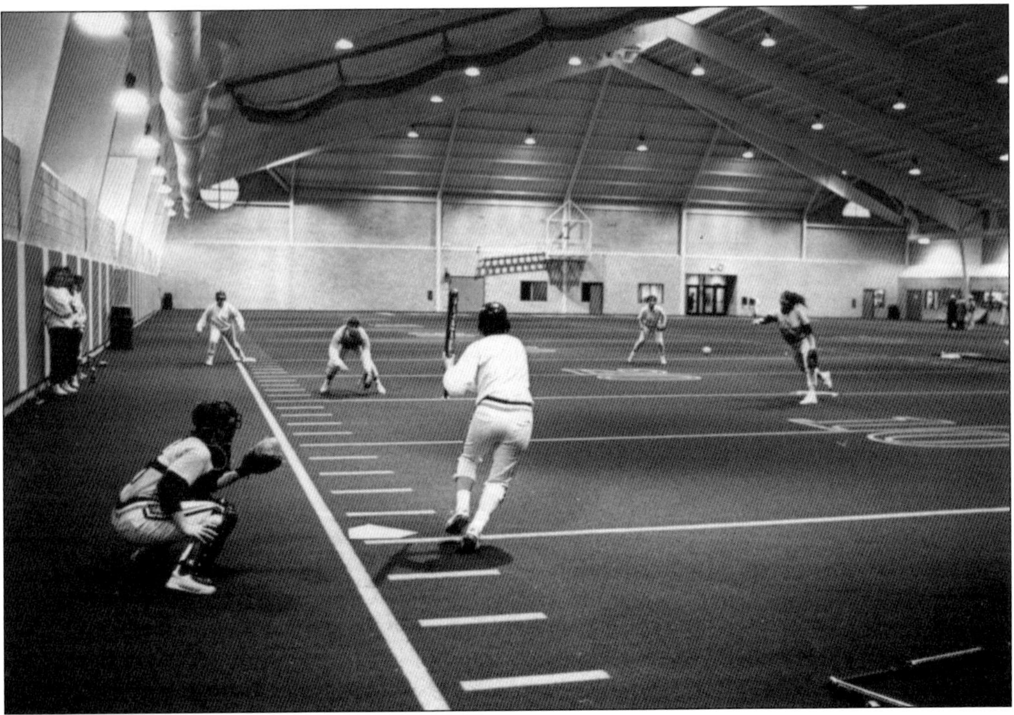

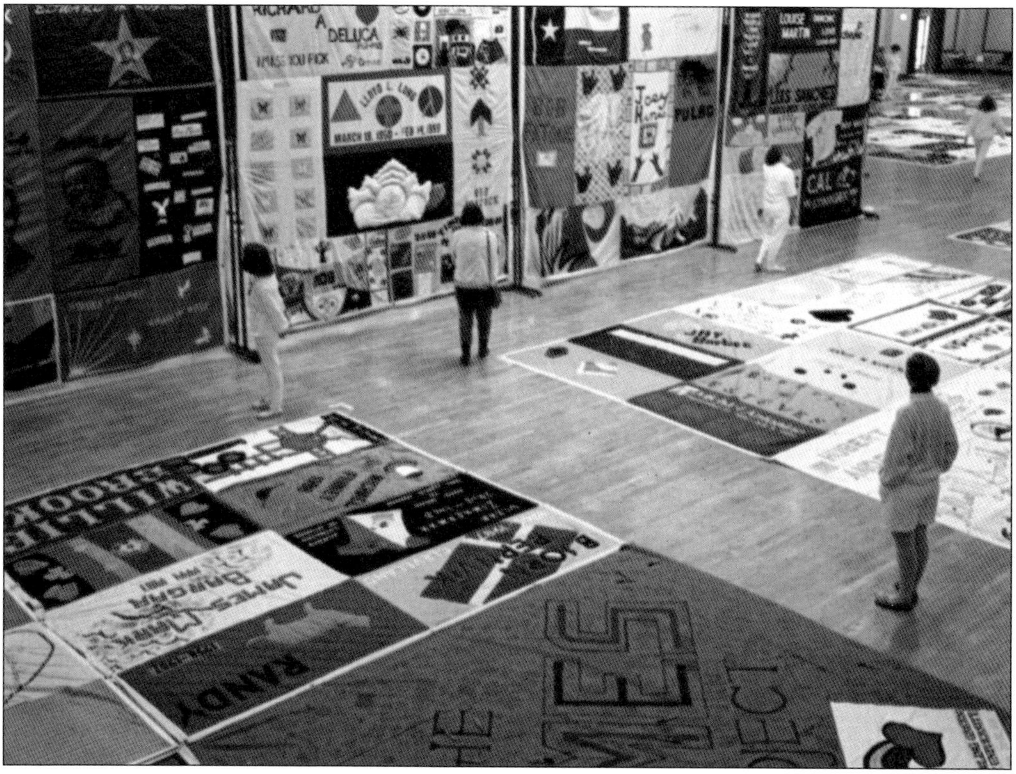

A special exhibit of the Names
Project AIDS Memorial Quilt was
held in the BGSU Student Union
in 1993. The quilt was created
in 1987 as a memorial for those
who died of AIDS and has been
exhibited all over the country.

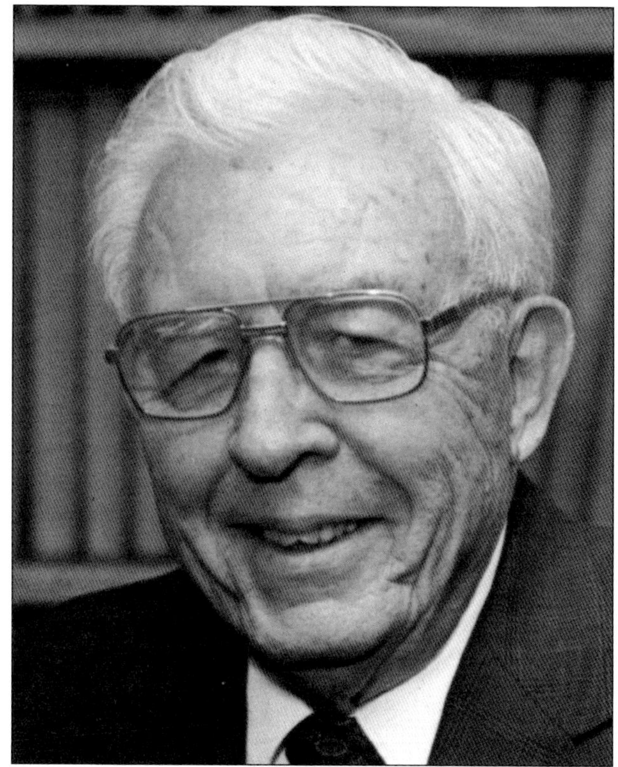

Wesley K. Hoffman came to
Bowling Green in 1965 to
command the Air Force ROTC
at the university. After retiring,
he served on the faculty of the
geography department. He
received his master's degree in
1971 from BGSU and was awarded
an honorary doctorate of public
service in 2000. He served as the
first municipal administrator for
the city in 1974 and as mayor
from 1992 to 1999. The Wesley K.
Hoffman Scholarship in aviation
studies was created in his honor.

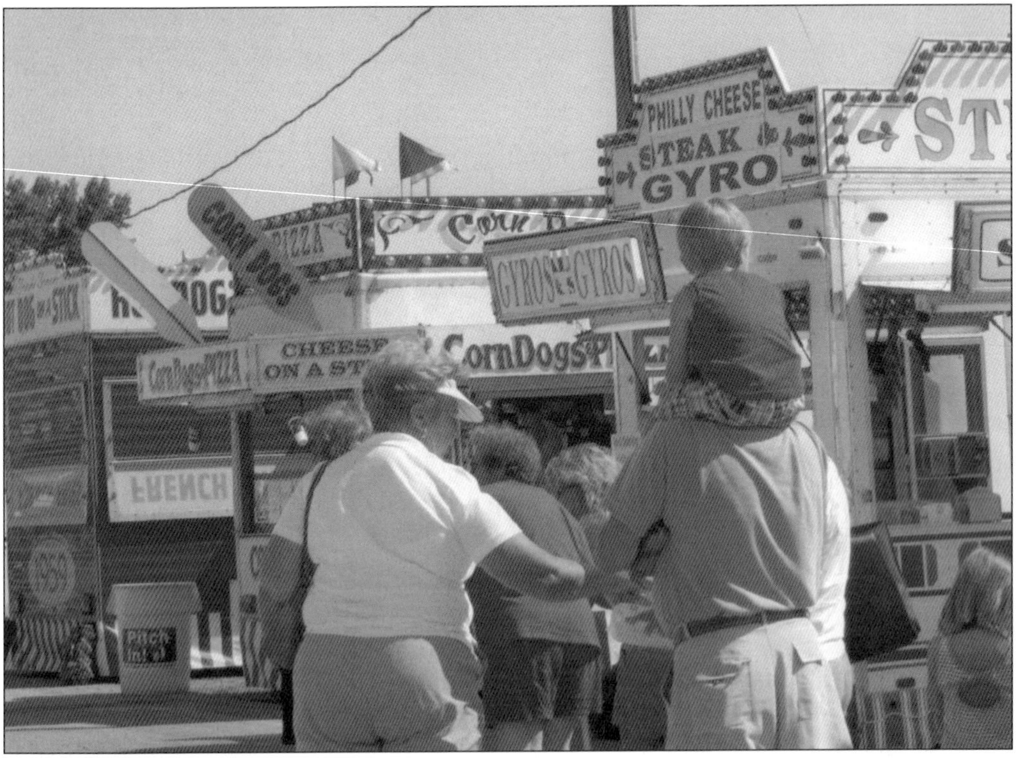

The Wood County Fair was permanently moved to Bowling Green in 1881. The fairgrounds were located at the site of the city park, and the fair was held there until 1927, when the event was discontinued. A group of area residents interested in starting a fair again successfully sponsored an event at the city park in 1951. A year later, a fair was held on land purchased by the recently established Wood County Fair Board. The fair, which is located on Poe Road, offers entertainment, livestock, and special auctions, displays, exhibits, rides, and a wide variety of food. (Courtesy of Marilyn Levinson.)

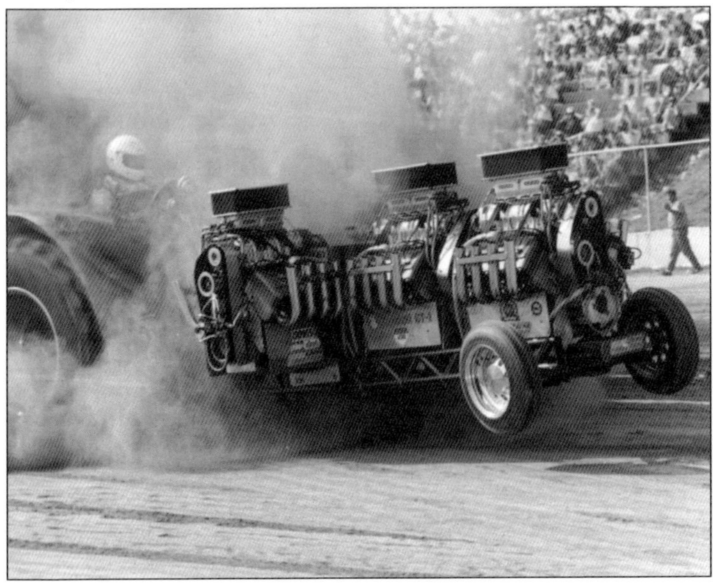

The first tractor pull to take place on the Wood County fairgrounds was held in 1962. The National Tractor Pull Championships came to Bowling Green in 1967 and continue to be a popular attraction among BGSU students and local residents. The first-place winner at the 27th Annual Championship in 1993 was Mike Piper with his 8.8 L Arias-powered "Just Add Dirt" modified tractor.

The first student-organized BGSU Dance Marathon for the Children's Miracle Network was held in 1996 and raised $45,476 for the Children's Miracle Network. The activity, which is held annually, includes participants from the local community.

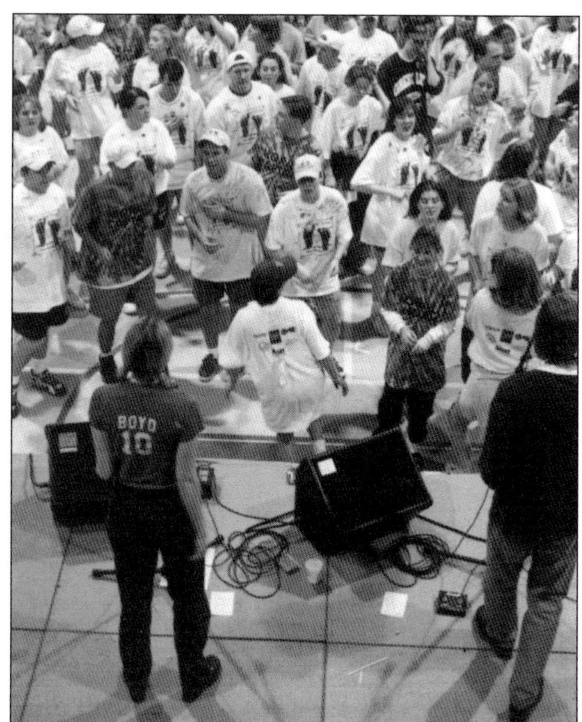

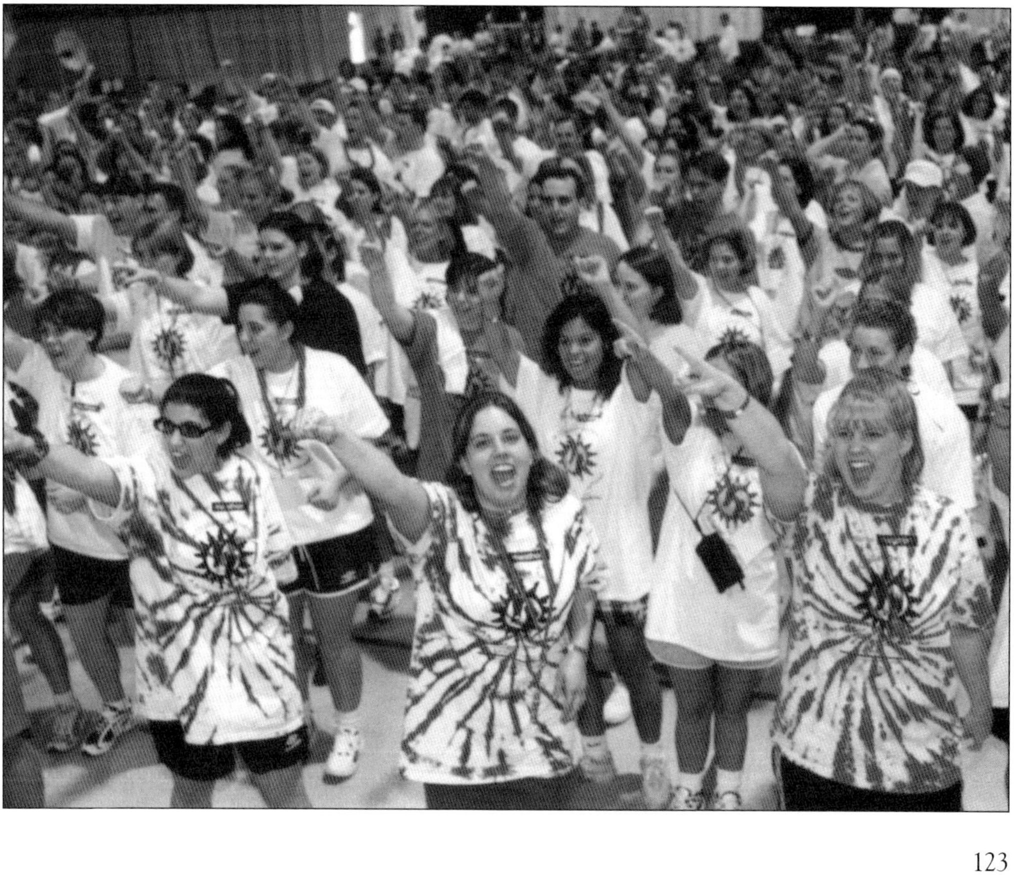

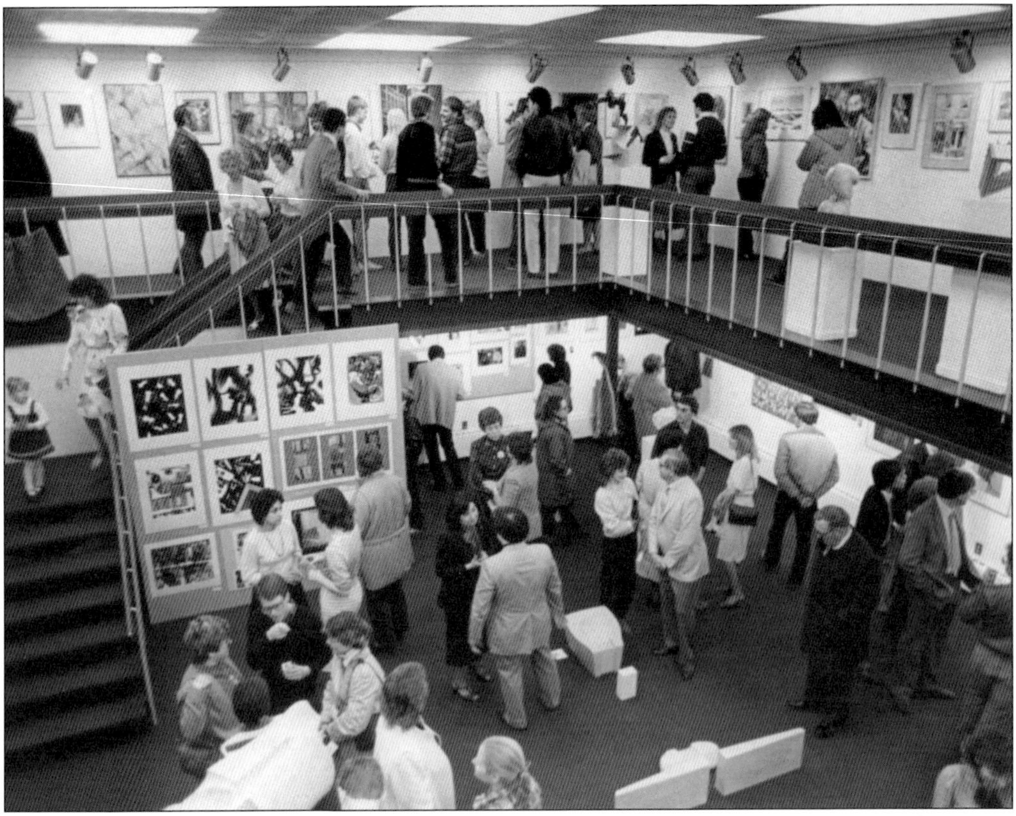

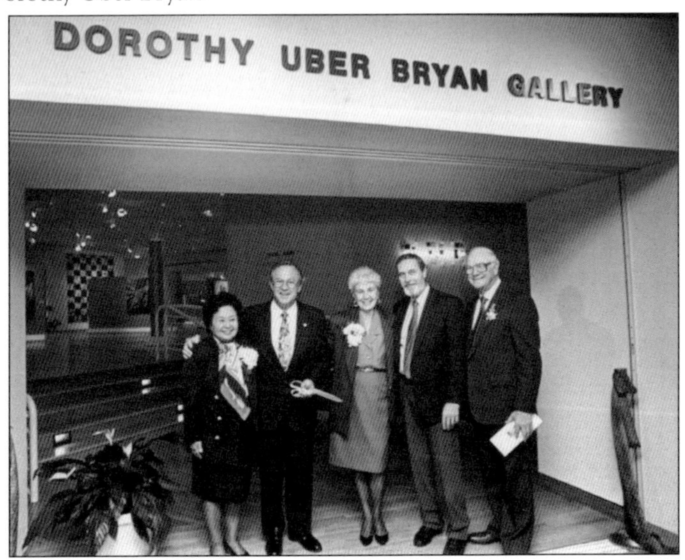

The Fine Arts Center, which was first opened in 1950, houses the School of Art. Subsequent renovations added specialized studios for drawing, sculpture, glass, ceramics, jewelry design, oil painting, and print classes and galleries for student and local resident artwork exhibits. The Willard Wankelman Gallery (above) was named in honor of the former School of Art director in 1998. The Dorothy Uber Bryan Gallery (below) was completed in 1992 with funds donated by Ashel and Dorothy Uber Bryan.

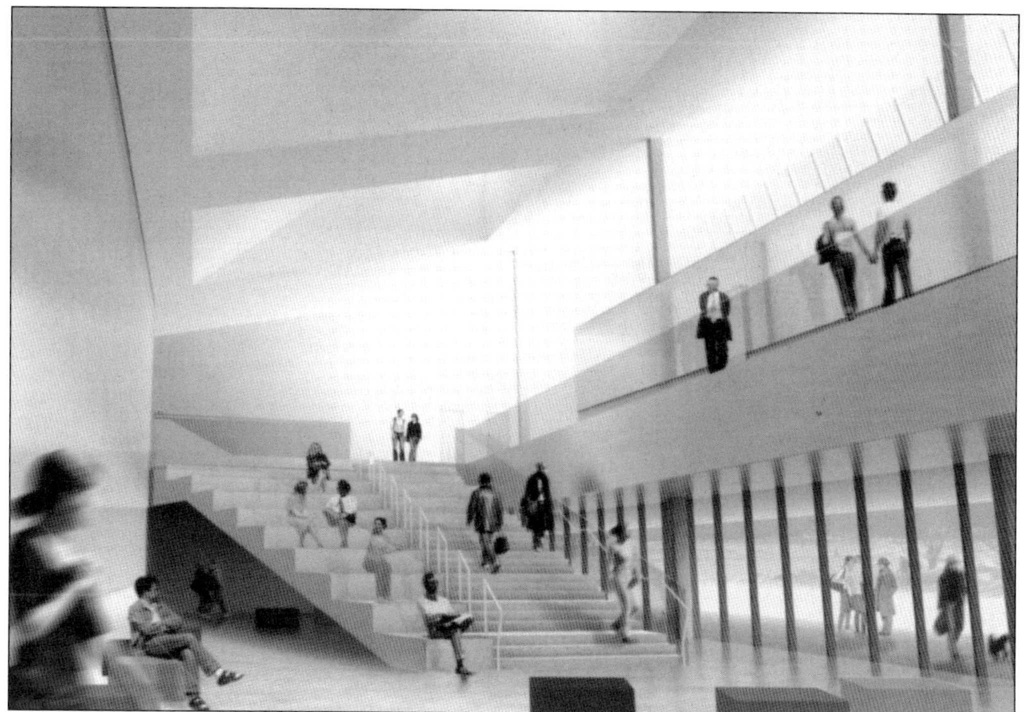

The Wolfe Center for the Arts, named for Mary and Frederic Wolfe, provides a space for collaborative environment for the fine and performing arts. The center features film and theater studies classrooms, the Thomas B. and Kathleen M. Donnell Theatre, which houses the main stage, Eva Marie Saint Theatre, the Margit Bloch Heskett classroom and dance studio, a sound stage, departmental offices, collaborative studios for vocal music and dance, and a student technology center. (Courtesy of Marilyn Levinson.)

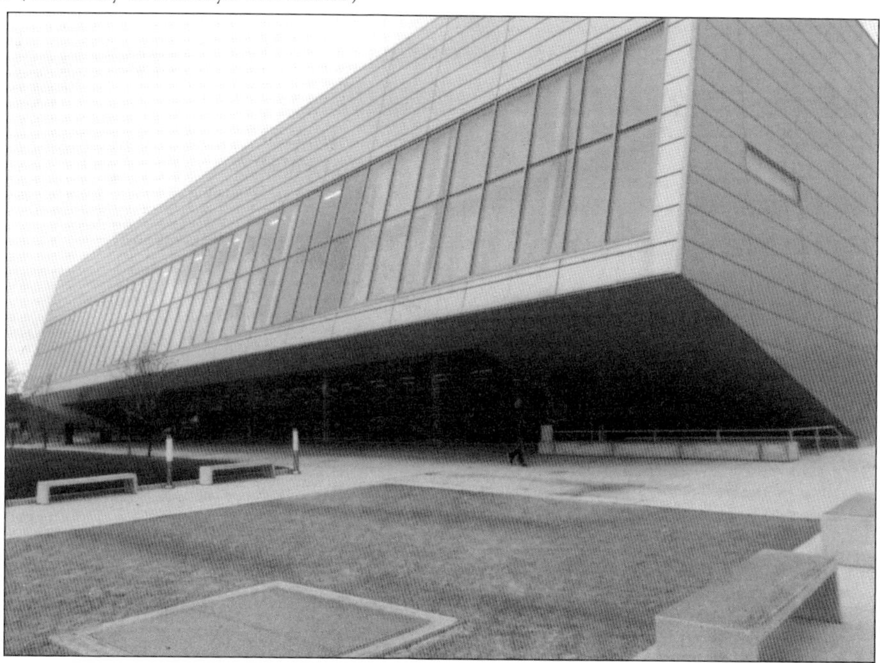

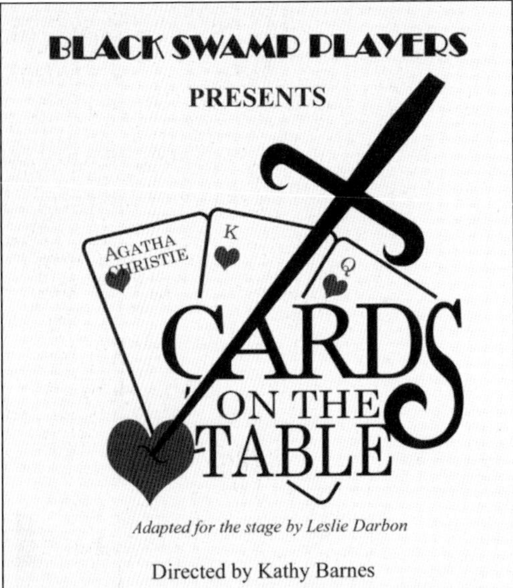

The Black Swamp Players, an active community theater group comprised of BGSU and other local talent, was established in 1968. The players have performed in many locations, including several Bowling Green schools, Veterans Memorial Hall in the city park, Woodland Mall, and currently at the First United Methodist Church. A Young People's Theater Program for junior high school students was established by the players during the 1975–1976 season.

BGSU and the City of Bowling Green joined together in 2013 to support equity, diversity, and inclusion in the communities. The national Not in Our Town campaign was begun in 1995 as an outtake of a PBS documentary related to hate crimes in Billings, Montana.

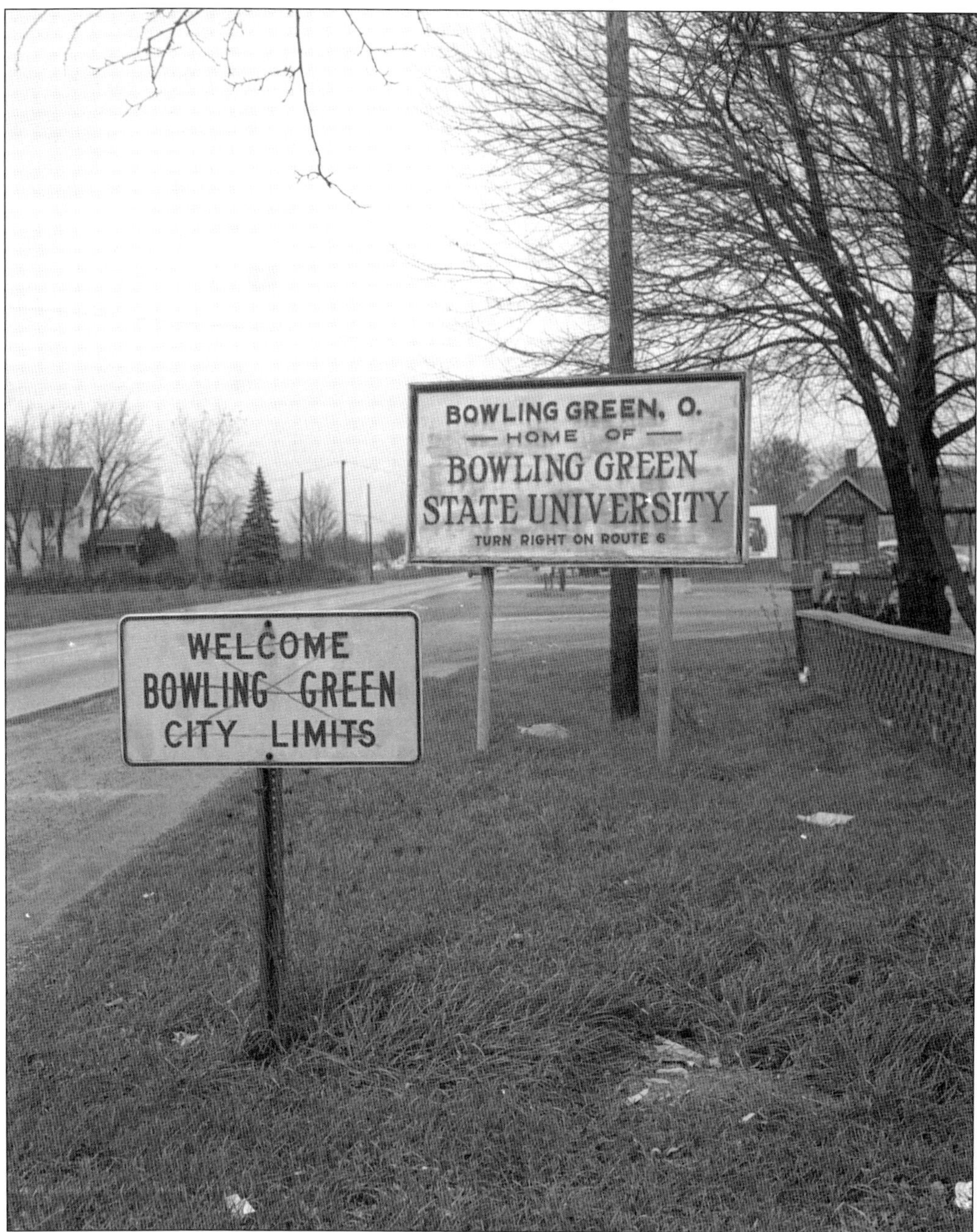

Bowling Green City Limits have been adorned with signs welcoming visitors and acknowledging, with pride, that the city is the home of Bowling Green State University. The mutually beneficial relationship between town and gown has existed for more than 100 years.

Discover Thousands of Local History Books Featuring Millions of Vintage Images

Arcadia Publishing, the leading local history publisher in the United States, is committed to making history accessible and meaningful through publishing books that celebrate and preserve the heritage of America's people and places.

Find more books like this at
www.arcadiapublishing.com

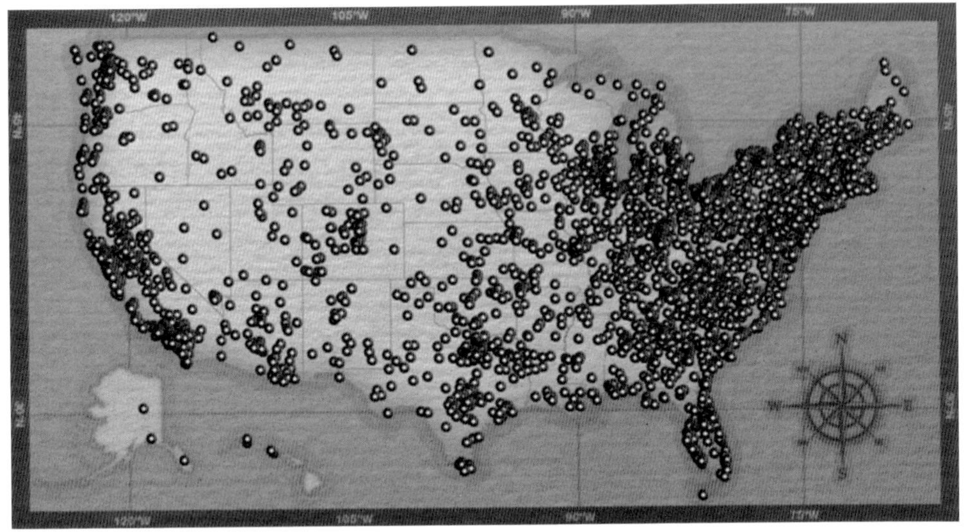

Search for your hometown history, your old stomping grounds, and even your favorite sports team.

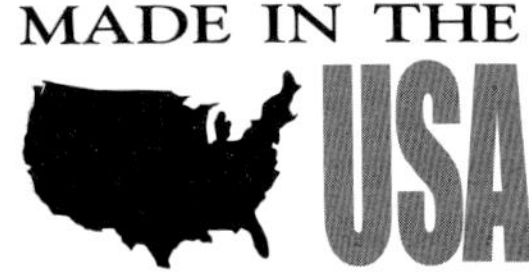